As a result of this, many [of] his disciples returned to their former way of life and no longer accompanied him. Jesus then said to the Twelve, "Do you also want to leave?" Simon Peter answered him, "Master, to whom shall we go? You have the words of eternal life. We have come to believe and are convinced that you are the Holy One of God." Jesus answered them, "Did I not choose you twelve? Yet is not one of you a devil?" He was referring to Judas, son of Simon the Iscariot; it was he who would betray him, one of the Twelve.

— Jn 6:66-71

HOW CAN YOU STILL BE CATHOLIC?

50 Answers to a Good Question

Christopher Sparks

Available from:
Marian Helpers Center
Stockbridge, MA 01263

Prayerline: 1-800-804-3823
Orderline: 1-800-462-7426

Websites: thedivinemercy.org
marian.org

Imprimi Potest:
Very Rev. Kazimierz Chwalek, MIC
Provincial Superior
The Blessed Virgin Mary, Mother of Mercy Province
May 1, 2017

Nihil Obstat:
Dr. Robert A. Stackpole, STD
Censor Deputatus
May 1, 2017

ISBN: 978-1-59614-399-9

Cover image: A.J.J. Meyer Photography

Cover and page design: Curtis Bohner

Printed in the United States of America

MARIAN PRESS
STOCKBRIDGE   MA 01263

Dedication

To Jesus, the Divine Mercy; Mary, the Mother of God; and St. Joseph, Universal Patron of the Church, who have always had my family in their care. And to my family — wherever you are, I am home. Through you, I have the faith I profess on these pages, and a life worth living. Thank you. I love you.

Contents

Introduction
"How can you still be Catholic when ... ?"

Catholics get asked that question a lot. Sometimes, we may even ask ourselves the same question. In the age of information overload and a thoroughgoing postmodern cynicism about any and all institutions, Catholics face an overwhelming tide of opinion and commentary about our faith and our Church. Often, the attention is negative. We hear jokes about priests and altar boys, get dismissed because of Pius XII and the Church's record during World War II, or face puzzlement from people who just don't understand how we can believe "that stuff." (And "that stuff" is a moving target, depending on whatever element of the Church's teaching or practice is found incomprehensible today).

It happens a lot. And, to borrow an image from Venerable Fulton Sheen, we often face challengers who behave like Pontius Pilate. Pilate asked Christ, "What is truth?" and didn't stay to hear an answer. All too often, the world throws down the gauntlet to Catholics and walks away without giving us a chance to respond. But I have a secret to share with you: There are answers, often very good answers, to each and every question asked in this book, and to every question the Church will ever be confronted with.

There are good answers for a very simple reason: Catholicism is true.

Not because I say so, or because the pope or the bishops or the cardinals say so, but because the Catholic faith tells the

11

truth about the nature of reality. Many brilliant minds and terrible sinners, many bright lights and wounded souls have challenged the Church and come to the dreadful, wonderful realization that the Church matters and cannot be simply laughed out of the room or dismissed; that the Church is the repository of saving truth; that she is, in fact, the Mystical Body of Christ, the salt of the earth, the light to the nations, a city set on a hill, a people set apart. This is true, all of it — and since it is true, no matter what challenges may come, no matter how awfully we Catholics may live the faith (for the faith is always better than we are), the Church will abide, will endure, until the end of all things.

So take heart, all you Catholics looking for answers to the questions you have been asked, or are being asked. Be curious, all you anti-Catholics or non-Catholics who have picked up this book seeking to find out if the Church has any answers to the seemingly unanswerable questions and challenges posed to her by modern scholarship, skepticism, and lifestyles. Take, and read; and then keep going, for here are some answers — very brief answers, to be sure, but it's a good start. For more information on any of the topics I've touched on, see Appendix A: Recommended Reading at the end of the book. It includes titles I've read, as well as official Church documents, works I've heard recommended, and books by authors I trust.

Fair warning — I am not a saint. I do not write these things because I am "good enough" or smart enough or gifted enough, no matter what my pride may tell me. I write these things because I do love Christ and His Church, however poorly, however imperfectly. I do believe the Catholic faith to be true, and the Church to be the Mystical Body of Christ. I believe, and so I also believe I am obliged to share with others this truth I have discovered. What sort of human being would I be if I thought I had found the font of faith, hope, and love, the repository of the Real Presence of Jesus Christ, true God and true man, and I failed to tell anyone else about it? As the famous magician and atheist Penn Jillette has said, "How much do you have to hate people to believe that everlasting life is possible and not tell them that?"

Jesus is the Way, the Truth, and the Life. Our world is in such terrible agony. Here is the answer to our problems, and more — the meaning of life, infinite love, and endless delight along the Christian mystical path and in the world to come. This, then, is worth sharing, if anything is.

So these aren't the words of a saint. I am merely a lay Catholic with an interest in his subject matter, a gift for putting pen to paper and having something at least halfway coherent come out, and enough time to write to get this sort of project done. Here are some basic answers to questions I've gotten from friends, family, and complete strangers, answers informed by the writings of saints and scholars, popes and pundits, from the whole heritage of Catholicism. So let a poor sinner introduce you to the reasons for the faith that is in him. I hope you'll be surprised and helped by what you find.

Pray for me — I'll pray for you.

Question 1:

How can you still be Catholic when the Church overall has so much dirty laundry?

Yes, let's go ahead and address the big picture: How can a person be Catholic when the Church has a lot of nasty moments in her history? It's true — we've had popes who've broken their vows of celibacy; the child abuse scandal; priests who were more focused on money and power than on God; financial scandals; and all manner of sins committed by Catholics. Yes, there's a lot of dirt. In fact, one could almost say that reading Church history is like reading the Old Testament.

How so? Well, like the Old Testament, the Church's history seems populated by as many sinners as saints. The people of Israel had a very checkered past of fidelity and infidelity, greatness and foulness, of beauty and strength as well as cowardice and calumny. God's chosen people didn't always choose God. Does that, in some sense, invalidate God's promises to them, or His choice? Not at all. Our God is a mighty savior, after all (see Zeph 3:17). The covenants made with the patriarchs and kings rested on God's fidelity, not just man's, and so they stand even to the present day. The Jews are and always will be the people of God, not because of their heroic sanctity, although they've certainly had heroes and men and women of great holiness. They will always be the people of God because of God's sanctity. God is faithful and true.

Similarly, a lot of people are still Catholic because we believe the Catholic Church to be God's Church, the Church Jesus founded on a rock (see Mt 16:16-19; Mk 3:16; Jn 1:42), just like a wise man building his house (see Mt 7:24-25). We believe this to be the household of God, the Church of God, which is the pillar and foundation of truth (see 1 Tim 3:15). We remain in the Church, not because every leader and member of the Church has always been perfect, but because we believe God's promise — that the gates of hell will not prevail against His Church (see Mt 16:18).

Does this mean it doesn't matter if Catholics are sinful, if some of our leaders have been corrupt, if we fail to live up to the faith? No! It *does* matter. It matters a lot. We are all called to be saints. But sinful Christians shouldn't come as a surprise. The faith is better than we are. God is better than we are. Yes, some people become great saints. They walk the entire Christian spiritual path and achieve heights of perfection that most of us only dream of.[1] But for the most part, Catholics prove the common saying, "The Church is not a hotel for saints, but a hospital for sinners," a saying that Pope Francis has updated and repeated often, calling the Church a "field hospital" for sinners. So don't be surprised when Catholics, even our leaders, sin! We're all potential saints in progress, not perfect now. We preach a Gospel that we still haven't lived up to. Why do we preach it? Not because we're equal to it, but because we believe it to be true.

And yet we *are* equal to it. Indeed, the Gospel is meant for the sick, for the sinner, for the broken, the fallen. The Gospel is the Good News of God's salvation for sinners, for fallen humanity. Jesus comes to seek the sheep that have gone astray. Is it any surprise that His sheep would stray again and again and again? Holiness takes time, a lot of help from God, and persistence in repentance. We have to keep saying, "I'm sorry" and "I love you" to God. He keeps saying, "I love you" to us.

We can still be Catholic, still be in a Church with a lot of dirty laundry, because a lot of that dirty laundry is our own. We are the sinners that the Church has been waiting for, that

Christ has gone looking for. We are the sinners whose sins give rise to scandal. How can we reject the Church because of the sins of our brothers and sisters? Our brethren have just as much cause to reject the Church because of our sins. Pope Emeritus Benedict XVI once said that part of the reason we are to love our neighbors is because they have to put up with us.

All Catholics are challenged to be saints. The Second Vatican Council made that abundantly clear.[2] That's the standard the Church holds us to: holiness. Have many Catholics fallen short in the past? Yes. Should this drive me away? No — I am not always so holy myself. Who am I to run from a Church full of sinners? That's exactly the sort of Church where I belong. And when did Christ ever promise a perfectly pure Church here on earth? Never.

Instead, He said, "Again, the kingdom of heaven is like a net thrown into the sea, which collects fish of every kind" (Mt 13:47), both bad and good. It is by letting ourselves be caught by the fishers of men, by Christ through His Church, that we are offered the way to holiness and eternal life.

Let's make it even clearer that corruption and sin in the Church should come as no surprise. Consider what happened to Jesus Himself. Jesus was betrayed by Judas, one of the Twelve Apostles — one of the men who were chosen to be the patriarchs of the new Israel, the Church[3] — and abandoned by the rest of His followers when He was seized. Only John and Christ's female disciples stayed close throughout Jesus' Passion. Jesus was convicted of blasphemy by the chief priest and the Sanhedrin, all men sworn to His service, since He is the God of Israel. Jesus was convicted by the guardians of law and order, the Romans, even though Pontius Pilate said that he could find no fault in this man. Jesus was methodically betrayed by many of the guardians of justice and the servants of sanctity of His time. These were the actions of the leaders of the Jewish religion and the leaders of the nascent Church of Jesus Christ when Jesus Christ was walking the earth. Why would we be surprised when leaders and members of the Church behave badly today?

Does this mean we are supposed to give up on getting better? Does this mean we should just accept our sinfulness? No. Jesus also said, "Be perfect, just as your heavenly Father is perfect" (Mt 5:48). How can this happen? Because Jesus brought the cure: Himself. He is the Way, the Truth, and the Life, and is present down through the ages in His Mystical Body: the Church.[4] We Christians are the Body of Christ.

And this has been proven, time and again, when saints have risen up from the ranks of the sinners in the Church. Saint Francis of Assisi was once a playboy. Saint Augustine had a mistress for many years before his mother's prayers and the preaching of St. Ambrose of Milan converted him. Saint Ignatius was a vain Spanish courtier and soldier until a cannonball broke both his legs, forcing him into bed long enough for reading and meditation to change his life. The list goes on and on of lives transformed by the grace available through the Church. As Oscar Wilde wrote, "[E]very saint has a past and every sinner has a future."[5]

Jesus said, "Those who are well do not need a physician, but the sick do. I did not come to call the righteous but sinners" (Mk 2:17). If the Church were not a hospital for sinners, I should have no hope — I need the cure just as much as every bad pope, bishop, or priest, every failed nun or religious brother.

There are many sinners in the Catholic Church, yes — we who are within the Church are sinners in treatment, sent forth to bring more sinners in. Welcome to the Catholic Church — there are sinners in every pew, and the Savior waits in the tabernacle.

Question 2:
How can you still be Catholic when they arrogantly think they are the one true religion?

That claim is arrogant only if it is not true.

Think about it. If some random guy on the street says, "I am the president of the United States," we wait for him to tell the rest of the joke. If he doesn't, we know something is wrong — unless we suddenly notice the Secret Service agents everywhere, the long black cars, the whole panoply of the presidency surrounding him. Then we realize that, strange as his claim seemed, we're talking to the president of the United States.

Similarly, Catholicism's claims are arrogant, impossible, insane, and demonic if they are not true. But if they are true — if God exists, is eternal love, and became incarnate to breathe divine life into us after we'd bent the created order by a primordial Fall — then there's no help for it. Sane, rational people, confronted with this reality through reason and evidence, must accept the way the world really is, whatever way that may be.

See, we *know* that the world has to be working under some particular set of rules, put in place by some particular Creator (even if that "Creator" is blind chance, or the fluctuation of a vacuum, or rules arising from the nature of things). There must be some claim about the universe that can be made and is true. For the sake of argument, that set of rules might be, "There are no rules." That set of rules might be the laws of Hinduism or Islam or the rules might be something that no religion has yet hit upon — but the world operates in some particular way. (I obviously believe the world works as depicted in Catholicism.) Some claims about the working of the world are therefore true, and others are not.

As Aristotle said, "To say of what is that it is not, or of what is not that it is, is false, while to say of what is that it is, and of what is not that it is not, is true."[6] Some claims about the nature and purpose of all things must be true, and anything that contradicts those claims will be false. Why? Because the world is a certain way. Any statements that go against this certain way are untrue, are statements that do not conform to reality. So the question is not, "How can a religion be so arrogant as to claim to be the one true religion?" The question is, "Who has got it right, if anyone?"

I know that this goes against every bone in most modern bodies. If someone is right, that means other people are wrong, and that's judgmental, premodern, and intolerant — right? And with so many religions in this world to which people are so strongly attached, you'll have to tell a lot of people that their deeply held beliefs are wrong.

The thing is, many people have no problem telling others that their deeply held beliefs are wrong. I've been told over and over again, "Catholicism is true for you, and I'm happy for you. But (*insert religion/philosophical position here*) is true for me." If Catholicism is only "true for me," then I'm outta here. As St. Paul said:

> If there is no resurrection of the dead, then neither has Christ been raised. And if Christ has not been raised, then empty [too] is our preaching; empty, too, your faith. Then we are also false witnesses to God, because we testified against God that he raised Christ, whom he did not raise if in fact the dead are not raised. For if the dead are not raised, neither has Christ been raised, and if Christ has not

been raised, your faith is vain; you are still in your sins. Then those who have fallen asleep in Christ have perished. If for this life only we have hoped in Christ, we are the most pitiable people of all (1 Cor 15:13-19).

So Christianity is a worthwhile faith only if its claims about reality are more than subjective statements of faith. Christianity is worth anyone's time only if those claims are true for all people, believers and nonbelievers, because Jesus was real, was really the Son of God, really did what the Gospels say, and truly saved us from our sins. Christianity is worthless if it is only "true for me."

Flannery O'Connor, the great southern writer, was once at a dinner party. Toward the end of the party, the subject of the Eucharist came up. One woman, a Mrs. Broadwater, said she thought of it as a symbol. O'Connor later recorded her own response in a letter: "I then said, in a very shaky voice, Well, if it's a symbol, to hell with it." She wrote that this was all the defense she could muster at the time. "It is the center of existence for me; all the rest of life is expendable."[7] Why? Because the Eucharist really is the Body and Blood, Soul and Divinity of Jesus Christ, present under the appearances of bread and wine.

That is what is at stake here — the center of existence. The meaning of life, the universe, and everything. Claims about the meaning of all things cannot simply be "true for me." If they are only "true for me," then they are false and I am deluding myself. Further, Jesus did not leave us the easy way out of saying, "I'm the Son of God if you believe it. I am whatever you believe me to be, whatever feels right for you." No, Jesus is not a Rorschach blot upon whom we can project whatever we wish. His claims are very direct, very specific, summed up when He says, "I am the way and the truth and the life. No one comes to the Father except through me. If you know me, then you will also know my Father. From now on you do know him and have seen him" (Jn 14:6-7). If the Church is right about the Eucharist, about Jesus, about the human person, about the nature of reality, and about our origins and destiny, then that is dramatic. That is powerful. That is, above all else, hopeful. We come from absolute, eternal life and love, and we are intended to return to absolute, eternal life and love.

So we return to the question. "How can you be Catholic when they [Catholics] arrogantly think they are the one true religion?" The Catholic Church does not arrogantly think Christianity is the one, true religion — she *inevitably* thinks Christianity is the true religion. Further, the Church is very clear that she recognizes true elements in other religions. She doesn't simply dismiss everything every other religion has to say. As the Second Vatican Council says in its decree on non-Christian religions:

> The Catholic Church rejects nothing that is true and holy in these religions. She regards with sincere reverence those ways of conduct and of life, those precepts and teachings which, though differing in many aspects from the ones she holds and sets forth, nonetheless often reflect a ray of that Truth which enlightens all men. Indeed, she proclaims, and ever must proclaim Christ "the way, the truth, and the life" (John 14:6), in whom men may find the fullness of religious life, in whom God has reconciled all things to Himself.[8]

The question, though, is always one of truth. We honor the truth taught by the other religions — not something "true for me," but truths that are universally applicable, like the litany of moral laws listed as the *tao* by C.S. Lewis in *The Abolition of Man*.[9] No matter who teaches it, we say yes to truth, knowing that all truth points back to God, the Source of all truth. Truth is one. Anyone who follows the truth all the way back will discover that Jesus is Lord, a doctrine we preach with unalterable clarity.[10] There is no other name by which humans are saved (see Acts 4:8-12), though non-Christians may find their

way home to Heaven, as did the Old Testament saints and the
Holy Innocents slaughtered by Herod's forces in pursuit of
the Christ Child.[11]

How can a non-Christian enter the Kingdom of Heaven if
Jesus Christ and His Church is the only way in? Think of it this
way: You can approach a walled city with a single gate from any
direction. Of course, it's easiest if you follow the main road, a
carefully paved, well-laid-out, well-marked highway; but you
can reach the city even if you come stumbling through a forest,
trek across a desert, slog through swamp and muck, or follow
faint trails and occasionally accurate signs, and have to avoid
traps with every other step. But there's only one way into the
city, through the one gate, so anyone who is to enter must pass
through that single gate.

Jesus is the Way, the Truth, and the Life, and apart from
Him, there is no entry into the Kingdom of Heaven — but
some who are publicly Christian on earth are far from Jesus,
and some who do not know His name know Him very well,
love Him deeply, and serve Him (see Mt 25:31-46), for they
serve Truth, Goodness, Beauty, Being, and Love — that is,
they know, love, and serve God (see Acts 17:22-23; see also
Mt 22:1-14; Rm 2:5-8). "Religion that is pure and undefiled
before God and the Father is this: to care for orphans and
widows in their affliction and to keep oneself unstained by the
world" (Jas 1:27). Some who think they are on the highway
to Heaven are instead passing swiftly to hell, and some who do
not know of the highway to Heaven will one day come face-
to-face with the one Gate, with Jesus Christ, who will welcome
them into the banquet.

Question 3:
How can you still be Catholic when the Crusades happened?

The short answer to the question is that, contrary to popular belief, the Crusades began as defensive wars responding to centuries of invasion by Islamic jihadis and to oppression of the native Christian populations throughout the Middle East and into Europe. So the Crusades make a lot of sense to me.

Also, I like the chivalric ideal; I like the goal of the strong protecting the weak, of the noble, holy knights doing battle for those most in need of aid. I like the papal project of taking men who might otherwise simply put themselves in the service of whatever local king might be willing to pay for bodies to attempt to assert himself against his neighbor, and inspiring them instead to risk everything in the name of protecting the holy sites of the birthplace of Christianity, in the service of Christ and His Vicar on earth, defending those who would practice Christianity against those who would prevent them.

Did we always live up to the ideal? No. But I think it a good ideal, nonetheless. The faith was, is, and will almost always be better than we are. The institutions spawned by that faith, including chivalric knighthood and the notion of a Crusade, are often meant to be far better than our sins and our folly allow them to be — though when saints arise, all good is possible.

But I know that all this will seem simply incredible to many people today. So back up with me here, and let's think through the question carefully.

This question is like asking a person, "How can you still be an American when America's wars happened?" An American will usually argue back, "Now wait a minute. Though there have been unjust actions by the United States in the past, it's certainly not true that every single American war or military action has been radically unjust or oppressive. Fighting Hitler was a just cause, for instance. Whether or not everything done in the course of World War II or the other wars in America's past was just does not negate the fact that American history is far from simply evil. It's true that, as General Sherman said, 'war is hell.' The less war the better. But there is such a thing as a just war."

The Church can say much the same of the Crusades. The Crusades, for many people, are synonymous with imperialism and unjust aggression. But to view them narrowly as a great stain on the history of the Church overlooks why the First Crusade was called to begin with.

According to the records of his address, Pope Urban II called the First Crusade in response to four main consider-ations: (1) to rectify disorder and bring about reform in the Western Church; (2) for the salvation of souls; (3) to bring aid to the Eastern Christians (both Byzantine and those in and around Jerusalem); and (4) to secure Jerusalem and the Holy Land against desecration.[12] He wanted to help end the culture of violence prevalent in Western Europe during that period, when the petty nobility waged seemingly ceaseless vendettas against each other.[13]

He was able to rally an army because the call to reclaim the Holy Land resonated with those who gathered to hear him speak. That crowd and the army that was raised did not simply arise in a vacuum. Both responded to Urban II because what he said resonated with Europe's experience of Islam in the first Christian millennium.

So, what had been Europe's experience of Islam before the First Crusade? To put it very bluntly: It was centuries of violent jihad and invasion that then prompted centuries of Crusades. Andrew Bostom in *The Legacy of Jihad* gives a sense of the extent of the centuries-long war, occurring across the length and breadth of Europe as well as the historically pagan, Jewish, and Christian lands of North Africa and the Middle East, between the forces of the Islamic caliphs and the indigenous populations. The Eastern Roman Empire, with its capital at Byzantium or Constantinople, was at war with one Islamic group or another nearly continuously from the seventh century on, ultimately falling in the 1400s. Constantinople was renamed Istanbul. Spain was originally a Christian land before the invasions from the south in the 700s, a time when Rome itself was assaulted. For a period of a few years, one of the popes, John VIII, essentially paid protection money to prevent Rome from being assailed again. The Mediterranean was not safe for centuries, owing to Islamic piracy and its seasonal raids on European cities and ships.[14] The Spanish were probably such bloody and brutal conquistadors in the New World because they had become a people of blood and iron after a seven- or eight-century war of Reconquest (the *Reconquista*), fighting to regain their lands from the Islamic invader. This doesn't justify Spanish imperial brutality — not at all. But perhaps the Spanish experience of invasion and Reconquest explains it.

The First Crusade was called because Byzantium sent for aid, a few decades after having suffered a bloody civil war, precipitated when one of its emperors was taken captive at the Battle of Mantzikert. The First Crusade was also called because indigenous Christians had fled the Holy Land (as the Copts and other Christians are doing now in the face of persecution).[15] When they reached Christian lands, they told their coreligionists of the treatment they had received at the hands of Islamic rulers, once invaders and now permanent occupiers of many regions.

Now, Christians *must* take responsibility for atrocities committed and war waged in the name of Christianity, and surely troops fighting under the sign of the Cross committed atrocities in the course of the Crusades — including the sack of Byzantium and, at times, ill-treatment of Jewish communities. Spanish Catholics *must* acknowledge the anti-Semitism in their history, the Spanish Empire's prosecution of global war after 1492, and whatever other real failings of the Spanish hierarchy and faithful can be accurately identified. The Catholic Church is far from pretending that its members haven't committed evil acts in the name of the faith. In the Jubilee Year 2000, for instance, Pope St. John Paul II and many of the leaders of the Church did public penance on behalf of the Church, asking for pardon for the sins of Christians past and present.[16] Yes, people should hold Catholics accountable. After all, we are called to be perfect as the Father in Heaven is perfect (see Mt 5:48). People are doing us a favor when they make plain our failings. But do not make the mistake of assuming the Crusades were a simply imperialistic venture, unprompted by invasion, set in motion by greed, and entirely rapacious. Indeed, as Rodney Stark explains in *God's Battalions*, the Crusader states in the Holy Land required a significant, regular flow of resources from Europe to sustain themselves, and those who set out on a Crusade were often the great lords of Europe and their heirs, not those with nothing to lose.

Further, when people speak of the Catholic Church and the Crusades, they often speak as though the popes directed every action, called for every slaughter, and ordered every massacre. To what extent did the Church lead the Crusades? The popes traditionally called them, but the day-to-day leadership of any Crusade was given to a commander in the field, often a ruler or general. In those days before instant communications between the battlefield and the high command, the popes did not usually have oversight of the fighting from moment to moment. So the Church could be criticized for calling the Crusades, but the actual management of them was not normally directly in papal hands.

Should the Church have never called for war? After all, Jesus taught that Christians should turn the other cheek to those who persecute them (see Mt 5:38-40). Can Christians go to war in good conscience? The answer, for many years, has been yes — under certain conditions. Catholic thinkers have been the main developers of "just war" theory.[17] War is not forbidden in Catholic moral teaching, though it is carefully regulated and restricted. For instance, Pope St. John Paul II argued against America's invasion of Iraq, drawing on the Church's traditional teaching about what constitutes a just war.[18] There have been leading Catholics who have taken a stance against any war whatsoever, including Pope Paul VI[19] and Cardinal Ottaviani (speaking in light of the destructiveness of modern warfare),[20] as well as Servant of God Dorothy Day and the Catholic Worker movement. Such a stance is legitimate. But the Church has not traditionally condemned *all* wars.

Question 4:
How can you still be Catholic when they just want you to suffer and feel guilty about everything?

I can still be Catholic, even though "they" call for us to feel guilty for our sins and ask us to take up our cross and follow Jesus, because "they" are just repeating Jesus' teachings faithfully. And then after teaching a hard morality aimed at perfection, in the Sacrament of Reconciliation the Church says through the priest, "I absolve you from your sins in the name of the Father, and of the Son, and of the Holy Spirit." The Catholic Church offers us hospitals, scientific research, and works of charity as means of alleviating human suffering, as well.[21] These are rather odd actions from the Church if she truly wants her followers and the rest of the world to just suffer. Indeed, the works of mercy are all about feeling compassion for the suffering of other people and going forth to do something to alleviate that suffering. Among the works of mercy is forgiveness extended to others. Surely, if the Church simply wanted people to feel guilty, there wouldn't be such an emphasis on forgiving other people as God forgives us!

At the same time, Jesus taught extensively about sin. He was given His name (Jesus, from the Hebrew *Yeshua*, meaning "Yahweh saves," as the NABRE explains) because He would save people from their sins (see Mt 1:21). He came to save the lost (see Lk 19:10), not the people who were "doing just fine, thank you very much."

The Pharisees and their scribes complained to his disciples, saying, "Why do you eat and drink with tax collectors and sinners?" Jesus said to them in reply, "Those who are healthy do not need a physician, but the sick do. I have not come to call the righteous to repentance but sinners" (Lk 5:30-32; see also Mk 2:17).

Jesus showed that He had the power to forgive the sins of other people when He healed the paralytic man, saying, "Which is easier, to say to the paralytic, 'Your sins are forgiven,' or to say, 'Rise, pick up your mat and walk'?" (Mk 2:5-10). That power was passed on in the upper room after the Resurrection.

[Jesus] said to them again, "Peace be with you. As the Father has sent me, so I send you." And when he had said this, he breathed on them and said to them, "Receive the holy Spirit. Whose sins you forgive are forgiven them, and whose sins you retain are retained" (Jn 20:21-23).

Further, the Baptism which Jesus brought is for the forgiveness of sins.

Peter [said] to them, "Repent and be baptized, every one of you, in the name of Jesus Christ for the forgiveness of your sins; and you will receive the gift of the holy Spirit" (Acts 2:38).

And there is much more where that came from. The New Testament is about nothing if not the sinfulness of humanity and God's saving mission to redeem us all from our sins. So yes, we are supposed to feel guilty about our sins. Why? Because the *feeling* of guilt is supposed to correspond to *real* guilt. Feeling guilty is being honest with myself, recognizing my sin, but we are not supposed to get trapped by our guilt. We are supposed to accept the forgiveness extended by Jesus and cooperate with His grace to become the sons and daughters of God we were meant to be. Look at the New Testament and see how many times it emphasizes that Jesus came to forgive our sins!

As Archbishop Fulton Sheen explained at great length in his little masterpiece *Peace of Soul*, true peace is not obtained by denying sin or refusing to feel guilt. Peace comes when we recognize that we have done wrong, confess our sins, and receive forgiveness from someone empowered to forgive us. We return to a right relationship with God, our neighbor, ourselves, and the world. To feel a healthy sense of guilt is not to be morbid about one's own wretchedness, but to recognize the true state of one's soul. All the saints were quite clear about what wretched sinners they were, but they were also clear that God loved them infinitely, absolutely, and that He desired all to be saved. They knew that they had fallen short of the glory of God, and that they were infinitely valuable, beloved children of a merciful Father who called them home to Heaven.

God *wants* us to experience eternal bliss. God *wants* us to go to Heaven. That's the entire point of Jesus' Incarnation.

Now, people really can go to hell for all eternity. God is perfectly just and takes our free will more seriously than we do. But God doesn't want us to go there. Jesus came to save us from hell, not send us to it. "For God did not send his Son into the world to condemn the world, but that the world might be saved through him" (Jn 3:17).

So Jesus teaches that we have sinned, He came to bring salvation, and we are meant for Heaven. Good. What's all this about suffering? Again, it's what Jesus said.

> Then he said to all, "If anyone wishes to come after me, he must deny himself and take up his cross daily and follow me. For whoever wishes to save his life will lose it, but whoever loses his life for my sake will save it" (Lk 9:23-24).

We are called, not just to suffer in union with Jesus, but to die in union with Jesus. We are called to lose our life for Jesus' sake. That is a very hard teaching. What makes it worth it? Why do we even feel the need to listen to someone who asks us to die for Him?

His Resurrection. If Jesus truly rose from the dead, then we who are alive in Him will never die — that is, never pass out of communion with Him and other people. [22] We must follow Him, yes, even to physical death, but in the hope of the "resurrection of the dead and the life of the world to come." [23] In order to have a share in His Resurrection, we must accept a share in His Passion and Cross. In order to rise to everlasting life, we must pass through temporary suffering and death.

Why? Because it is in the suffering and death of Jesus on the Cross that the love of God is fully revealed — the radical, self-emptying love of the Son for the Father is shown in Jesus' absolute gift of self to the Father in atonement for the sins of the world. Love is revealed in sacrifice, in suffering. Love is revealed in death, in dying for a cause, for a person, for a nation, for a community. In J.R.R. Tolkien's *Lord of the Rings*, love for the Shire impels Sam and Frodo to go all the way to the heart of Mordor, to Mount Doom, to risk everything in order to overthrow evil and preserve what they love. Love moves God, the Three Persons of the Blessed Trinity, to act, to permit the created order to lay hands on the Son, to kill Him, to bury Him — and then the love of the Father and the Spirit raises the Son on the third day.

God's life, the only eternal life on offer, is unavoidably bound up with His love, and His love is absolute self-gift. We are invited into eternal life, which means we are called to share in the very life and love of God.

> His divine power has bestowed on us everything that makes for life and devotion, through the knowledge of him who called us by his own glory and power. Through these, he has bestowed on us the precious and very great promises, so that through them you

may come to share in the divine nature, after escaping from the corruption that is in the world because of evil desire (2 Pet 1:3-4).

So I think repentance is worth it, when the reward is God.

Question 5:

How can you still be Catholic
when they believe sex has
only one objective: to procreate?

I can still be Catholic because we believe that sex has its proper place only in marriage, and marriage has more than one objective. The Sacrament of Marriage aims at the good of the spouses, as well as the procreation and education of children (*Catechism of the Catholic Church*, 1601).

In other words, sex and marriage build families, and that is a very good thing. To build a family involves much more than simply having children. It also demands love between the spouses, kindness and affection, care and concern, daily acts of self-sacrificing love as well as gratefully receiving the gifts and self-sacrificing love of one's spouse.

To build a family demands lovers, really. The point of making love is to make lovers out of the man and woman, and then to make more people to love.

I can support that. I can believe a faith that teaches that building a family requires a husband and a wife who make love, and make a home, and make time for each other, and make time for their children. The family is built upon the marriage bond, says the Church, a permanent bond of giving and receiving selfless love, consummated by the sexual act. And that act speaks. Sex is body language, expressing total self-gift and total openness to the other. In order for the act to truly say,

"I give you everything I am and have, I welcome you entirely, and this sort of love is the meaning of life," it must be open to the possibility of children, whether or not each act of sex results in a new human life.

Now, immediately people will ask, "But what if you can't afford children right now? What if having more children would cause a hardship for the family that's already here?"

It is possible for people to be faithful Catholics, have a sexual life in the context of marriage that doesn't involve contraception, and still be able to space out births. Many people will immediately scoff and say, "Oh, the rhythm method." Nope — natural family planning, sometimes called organic family planning, is attracting more and more people to use it these days, for religious reasons as well as for health reasons or out of concern for the environmental impacts of artificial birth control.

And if practiced properly, it's as effective as artificial contraceptives. (See Question 8 for sources.)

Whether sex results in children or not, in procreation or not, then, the object of sex, according to the Church, is the formation of families. Yes, that grants sex huge meaning and significance — but hasn't sex always had those life-changing possibilities attached?

And families are at the very foundation of every society, training the adults in self-giving love now and preparing the children for lives of self-giving love ahead of them. In families, ideally, no one is left homeless or alone; all members have a place to which they can always return, where they will always be welcome, where they belong. And all of this is enabled and cemented by romantic love bringing together a man and a woman in marriage.

Note: This is true even in marriages where couples are infertile. Sex is the consummation of a couple's union, bringing them together in a one-flesh union, no matter whether or not children may result. Sex forms a family, even if the couple is naturally infertile and will never bear physical offspring. The two brought together in love are called on, as are all married couples, to be generous with their love, whether their generosity be directed toward adopted children, or their communities, or their extended families, or beyond.

Not all sex is necessarily procreative, but all sex is certainly meant to be creative, says the Church, to be open to life, in accord with the nature of the reproductive system, and to train people to become generous in love.

Question 6:

How can you still be Catholic when priests have abused little boys?

I can still be Catholic even after the sex abuse scandals because the faith condemns the crimes committed as severely as, if not more severely than, the rest of the world does. It is not normal for priests to abuse children. If abuse of children by the clergy were normal, there'd be no Catholics, because everyone would have fled the Church. The sexual abuse of children is not, was not, and never will be "normal."

How can I say this when "Catholic priest" and "pedophile" seem synonymous in so many minds these days? Simple. The numbers bear me out.

For instance, according to the John Jay College independent study commissioned by the United States Conference of Catholic Bishops (USCCB), "[t]he 'crisis' of sexual abuse of minors by Catholic priests is a historical problem. The count of incidents per year increased steadily from the mid-1960s through the late 1970s, then declined in the 1980s and continues to remain low."[24]

How low? Sociologist Philip Jenkins estimated that, judging from the scandals in the U.S., the highest respectable estimate of abusive clergy in the Catholic Church would be 5 percent, but the number is far more likely to be less than 2 percent.[25] Compare that with pedophilia in the general population, which has been estimated at around 4 percent.[26]

Further, a 2002 study of the general population found that child sexual abuse "constitutes approximately 10% of officially substantiated child maltreatment cases, numbering approximately 88,000 in 2000. Adjusted prevalence rates are 16.8% and 7.9% for adult women and men, respectively."[27]

The percentage of sexual predators in the priesthood is less than that in the general population.

And the sort of scandal that's come to light the past few decades is not the norm, either. While of course sexual sins including pedophilia have been present in the Church and broader society throughout history, reputable histories do not show a Church constantly plagued with the problem of priests abusing children. The John Jay study showed that the sex abuse crisis was a problem from a specific time period. What happened? "Social and cultural changes in the 1960s and 1970s manifested in increased levels of deviant behavior in the general society and also among priests of the Catholic Church in the United States."[28] In other words, the sexual revolution influenced the members of the Church, along with the rest of society.[29]

How could the sex abuse scandal occur? Because there were far too many bishops, priests, and religious superiors who were not obeying or not enforcing the law and teaching of the Church. George Weigel wrote about this aspect of the sex abuse crisis in his book *The Courage to Be Catholic*. In it, he identified the main source of the crisis as a failure of fidelity to the Catholic faith. In other words, Catholic teaching calls chastity good and lust bad; pedophilia a serious sin and incest forbidden; sex within marriage good and sex outside marriage bad; children a blessing; and human dignity of high concern. The Church forbids rape (see *CCC*, 2356). For centuries, canon law, the internal law that governs the Church, has been consistent in its condemnation of child abuse by clergy as a grave crime.[30]

Catholicism is not the source of these abusive actions. Nor is the priesthood, or priestly celibacy, despite what people often say. Indeed, by many accounts, most priests are quite happy in their vocation.[31] If celibacy were to blame, then there should be evidence that the rate of abuse by Catholic priests is a lot higher than that by teachers and other adults who have access to children but who, unlike priests, can get married. But no such evidence has surfaced.[32]

No — what happened was a combination of cultural changes in society[33] and in the Church, and mismanagement and sometimes outright dereliction of duty on the part of bishops and superiors, resulting in immense harm being done to far too many children. The Church has paid a heavy price for the sins of some of her priests, and will continue to pay that price — not just when it comes to credibility or finances, but most especially in souls. We are meant to be in the service of Jesus. We are meant to provide an open path to Christ, the source of the world's salvation and elevation into communion with God. We are not supposed to be the source of grievous harm.

A lot of Catholics are justly furious at the priests who committed these crimes. A lot of Catholics wouldn't mind seeing a lot more bishops losing their posts as a result of their failure to properly oversee their priests and to react promptly when scandals did break out. Even in times when pedophilia was seen by the psychiatric profession as treatable, the Church's teaching had not changed — so we are really without excuse for the grave harm that did occur. Our bishops and priests should have known better.

But the harm has been done. We can and must now take steps to try to make sure such a scandal doesn't happen again. The bishops are doing that, slowly but truly. The Catholic Church has taken, and is continuing to take, big steps to protect the children in her care at schools, parishes, and orphanages around the world — to make sure all other Catholic kids have the same safe experience I, and many other cradle Catholics, have had in the Church.[34] Examples include the implementation of the 2002 Dallas Charter for the Protection of Children and Young People by the U.S. bishops.[35] The charter has been imitated by the Church around the world, especially its zero-tolerance policy for sexual abuse. Under Pope Benedict

XVI, both as head of the Congregation for the Doctrine of the Faith and then as pope, the process of removing abusers from ministry and even from the priesthood sped up significantly.[36]

Some may say, "That's all well and good, but people have been irreparably hurt. How can the Church ever make up for it?" I'm not sure if we can, this side of death. God will be the ultimate judge, after all, of everything that's been done by His servants and His betrayers. He will be the ultimate source of healing for the victims and the ultimate source of accountability for the bishops and priests of the Church. I have faith in the justice and the mercy of the living God, and so I believe that both victims and predators will get precisely what they ought from a just and loving God.

This may sound like cold comfort. I grant that. But I believe this to be true, and so I am compelled to say it in response to the question. How am I Catholic after we've endured such a betrayal of Christ and the faith by so many? Because I believe that evil does not have the last word. God, who is utterly good and true, who is Love and Justice, Source of all being, will see justice done in the end and will have mercy on us. Because I believe that God's grace is more powerful than the hurts we experience and the crimes people have committed. Because I believe that the Church is more than the story of the sexual abuse crisis. The Church turns lead into gold by the alchemy of the Holy Spirit. She makes saints of sinners, washing us in the blood of the Lamb, offering the bread from Heaven and the wine of eternal life, sealing us with the fire of the Holy Spirit, and laying before our feet the Way, the Truth, and the Life (Jn 14:6). In this hospital, all are welcome, and all may be healed.

Sometimes in this hospital for sinners, the patients hurt each other — not just in huge ways like sexual abuse but, all too often, in small, petty ways. People can be cruel, or ignore the needs of their neighbors, or struggle for power rather than decide to serve. We are all ill here, after all. We're all walking a long road to health and holiness. Sometimes our illnesses are contagious and spread to others. Sometimes our illnesses are such that we don't notice the damage we are doing to those around us. But we are all ill here, being healed and transformed by grace — to leave the hospital because there are sick people there doesn't make sense.

Question 7:
How can you still be Catholic when homosexuality is clearly genetic?

Well, it's not *clearly* genetic, not yet. Identical twins aren't always both gay, for instance (though that's not dispositive). Further, if homosexuality were strictly genetic, one would expect it to disappear or at least become rarer with each generation, since men with male lovers and women with female lovers aren't going to pass the gene on to offspring in the ordinary course of things.[37] But really, all that's a side issue.

Put the question another way, though. "How can you still be Catholic if gay people are simply born that way?"

Granting the premise of the question: Quite simply, because Catholicism teaches me that gay people are beloved by God, just as all other human beings are loved by God. The fact that we are tempted toward a particular sin doesn't mean that God clearly does not love us, or that God condemns us. God died for us. He sent His only Son to rescue us all, to make sure that sin didn't necessarily mean hell, to give us hope and a way out of the valley of death.

God didn't come for the perfect and the pure — He came for the fallen human race. And so, because He did come, there have been perfect and pure people — the Blessed Virgin Mary; St. Joseph; St. John the Baptist. Because of God's grace, given through the Incarnation of His Son, Jesus Christ, we have hope, and a path open to us to reach Heaven.

I can be Catholic because the Church has room for all of us who are born with certain predispositions to forbidden things: to gluttony or lust or sloth or wrath. It's not as though all the people who aren't gay have all their ducks in a row; it's not as though straight people are perfectly pure and wholly healthy! The Church is full of folks, gay and straight, whose desires don't track with the commandments of God. By God's grace, we all also have a way back to the love of God and the fellowship of the Holy Spirit.

I can still be Catholic because the Church doesn't condemn gay people. To condemn an action as a sin is not the same as to condemn those who are tempted to that sin or who perform that sin as somehow less than human, as unworthy of human dignity, or to deny them the same personal worth as every other human being. We are, all of us, fallen, save the two great exceptions: Jesus and Mary. Everyone is tempted to something damnable, whether that be gossip, or gluttony, or wrath, or pride, or some other sin. The Church offers the same remedies to gay people that she does to every other human being under the sun: true teaching about faith and morals, and the medicine of Confession for when we fail to live up to the high standards of the Catholic faith and Catholic morals.

Bishop Robert Barron expressed this so well in his 2017 interview with David Rubin: it's not as though the Church simply washes her hands of those who don't live up to the moral teaching of the Bible and the Tradition. Not at all. We are called to sanctity by Mother Church, and we are also offered extreme mercy.[38] That call is for all of us, no matter our temptations, no matter our weakness, no matter our sins, our past, or our failings.

By God's grace, it is possible for us to live like saints, if we cooperate with that grace. This is not at all to say, "Pray and God will fix everything instantly." Prayer is not an infallible immediate escape from temptation — look at the dark nights experienced by the saints. They prayed, and yet because they were being purified, their prayers did not immediately, obviously bring light to their dark nights. Indeed, they were sometimes closest of all to God when the darkness seemed deepest. Prayer is a communion with God, a sharing in His life and love, not a magic spell or a silver bullet cure for what ails us. It is love, and life, and truth being shared between persons, not an on-off switch.

Because that's true, being Catholic doesn't mean we expect to instantly conquer all temptation. Yes, we are called to "rectification of the will," or repentance and a firm resolution never to sin again. But the Church knows that we need a great deal of help along the way. Part of God's grace, given through the Body of Christ, the Church, is the Sacrament of Confession. This indicates that the process of walking on the path toward obeying God perfectly, toward loving God with His own divine love, the Holy Spirit, will involve coming to God again and again when we fail. We are also given God Himself through the Eucharist, through the Word of God, through the fellowship of the Body of Christ, through the prayers of the saints and sinners with us in the Church, through God's providence working in our lives, through so many things. We are given much help to live a full life in obedience to God, if only we take advantage of His many gifts.

All of that is part of the Catholic faith, and so there's room in the Catholic Church for saints and sinners, for those with a perfectly trained will, rightly ordered desires, and an enlightened intellect, as well as those of us with a weakened will, disordered desires, and a darkened intellect. The Church holds weeds and wheat, good fish and bad, those who have been transformed by God's grace and those who are just beginning to walk with God. And part of the drama of life, as Chesterton once said, is that those who are good may yet fall, and those who are bad may yet become the greatest of saints.[39]

Catholicism has a remarkably balanced realism about it, you see. Many denominations within Protestant Christianity hold to the theology of "once saved, always saved," with something of an accompanying expectation that if you are truly a Christian, you will be living a perfect life now. It owes something to Calvin's version of the theological teaching of predestination, that those who are destined for Heaven by God's will from before they were born will live so as to make that destiny manifest. Similarly, those who are predestined for hell will live in ways that make their predestination clear.

That's not the Catholic understanding at all. Throughout our history, we have had deathbed converts, including Oscar Wilde, the famous writer who was dragged before a court because of his gay affair with Lord Alfred Douglas. Wilde's life was ... well, wild. He died a Catholic, having received the Sacraments, and so is probably either in Purgatory or in Heaven at this point. (This is to say, not that only publicly professed Catholics are in Heaven,[40] but merely that, given the teachings of my faith about the Sacraments, I believe Wilde is almost certainly on the road to Heaven, if he has not already arrived.)

I can still be Catholic because the Church has room for gay people. Gay people, like every other group of people on the face of the earth, are called to carry crosses (see Mt 16:24), to die to self in order to live in Christ (see Lk 9:23). Different people do this in different ways. But everyone is called to self-gift, to let the old man of sin be crucified with Christ, and to put on the new man in Christ (see Col 3:3-17). Everyone, all of us — we all have the universal call to holiness.[41] Do I always do this well? No. I am often a sinner. Thank God for Confession. Are Catholics often perfectly responsive to the grace and truth of God? No. All too often, we give scandal through our sins and failures. But the call is there, as are the grace and strength needed, and the forgiveness for when we fall.

Question 8:

How can you still be Catholic when the Church continues to forbid birth control?[42]

For a variety of reasons.

To begin with, not all forms of family planning are forbidden by the Church. It would be a mistake to assume that a ban on artificial contraceptives means Catholics have no say in how many children they have. Though many people disparage natural family planning, it works, according to the testimony of many who use it, and according to a growing number of scientific studies. A 2007 study found that the fertility awareness method (or the "sympto-thermal method") "is a highly effective family planning method, provided the appropriate guidelines are consistently adhered to." The women in the study who reliably used the method had an unplanned pregnancy rate of 0.6 per 100 women.[43] The Standard Days method, developed by researchers at Georgetown University Medical Center, "so effectively meets the needs of users that they continue to rely on it for years."[44]

Second, take a look at the predictions made by Paul VI in his 1968 encyclical *Humanae Vitae* (*On the Regulation of Birth*), in which he reiterates the Church's unchanging ban on the use of artificial contraceptives. A 2012 article in *Business Insider* pointed out that the Holy Father had identified four consequences of a civilization's accepting contraception as an ordinary means of controlling pregnancy:

- General lowering of moral standards
- Rise in infidelity and illegitimacy
- Reduction of women to objects used to satisfy men
- Government coercion in reproductive matters

The article concludes, "Does that sound familiar? Because it sure sounds like what's been happening for the past 40 years."[45]

And it doesn't sound good. Are these the direct consequences of the widespread use of contraception? Not necessarily. But can it be argued that easily available contraception made a huge difference? I think so. I doubt the sexual revolution could have taken place without the invention of the pill and other, new forms of contraception [46] Why would these consequences result from widely used contraception? Well, sex is an organic act. It involves the use of the reproductive systems of two individuals to form a biological unity. As has been noted by bioethicist Dr. Patrick Lee and many others, the reproductive systems of men are incomplete without the reproductive systems of women — there's only one known example of a virgin birth in humans, and that required divine intervention. In short, biologically speaking, a man and a woman must form a biological unity in order to reproduce, to achieve the end toward which the system is directed. Artificial forms of contraception disrupt the biological integrity of human intercourse.

And in that integrity we find the goals of marriage: "the good of the spouses and the procreation and education of offspring."[47] The good of the spouses — two human beings bound together by love and intimacy. Procreation — the intimacy that leads to further life. Education of offspring — the two parents, bound by the ties of love and fidelity, raise the child or children. Contraception breaks all this apart, as professor of moral theology Dr. Janet E. Smith has noted.[48]

So as contraception has disrupted the organic unity of marriage and sexuality, the consequences predicted by Pope Paul VI have become endemic in our modern society. Contraception makes it easier for people to have sex without consequences, helping to lower moral standards in an age in which what's good is "what seems good to me" and reducing the chances that adulterous sex will produce offspring. A man is having sex, not necessarily with the woman who will be the mother of his child, but only with the object of his attraction. And the government — well, the U.S. has a history of eugenic policies already.[49] China had their one-child policy for decades and is beginning to reap the fullness of all the associated problems,[50] and India famously had forced sterilization programs in the 1970s.[51] Why couldn't it happen again?

Does this mean that couples who are infertile are, in some way, in a lesser marriage? No — not all sex needs to be fertile sex, but all sex needs to be open to human life. Sex is also meant to be joyful, to be something in which a couple can delight, and an act that helps bring them together as lovers, partners, and friends. Not for nothing does the Christian mystical tradition see in lovers' embrace the foreshadowing of Heaven.[52] But sex is intrinsically, inherently aimed at procreation, as well, and that connection to procreation guides sexual morality. That is, we are to use our reproductive systems according to the end for which they are designed. We are to use our reproductive systems in a reproductive manner — even if we are not fertile at the time. It is perfectly permissible, according to the Church, for couples, respecting the natural cycles of fertility that women experience, to plan their families and space out the births of their children. Such natural family planning promotes chastity, self-control, communication between the spouses, and mutual respect and love as they act as good stewards of each other and their resources. It's certainly not without its burdens, but many of those who practice it insist it's not without its blessings, as well. See Appendix A: Recommended Reading for more.

Question 9:
How can you still be Catholic when they want you to have so many babies in a world that's already overcrowded?

First and foremost, the Church permits natural family planning (NFP), also increasingly called organic family planning. NFP involves methods of spacing births through tracking a couple's fertility — no artificial contraceptives or methods are required (see Question 8, page 46 for more). The Church demands, not unfettered fertility, but rather openness to human life and awareness that children are a gift, not a curse. Heck, a large chunk of the Church is composed of people bound to celibacy by vows — the Church is not demanding that every Catholic go forth and reproduce!

At the same time, the Church does teach that married couples are to be open to new human life. They are to welcome children as gifts from God.

That just makes sense to me on a gut level. Of course children are a gift! Look at the sadness felt by many infertile couples, or couples who have difficulty conceiving. It's a blow to them to be denied this particular gift. Look as well at the many large families who do experience new children as gifts. I always think of my mother's family when this comes up. My mom was the seventh of 11 children. If my grandparents had not been open to life — if they had stopped at, say, anywhere from one to six children, my mother would never have been born, and then I wouldn't be here either. My grandparents loved their children, all of them, as evidenced by how heartbroken the whole family was when my grandfather died just before I entered the sixth grade, and when my grandmother died in 2015.

For them, children were a gift. And their children have been gifts to the rest of us, as well. My grandparents' children — my mom, aunts, and uncles — have been teachers, lawyers, a university professor, a state representative and senator, and much more, besides. Tell me: Which of their lives, families, and contributions should we all have done without in the name of preventing overpopulation?

Now, certainly we all have a responsibility to be good stewards of the natural world, of the environment and the resources that are given to the whole human race by God. All that is part of Catholic teaching, most recently expressed through Pope Francis' encyclical *Laudato Si'* (*On Care for Our Common Home*), which drew heavily on earlier teaching from Pope Benedict XVI and St. John Paul II, among other sources. Certainly, responsible stewardship involves a concern for ensuring we don't simply deplete natural resources without renewing them, and for seeking renewable resources to use instead of nonrenewable ones.

Much of that can be tended to through scientific innovation, through new and improved farming methods, through better systems of distribution of goods and services across the world to meet the needs of the human race.

But in order for that sort of innovation and implementation to happen, we will need workers. We will need labor, both skilled and unskilled, both highly trained and able to do the most basic of tasks. And when the population in a society contracts, there's a real shortage of labor. The elderly become a much greater proportion of the population, and the young, a much smaller.

Thus, nations such as Japan and Russia are facing crises as their populations contract. A number of communities across these countries are asking hard questions about where the next generation of workers will come from, and who will give birth to the next generation. Demographic decline has consequences for the existence of towns and villages, as well as the political integrity of regions within the countries or even the countries themselves.

Why is it, by the way, that when we look at the possible problem of overpopulation, our first thought is how to remove persons from the equation? Right there is a significant problem from the get-go, for persons are far more valuable than any given stockpile of resources. People before things, always. Why do we prioritize removing human potential before figuring out how best to maximize the potential of existing resources? Perhaps our successful attempts at population control to date have removed precisely the minds and hearts we need to solve these problems. Perhaps we have aborted or contracepted the inventor who would have made possible travel to other worlds, and thus solved the issue of where to put people. Or perhaps we have aborted or contracepted people who could have cured any number of debilitating illnesses, and thus enabled far more of the population to produce, to visibly contribute, for far longer. Or perhaps we have aborted or contracepted the persons necessary to figure out the best renewable fuel.

Getting rid of people is not a solution to this sort of problem — if, indeed, it is a problem.

Yes, there are any number of major environmental challenges facing the human race today as a result of pollution. Yes, we absolutely need to be better stewards of the earth, both individually and as a community. Yes, yes, and yes. But is the problem the sheer number of human beings making use of the world, or is it the way in which we make use of the world?

Question 10:

How can you still be Catholic when Mary is elevated above God?

That's easy — she's not. She's a very important person, a very important woman. In fact, she is the greatest of all creatures, and she is blessed among all women. But she is infinitely less than God. Why? God made all the created order *ex nihilo*, from nothing. All of creation depends on God to keep it in existence. If for a moment He should let go, we would all slip back into nothingness. If God didn't sustain Mary's existence, she would instantly pass away as though she had never been. She is utterly dependent upon God for everything she is and everything she has.[53]

And what does she have? She has the grace and privilege to be the *Theotokos*, the God-Bearing one. She is the Mother of Jesus Christ, and Jesus Christ is God incarnate, the Son of the Father in the flesh. All her extraordinary privileges, the graces that elevate her above all other women, come from her Son. All grace comes through Jesus Christ; Jesus Christ comes through Mary by the choice of God and her acceptance of His will. So all grace comes to us through Mary.

Does that make her Jesus' equal? Of course not. The creature can never attain absolute equality with the Creator. Again, Mary is completely dependent on God. Without Him, she would cease to be. But she was the true Mother of Jesus Christ, and Scripture tells us, "He went down with them and came to Nazareth, and was obedient to them; and his mother kept all these things in her heart" (Lk 2:51). Savor the weirdness in that sentence — He was obedient to them. Jesus was obedient — to whom? To Joseph and Mary. God almighty was obedient to a pair of humans. He honored them as a father and a mother.

Which means what? Which means this pair is extraordinary. These two human beings are righteous, because God is not about to obey someone telling Him to commit a mortal sin, or a venial sin, or any kind of sin. Jesus was obedient to Joseph and Mary, and "Jesus advanced [in] wisdom and age and favor before God and man" (Lk 2:52). Jesus, who was both fully man and fully God, grew up and became a wise and blessed human by obeying His parents.

So under these circumstances, we can say that God placed two humans over Himself. God chose to submit Himself to these two people. The Son chose to accept them as parents, the Father agreed that Joseph and Mary would be good icons of His own love to the Son, and the Holy Spirit overshadowed Mary so that she would bear the Son. And these humans raised Jesus right; He advanced in wisdom, age, and favor before God and man.

So Mary and Joseph are created beings, totally dependent upon God for their existence and every good thing they have. And yet they were also placed in a position of authority, of stewardship over the Second Person of the Blessed Trinity. They raised Jesus. They taught Him how to walk, how to talk, how to live in their society, how to obey the law, and so on. They taught Him. They taught God.

Joseph and Mary must have been extraordinary individuals, aided immensely by the grace of God, specially blessed and gifted for their extraordinary roles — parents to Jesus, the Son of God! — to which they were called by the messages of angels.

And she who is the Mother of Jesus, the Child "destined to rule all the nations with an iron rod" (Rev 12:5), has other "offspring, those who keep God's commandments and bear witness to Jesus" (Rev 12:17). Who are these other offspring? They are the people who profess Jesus and keep God's commandments. They are Christians.

The Mother of Jesus is the Mother of the members of the Body of Christ — the Mother of all Christians. And God requires us to "honor your father and your mother, that you may have a long life in the land which the LORD your God is giving you" (Ex 20:12). So we are required by God to honor our Mother in Christ, who is Mary. But here's the weird thing. Mary is the Mother of Jesus, who is God in the flesh, fully God and fully man. By God's own commandment, God must honor Mary.

And the woman of Revelation 12 is certainly highly honored — by the cosmos, in fact, for she is "clothed with the sun, with the moon under her feet, and on her head a crown of twelve stars " (Rev 12:1). God has adorned His Mother in the splendors of the created order in this vision given to John on Patmos. But note: She is dependent on God and God's gifts. Her exaltation comes from her love of God, her love of Jesus and of His heavenly Father.

And what are the characteristics of someone who loves Jesus? Jesus said, "Whoever has my commandments and observes them is the one who loves me. And whoever loves me will be loved by my Father, and I will love him and reveal myself to him" (Jn 14:21).

This passage tells us a lot! Clearly, someone who loves Jesus is someone who follows His commandments. Someone who loves Jesus is also loved by the Father. The Son loves those who love His Father, and so the Son will reveal Himself to those who love the Father by keeping the commandments of Jesus, who is the Word of God Incarnate.

In short: The extent of God's revelation of Himself to us depends upon our obedience out of love.

So what does that tell us about the one person in human history to become the Mother of the Son of God? The Mother of Jesus is she whom God loved, to whom He revealed Himself most fully, which means that Mary must have loved God, which means she must have kept God's commandments. She must have been deeply, totally obedient to God's commandments, totally loving God for such a complete revelation as this — indeed, wholly holy.[54] For Jesus is the complete revelation of God, the very presence of God. He said, "Whoever believes in me believes not only in me but also in the one who sent me, and whoever sees me sees the one who sent me" (Jn 12:44-45; see also Jn 5:19; 14:7-14). And the first human to receive this divine revelation was Mary, who becomes the Mother of Jesus.

"Most blessed are you among women, and blessed is the fruit of your womb. And how does this happen to me, that the mother of my Lord should come to me?" (Lk 1:42-43). Elizabeth was filled with the Holy Spirit and cried aloud a testimony to Mary's holiness, to the blessing that was upon her, that she was unique among all other women. Elizabeth recognized that here was the "mother of my Lord," the Mother of God — and that it was a singular honor and privilege that the Mother of God should come to her.

Mary replies, "My soul proclaims the greatness of the Lord; / my spirit rejoices in God my savior. / For he has looked upon his handmaid's lowliness; / behold, from now on will all ages call me blessed. / The Mighty One has done great things for me, / and holy is his name" (Lk 1:46-49). She is the singularly blessed woman, so blessed that "all ages," all generations, shall call her blessed — and that blessing comes from God. She is not exalted *above* God, but she is exalted *by* God. She is not honored *above* God, but she is honored *by* God. She is not loved *more* than God, but she is beloved *by* God. And so all generations shall call her blessed.

Question 11:
How can you still be Catholic
when there is no reason a woman
cannot be just as good a priest as a man?

If you assume there is no fundamental difference between a Catholic priest and any other minister of any other Christian denomination, then it makes sense that a male-only priesthood would seem ludicrous and antiquated. After all, women can preach. They can say the words and make the gestures for the liturgy. They can be pastoral and can care for the needs of their congregations. Heck, some women would certainly do all these things far better than many men! But the Catholic Church has never reduced the priesthood to something simply involving saying words, making gestures, and being present to the congregation.

First, the Church's reasoning on this issue is laid out in St. John Paul II's apostolic letter *Ordinatio Sacerdotalis (On Reserving Priestly Ordination to Men Alone)*. He concludes the document with the following:

> In order that all doubt may be removed regarding a matter of great importance, a matter which pertains to the Church's divine constitution itself, in virtue of my ministry of confirming the brethren (cf. Luke 22:32) I declare that the Church has no authority whatsoever to confer priestly ordination on women

and that this judgment is to be definitively held by all the Church's faithful.[55]

In brief, *the Church has no power to ordain women.* It's not a matter of choice on the part of the pope or bishops — it's not up to them. We cannot change the teaching. We cannot change the practice. We cannot touch this issue. It is, quite simply, impossible. Why? We can't do it because Jesus didn't authorize it.

The document lays out the unchanging witness of the Church down through the ages on this point, stemming from Christ's own choice of His apostles:

> [T]he Gospels and the Acts of the Apostles attest that this call was made in accordance with God's eternal plan; Christ chose those whom he willed (cf. Mk 3:13-14; Jn 6:70), and he did so in union with the Father, "through the Holy Spirit" (Acts 1:2), after having spent the night in prayer (cf. Lk 6:12). Therefore, in granting admission to the ministerial priesthood, the Church has always acknowledged as a perennial norm her Lord's way of acting in choosing the twelve men whom he made the foundation of his Church (cf. Rev 21:14). These men did not in fact receive only a function which could thereafter be exercised by any member of the Church; rather they were specifically and intimately associated in the mission of the Incarnate Word himself (cf. Mt 10:1, 7-8; 28:16-20; Mk 3:13-16; 16:14-15).[56]

The 12 men, called to be apostles, stand as the 12 patriarchs of the new Israel, the Church, the kingdom of the Son of David, following Jesus, the New Moses, as He leads them to the Promised Land of the Church.[57]

This also leads us to look at the precedent set in the Old Testament. At no point did the Jews ever have priestesses. Was this a mere cultural restriction? If it was, it certainly was an odd one, since the ancient Israelites were surrounded by people who did have priestesses. Look at the time of Jesus — the Romans had priestesses. And even surrounded by examples of priestly women, Jesus and the Jewish tradition both continued in handing on priestly orders solely to men. This association of the priesthood with masculinity, then, is something that continues from the Chosen People to the Catholic Church, as well as the Eastern Orthodox churches.

In the Sacraments of Marriage and Holy Orders, gender matters at a deep, fundamental level. In the same way that the Church could not perform a valid sacramental marriage for two men or two women, so the Church cannot ordain a woman as a priest.

What is it about masculinity that is so essential to priesthood?

Simply, in the Judeo-Christian tradition, there is an essential connection between priesthood and fatherhood — and fatherhood is inextricably tied to masculinity.

The renowned Catholic apologist Dr. Scott Hahn explains that, according to Scripture, there is an ancient connection between priesthood and fatherhood.[58] This connection is evident throughout the Old Testament, beginning with Adam and his unique call from God to tend and keep the Garden of Eden.[59] Adam is given a priestly/paternal role from the very beginning, standing as the first in a long line of biblical patriarchs whose roles as fathers of peoples included being the priests speaking to God on behalf of their people.[60] The connection between paternity and priesthood continued throughout the Old Testament[61] and was affirmed by Christ in the New.[62]

Priesthood, in the Scriptural understanding, is inextricably linked with paternity. How do we know that this teaching doesn't denigrate women? Very simply, as St. John Paul points out, because there is no evidence whatsoever that the Blessed Virgin Mary ever served as an ordained priestess.[63] She is understood by Catholicism to be the greatest of all created beings. Therefore, if any woman should have been qualified to be a priest, it would have been her. And yet she was not an ordained priestess.

Now, even after reading all this, I'm sure there are a lot of people saying, "But this is just wrong! Women are equal to men and can do anything a man can do!" This is true to a certain extent. Women are just as smart, just as capable, and just as fully citizens as men, no matter what passing cultural norms may try to say. Indeed, some of the Church's greatest and most influential saints are women! Look at St. Catherine of Siena, St. Thérèse of Lisieux, St. Faustina Kowalska, or Mother Teresa, for example. But women are not totally interchangeable with men. There are fundamental differences between the sexes. For instance, no man may be a mother, and no woman may be a father.

Is this meaningless "biologism"? Ask anyone who grew up in a household with a father and a mother in a stable, healthy, loving marriage: Were there no meaningful distinctions between their mother and father? Did it matter at all whether the parent at hand for certain situations was their father or their mother? I bet you their answer would be the same as mine: There are fundamental, essential differences between fathers and mothers.

And priesthood is a job for fathers. Not because *I* say so, but because Moses and Jesus said so by their choice of priests. But why? I can't speak definitively on this, but I suspect it has something to do with the reason why God chose to have His Son become incarnate as a man, and the reason why the Lord's Prayer is the Our Father, not the Our Mother. Many Christians today will argue that the choice to speak of God as Father in the Gospels indicates that Jesus wasn't free in the face of the dominant culture. He was a man of His time, and so He called God "Father." I find that totally unconvincing since I believe Jesus was God in the flesh, and God in the flesh doesn't particularly need to listen to the dominant culture to take cues on how He will speak of the Divine Persons. God in the flesh knows very well who exactly God is, and the Son will call the Father whatever the divine will pleases, thank you very much. And so Catholic priests are men, are fathers, who stand *in persona Christi capitis* (in the person of Christ the Head), and the Son is the face of the Father's mercy.[64] And, for some reason known to God, the face of the Father's mercy is a male face, now and into eternity.

Does this privilege men above women? I don't think so — if anything, it gives men an awful lot of responsibility to be as meek in carrying their crosses as Jesus, to serve their wives as self-sacrificingly as Jesus serves His Church, and to embody the Beatitudes for their family, friends, and enemies. Indeed, there's reason to believe that women are presented in Scripture as the crown of creation, the peak of the whole process. That interpretation is suggested by Eve's being the last of the creatures to be made (see Gen 2) and reinforced by the Catholic doctrine that the Blessed Virgin Mary, by the grace of God, is the greatest of all created beings, higher than the angels, second only to God, though infinitely less than God. The Blessed Virgin Mary is known to all of us who love her and ask for her prayers as a powerful intercessor, for she is the *gebirah*, the Queen Mother in the eternal kingdom of the Son of David.[65] And it's good to be the queen!

As St. John Paul II worked to make plain, women have a very high place in Catholicism properly understood and lived, one that offers them a wide scope within which to bring their gifts to bear. Am I suggesting that women are fully integrated into the life and offices of the Church to the full extent of their capabilities? In my opinion, no, not yet. I think there's a lot of room for women working as theologians and philosophers and canon lawyers throughout the institutional life of the Church; lots of room on the USCCB's advisory boards and in other positions; lots of room on Vatican committees, in dicasteries (the different "departments" in the Vatican curia working for the pope), and so forth.

I hope also to see a renewal of the religious orders of women, especially the reemergence of great convents and abbeys with mother superiors and abbesses who are responsible for the spiritual health and well-being of as many people as some bishops. I think there needs to be the creation of many more lay movements where men and women labor side by side in the works of mercy, for the New Evangelization, and for the coming of the life and love of God into the hearts and minds of people the world over. I think that women have only begun their labors, as have many men, and that we all need to pour ourselves into the hands of Jesus and Mary to love the world back into life, for so much is burning and dying through all of our sins.

Question 12:

How can you still be Catholic when Christ says to take care of the poor and yet the pope lives in a mansion?

I can still be Catholic when the Holy Father lives in the Vatican because, most basically, the Church is larger than the Vatican and the Holy Father. Yes, the Holy Father is the head of the Church on earth, the Vicar of Christ, the delegate of the Second Person of the Blessed Trinity. But he is not the only member of the Church, or even the most important member of the Church (that honor would go to Christ, then to the Blessed Virgin Mary).

And the Church (including the Holy Father) does take care of the poor. The list of Catholic charities across the world can seem endless (to name just a few: Catholic Relief Services, Caritas Internationalis, the Knights of Malta, Catholic Charities USA, the St. Vincent de Paul Society, the Jesuit Refugee Service, the papal almoner's office), and more spring up all the time. There are also countless consecrated religious serving those in need in a variety of capacities, performing the works of mercy, and doing the will of the Lord (think of Mother Teresa's Missionaries of Charity, to name just one).

Now, does the Holy Father need the Vatican in order to exercise his ministry? No, it's not indispensable. The Vatican matters because it houses the Successor to St. Peter and the exercise of his ministry. There are historical, architectural, and artistic reasons to value the Vatican, as well, but most of those emerge because of its connection to the papacy.

Which brings us to another reason why I'm Catholic when the Holy Father is housed and works at the Vatican: He's got to live and work somewhere.

And where he is, there will be a lot of other people. He's the head of the Universal Church, a Church that needs to keep track of who has received which Sacrament, especially when it comes to Holy Orders and the ordination of bishops; a Church that will need people at the top to be able to handle requests for assistance, for support, for missionaries and priests and catechists and supplies. The Holy Father is the linchpin of the unity of the Catholic Church, which means he needs theologians and scholars to advise him, to help preserve the memory of past decisions, of conciliar teaching, of the origins of the Scriptures and Tradition, of the authentic ways to celebrate the Sacraments and say the prayers of the Church. He needs libraries and archives. He needs a great many things to perform his office, his ministry, and his role well.

And we've got the Vatican. So why not use it?

Indeed, in some ways, it may be cheaper to use the present arrangements than to try to put the whole apparatus in a modern office building or build anew. Further, the Vatican's being in Church hands means that the public has access to the treasures of the Vatican museum and St. Peter's Basilica. We, the general public, might not ever see these things again if they were all sold off into private hands. Which would you rather see happen: the poor being able to access these treasures of art and architecture, or the money from the sale of the art and architecture of the Vatican being used to feed people for a day?

No, the Vatican isn't the sort of thing that tends to cause me scandal. It's a family heirloom at this point, a nice memento of previous popes and fellow members of the family of God in the Church. It's beautiful and serves a purpose. It's a touchstone in a changing world, a sign of stability, permanency, and the power of God, on which the faith truly rests, rather than on the strength of humanity.

If the Vatican is ever destroyed or taken away, fine. One symbol of the endurance of the Church will be gone, but the faith will stand. It's always sad to lose nice things, but we'll be fine without it. We were fine without it for the first millennium or so of Christianity, after all. Our faith rests, not on a building, but on Jesus Christ.

If that's so, why do we build elaborate cathedrals and basilicas like St. Peter's in Rome?

For the same reason that Solomon's Temple was such a grandiose proposition (see 1 Kgs 6; 2 Chr 3) or the Magi brought gold, frankincense, and myrrh for an infant (see Mt 2): We're giving gifts to God. Beautiful architecture and art in our houses of worship are equivalent to the gift of the sinner who brought a jar of the most expensive ointment and anointed Christ (Lk 7:37-50; Jn 12:3-8). Jesus commended the action, even though the money could have been used for the poor instead of for such expensive perfume that now had all been used — and on His feet!

Why? God is worthy of our best work; of our time, talent, and treasure. Adorning the houses of worship is worthy and noble.

Yes, the Vatican is a palace, and not all worship space. But again — it's a family heirloom, and I value family heirlooms, even if they're big and don't fit modern tastes or sensibilities. And across the centuries, the Holy Fathers have put it to good use for the poor and displaced. For instance, under Pope Pius XII, the Vatican served as a safe refuge for Jews and those being hunted by the Nazis occupying Rome.[66] Under St. John Paul II, the Missionaries of Charity established a homeless shelter within Vatican City.[67] Under Pope Francis, showers and a barber chair have been set up for the homeless in St. Peter's Square.[68]

All this, and more. Not bad for a family heirloom!

Question 13:
How can you still be Catholic when you have to believe that everything the pope says and does is "infallible"?

Simple answer. We don't. How can I say that? Because infallibility applies in rather narrowly defined circumstances, certainly not to "everything the pope says and does."

Let's take this one step at a time. What does papal infallibility mean, according to the Church that claims it exists?

This teaching was defined by Vatican I (1869-1870) in the dogmatic constitution *Pastor Aeternus* (*The Eternal Shepherd*).[69] To summarize: The pope speaks infallibly under limited circumstances. He must be exercising his full apostolic authority — speaking *ex cathedra*, from the chair of Peter. (It's not a physical chair; the pope speaking *ex cathedra* is like the president exercising his office). The pope must be speaking on a matter of faith, morals, or both.

That's about it when it comes to the pope infallibly defining dogma. Where does this come from? Says Vatican I, from "the divine assistance promised to him in blessed Peter, that infallibility which the divine Redeemer willed his Church to enjoy in defining doctrine concerning faith or morals." It comes from the "power of the keys," the power to bind or loose in Heaven and on earth, given by Christ to Simon Peter, the first pope, and Peter's successors. Each has served in turn as the prime minister in the new and everlasting Davidic kingdom of Jesus, the Son of David, like the prime ministers of the Davidic kingdoms of old, who held the keys to everything in the kingdom, and who could bind or loose in the name of the king (see Is 22:20-24)

We get a first glimpse of papal infallibility when Peter answers Jesus' question, "Who do you say that I am?"

> Simon Peter said in reply, "You are the Messiah, the Son of the living God." Jesus said to him in reply, "Blessed are you, Simon son of Jonah. For flesh and blood has not revealed this to you, but my heavenly Father. And so I say to you, you are Peter, and upon this rock I will build my church, and the gates of the netherworld shall not prevail against it. I will give you the keys to the kingdom of heaven. Whatever you bind on earth shall be bound in heaven; and whatever you loose on earth shall be loosed in heaven" (Mt 16:16-19).

Peter answers truly, giving an answer that "flesh and blood has not revealed" to him, but which comes from God. He is the rock on which the Church is built, and hell shall not prevail over the Church. The Church is "the household of God, which is the church of the living God, the pillar and foundation of truth" (1 Tim 3:15). If the Church is the pillar and foundation of truth, and it rests on the foundation of Peter the Rock, then Peter must be enabled by Christ to teach truly, or else that whole Church shall fall.

So papal infallibility undergirds an even broader infallibility: that of the Catholic Church. Did the understanding of the Church's ability to teach infallibly predate Vatican I? Yes.[70]

How can anyone speak infallibly, though? You may as well ask how anyone can perform miracles! It's all by the gift of God. The Catholic faith involves accepting God's intervention in human affairs. That's what the Incarnation of Jesus was all about! So people will work miracles by the power of the Holy Spirit, and popes will be infallible by a special grace attached to their office. If one accepts miracles, then why not infallibility? If one believes in the Incarnation, then why not in special gifts and graces given to the ministers of Jesus Christ?

Now, many people mistake infallibility for impeccability. These are two dramatically different things. Infallibility means that the teaching of a pope will not be wrong, given certain special conditions listed above. Impeccability means that a person will not sin. But popes can and do sin — and they admit it! Saint John Paul II went to Confession on a regular basis. Pope Benedict XVI and Pope Francis have done the same. There's no point in going to Confession if you think you never sin! The popes acknowledge that they are sinners and seek forgiveness from Jesus through the ministry of Christ's priests, just like the rest of the Catholics. Heck, every time the pope says Mass, he has to participate in the penitential rite, just like the rest of us. In one form, we pray, "I confess to almighty God and to you, my brothers and sisters, that I have greatly sinned, in my thoughts and in my words, in what I have done and in what I have failed to do, through my fault, through my fault, through my most grievous fault … ." If the Holy Father is supposed to be without sin, what on earth is he doing praying such a prayer?

It's worth noting that the Holy Father can and does exercise his authority in ways other than infallible, *ex cathedra* pronouncements. He has "full, supreme, and universal power over the Church," after all![71] He makes all sorts of administrative decisions and rulings that affect the lives of Catholics in various parts of the world, such as appointing bishops, creating cardinals, issuing different instructions regarding liturgical practices or customs, and a great deal more. Further, there are often a number of different levels of authority in play in the Holy Father's exercise of his teaching office, according to Dr. Robert Stackpole, author of *The Papacy: God's Gift for All Christians*. These include:

- the infallible extraordinary magisterium (*ex cathedra* papal pronouncements and doctrinal definitions of ecumenical councils accepted by the papacy as such);

- the infallible ordinary magisterium (teachings by popes on faith and morals addressed to the universal Church and held to be important for all the faithful to believe — especially ones that have been repeated at that level — and that have been at least tacitly echoed by the Church's bishops spread throughout the world);

- and the fallible ordinary magisterium (teachings on faith and morals not having all the requisite characteristics of the previous categories); for these, we are still duty bound to give the Holy Father the benefit of the doubt on account of the presumption of guidance of his office by the Holy Spirit, but well-informed, respectful dissent is possible.[72]

Generally, we are to obey the Successor to St. Peter when he teaches us, even when he's not speaking infallibly, using the full power of his office. Why? Because he's our earthly father, delegated by Jesus to be His Vicar — His representative — on earth.

Further, he's the Holy Father, holy by reason of his office, certainly, and hopefully (but not necessarily) by reason of his personal sanctity. The pope is consecrated to the service of God, which makes him holy in the Old Testament sense — that is, set apart for divine service. Some of those who were consecrated to divine service have behaved in unholy ways, like the sons of Eli (see 1 Sam 2:12-25); similarly, some popes have behaved awfully. Even the most holy of men would have a hard time always avoiding misusing the power of the papacy, and so we pray for the pope. He has a huge responsibility, an enormous burden of pastoral care.

We are to imitate him when he most fully imitates Christ. We are to pray for him whether or not he succeeds in being a saintly Holy Father. We are to love him, both as a brother Christian and as one who has been given spiritual paternity over us.

On a number of things, we may disagree with the Holy Father. For instance, Pope Francis is a card-carrying member of the Argentinian San Lorenzo de Almagro soccer team's club. There are many Catholics who are fans of other soccer teams. That's fine. Supporting a sports team isn't a matter of faith or morals! We can challenge the pope's choice of what food is the best, or his preference in movies, or his notion of which music is best. We can even, to a certain extent, ignore him. After all, many people go along very happily in their life of faith with their local parish, hearing about the pope only when he makes headlines. Not everyone reads papal encyclicals or checks the Vatican news, after all. Many Catholics get by with the Sacraments, prayer, good works, and the teaching of their local pastor. And that's fine, so long as we remember to pray for the Holy Father at Mass and every so often in our devotions!

So when the Church teaches that the Holy Father is infallible, I can still be Catholic because I don't find it far-fetched that the man with the job of being the Rock on which the Church rests (see Mt 16:18; Jn 1:42) would be given a special gift to protect him from teaching falsehood. If the Church is the pillar and foundation of truth (see 1 Tim 3:15) and the Church rests on Peter, then Peter surely must also be a pillar and foundation of truth (see Gal 2:9; Eph 2:20).

Question 14:

How can you still be Catholic when God doesn't exist?

I can still be Catholic because God *does* exist, something that we can know simply by looking at the world around us. Everything we come into contact with, everything we can find in the cosmos, is dependent on something else. Nothing in the entire universe has always existed. Every speck of matter, every bit of energy has a beginning. According to modern physics, time itself has a beginning, as does space.

So all of this wondrous universe is dependent — on what? It must have been caused by something completely outside itself — outside time. Time is something created, inextricably bound up with space. So the Creator, the creating agent, must be outside time (eternal), and also outside space. The Creator, the source of all the universe, must be capable of creating everything that we encounter inside time and space. Nothing comes from nothing, after all. You can't give what you haven't got. So the Creator must be capable of giving rise to humans and other life-forms, as well as all the magnificence of the inanimate cosmos. And the Creator must be sustaining us, moment to moment.

That's one argument for the existence of God, adapted from the work of Fr. Robert Spitzer, SJ, the author of *New Proofs for the Existence of God.*[73] In his book, he explores a number of new arguments arising from the most recent findings of physics to indicate that God made all things. He also draws from the perennial findings of philosophy to show that the deepest desires of the human heart point toward a creator, as well.

But a lot of people will not have the time or the patience to delve deeply into the arguments from science or philosophy. Indeed, the public spectacle of so many believers falling so far short of the faith we profess has probably left a lot of people impatient with merely reasoned arguments. Such people can probably agree wholeheartedly with what Cardinal Joseph Ratzinger (later Pope Emeritus Benedict XVI) said:

> I have often affirmed my conviction that the true *apologia* of Christian faith, the most convincing demonstration of its truth against every denial, [is] the saints, and the beauty that the faith has generated. Today, for faith to grow, we must lead ourselves and the persons we meet to encounter the saints and to enter into contact with the Beautiful.[74]

I couldn't agree more. The saints are the ones who most attracted me to the Catholic faith to begin with. When I was a little boy, I was given two books on the lives of the saints. I read those books repeatedly. I wanted to see the miracles described and know the people who worked them. I loved what I saw and heard in these people's lives — a total dedication to goodness, a total commitment to love and truth, a total selfless gift to God, which He then blessed and transformed into a massive gift to the people around them. These saints had figured life out! This was authentic human life lived right.

As I've grown up, I've come to discover how deeply we really do require saints. After all, a society of saints would be a healthy society, a whole society. Further, looking at the world today, you soon see that the problems humanity faces are overwhelming, impossible. We cannot dig ourselves out of this pit. We are not up to this challenge. Where then can we find hope? We find it in the discovery that the full human life, the sort of life that we all desire deep within our hearts, is the life of graced nature, the supernatural life made possible by the grace of God given through Jesus Christ. Humans share an innate desire to be saints. This is because to be a saint is to be living your divine adoption in the world today. To be a saint is to be back in the right relationship to the world, to yourself, to your neighbor, and to your God.

Look at the lives of the saints. Francis of Assisi, who transformed the world by being a poor, humble man. Patrick of Ireland, whose ministry and witness set the stage for the island of saints and scholars to "save civilization." Augustine of Hippo, whose life was transformed by the prayers of his mother, Monica; and whose writings serve as part of the foundation for Western Civilization. Benedict of Nursia, whose monasteries preserved the classics and served as fonts of grace for the conversion and healing of the nations. The apostles. Mary, the Mother of God. Stanislaus Papczynski. Jean Vianney. Padre Pio. Thérèse of Lisieux. Teresa of Avila. John of the Cross. Ignatius of Loyola. Brother Andre. Mother Cabrini. Damien of Molokai. The Christian martyrs from the earliest days to the present day. Faustina Kowalska. John XXIII. John Paul II. Mother Teresa. And on. And on. And on.[75]

See how their presence caused eruptions of grace and conversion, how their lives stand as signposts for changes in the course of history, how they handled problems and healed wounds that their contemporaries couldn't begin to touch. See how they stand as light to the nations, as the salt of the earth, as a city shining on a hill. See how these people did things that they could not have done on their own. See the grace and the power of God shining through their lives and witness, healing where it touches, transforming and elevating.

For further evidence of the existence of God, we can point also to the transcendental beauty unleashed into the world through the faith. People still flock to the cathedrals of Europe, to the art collections remaining wherever the Renaissance touched. People still listen in awe to the music generated by the faithful, and borrow from it to create their own. Beauty points right outside everyday life, or illumines everyday life with light from beyond the boundaries of this world. It reminds us of our heavenly home and the community of love into which we are invited.

Yet another argument for the existence of God comes from the personal experience of so many people whose lives have been touched and transformed by grace. There are more people than many atheists realize who believe in God because, well, they've met Him, thank you very much! Some of these people are former atheists, like the science fiction writer John C. Wright, whose conversion story is dramatic and powerful.[76] Others are people who've been believers and have personally seen miracles or met God, the saints, or the angels, and so are not likely to ever cease to believe in God. Consider the apparitions at Fatima and the Miracle of the Sun, which convinced tens of thousands of people that God was real and that the Blessed Virgin Mary had appeared to the children.[77] Look at the miraculous physical healings at Lourdes,[78] the miraculous conversion of the Americas by Our Lady of Guadalupe,[79] and Our Lady of Kibeho's miracles and prophecy of the genocide in Rwanda![80] Still other people have encountered the powers of hell and know better than to say there is no such thing as the devil. Many of those people have also seen the power of Jesus Christ deployed in exorcisms or prayers of deliverance, and so have every reason to believe in God and the Son of the Father.[81]

I can very easily be Catholic in the modern day because the evidence for the existence of God and the truth of the Catholic faith is overwhelming.

Question 15:
How can you still be Catholic when Catholics behave in such un-Christian ways?

I can still be Catholic when I'm in a Church full of sinners because, well, that's right where I belong. I am a sinner in need of a Savior, and Jesus is waiting for me in the Catholic Church, in every parish church, in the tabernacle and in the Mass, in the assembly of people and the Scriptures, in the Sacraments and the whole Mystical Body. I go where Jesus is. And where does He go? Who did He seek as His dinner companions and people to hang out with?

> ...[M]any tax collectors and sinners sat with Jesus and his disciples; for there were many who followed him. Some scribes who were Pharisees saw that he was eating with sinners and tax collectors and said to his disciples, "Why does he eat with tax collectors and sinners?" Jesus heard this and said to them [that], "Those who are well do not need a physician, but the sick do. I did not come to call the righteous but sinners" (Mk 2:15-17).

So He calls sinners — and what happens? The Kingdom of Heaven forms around the Son of Man. What is that kingdom like?

> Again, the kingdom of heaven is like a net thrown into the sea, which collects fish of every kind. When

it is full they haul it ashore and sit down to put what is good into buckets. What is bad they throw away. Thus it will be at the end of the age. The angels will go out and separate the wicked from the righteous and throw them into the fiery furnace, where there will be wailing and grinding of teeth (Mt 13:47-50).

We are gathered into the boat of Peter the fisherman, the fisher of men, and shall be sorted out at the end of the age. The nets of the evangelists are full to bursting with fish of all sorts, gathered from out of the stormy seas of this world. In other words, the Church holds both living saints and barely living sinners, the grateful and the ingrates, the good and the bad. We can do no less than our Master did before us. As the Gospels describe, Jesus eats with tax collectors and sinners. Even at the Last Supper, Judas eats food handed to him by Jesus right before he goes out and betrays the Son of God (see Jn 13:26-27).

But aren't we supposed to be better than that? Aren't we supposed to be the hands and feet of God in the world? Yes. All Catholics are called to holiness — every single one, whether we are a priest or a child, a housewife or a corporate executive, a nun or the Holy Father in Rome. Every single Catholic is called to become a saint. How do we do this? Not by our own strength, but by living in the Spirit of God — that is, by saying "yes" to the grace of God, "yes" to His love, "yes" to His divine life. Sometimes, that means we have to give up good things in order to put God in first place. Some people have to give up any romantic relationship, for instance, and follow God's call either as single Catholics in the world or as some form of consecrated religious or clergy. Others must learn to give up time with television, or the Internet, or their drug of choice, or their late nights at the bar, or any number of other sources of pleasure in the world in order to love God and their neighbor as they should.

It's not an easy road, because it's the road to Calvary. Jesus calls us to pick up our crosses and follow Him to our deaths. Why? Because we must die in order to rise again. "For whoever wishes to save his life will lose it, but whoever loses his life for my sake will save it" (Lk 9:24). The call to the Christian is the call to participate in the divine nature of our God, and our God is a consuming fire. He is total self-gift, the Father giving Himself utterly to the Son, and the Son pouring Himself out utterly to the Father, and the Spirit, also known as "Gift," is the divine Love being poured out. In order to enter Heaven, we must learn to live this great exchange of love and give ourselves utterly to God, so that He may give Himself utterly to us. It's like playing with fire — we shall get burned, and, burning, be saved (see 1 Cor 3:10-15).

We can live a divine life only by the gift of God. We can enter the eternal dance of the Trinity only if God gives us the strength to keep up. Sometimes, it takes a lifetime to learn the steps of the dance, to learn to make the utter self-sacrifice. At other times, the Lord God raises up great saints. Padre Pio, for example, made an extraordinary gift of self to God beginning in his youth. Saint Thérèse of Lisieux died in her 20s and was called by Pope St. Pius X "the greatest saint of modern times."

Are Catholics failures if we haven't yet achieved that level of love and virtue? Nope — we are failures only if we give up the fight. God gave us the Sacrament of Confession for a reason — so that we could use it, so that we could be raised from spiritual death, strengthened, and renewed to resume the fight. We are given the Sacrament of the Anointing of the Sick in order to have forgiveness and assistance in our illnesses and on our deathbeds. And Purgatory awaits as a final extension of mercy to those who do not make the complete self-gift in this life.

So God comes out to meet us even when we are sinners. He comes out to meet us in order to raise us up to become His sons and daughters. We are in the Church in order to be elevated. And it takes time and grace. We have to be purged of our sins and bad habits, illuminated by the grace of God, and united to Him in a perfect way. There are many people at many stages along the way still in the Church, and that's OK.

Mother Dolores Hart, a Benedictine nun living at Regina Laudis monastery in Connecticut, once said that living in a monastic community was like "being skinned alive." We have to learn to love our brothers and sisters in Christ as they are — as Christ loves them — even as we all try to become perfect as our heavenly Father is perfect.

As C.S. Lewis once put it, the key question to ask is, "If I, being what I am, can consider that I am in some sense a Christian, why should the different vices of those people in the next pew prove that their religion is mere hypocrisy and convention?"[82] Jesus came to save the whole human race, and so the whole human race is represented in the Church. Priests have heard confessions for centuries. In that length of time, how many murders do you think have been confessed? How many sexual sins? How many acts of anger, envy, pride, or sloth? How often do priests hear the confessions of those in prison, and of those who ought to be in prison? How often do you think priests must go on missions of mercy to people of terrifying depravity?

We should not be surprised when we encounter the great sinner in the next pew over, or even the merely annoying sinner. Rather, we should thank God for His mercy — to us all.

Question 16:

How can you still be Catholic when the Church draws such a hard line on the life issues (abortion, for example) with no room for mercy?

If you remember nothing else from this book, remember this: God loves you. He loves you absolutely, endlessly, completely. He knew everything you would do in your life when He was suffering in the Garden of Gethsemane, and still He chose to go to the Cross, to His Passion and Death, rather than lose you. He loves you. Oh, how He loves you! So no matter what you have done, no matter what you have been or seen or been a part of, know: God loves you. If I have not managed to teach that truth, this book is worthless.

Now: I can still be Catholic because the Church *does* offer mercy, even when she's dealing with a matter of life and death. Absolution for the sin of abortion has always been available in the Catholic Church, though at times it's been restricted. At one point, one had to seek absolution for abortion from the local bishop. Why? I think the purpose was to ensure that the local bishops would hear about the existence of the practice in their diocese and be able to take pastoral steps in response. Now, though, those restrictions are gone: In the wake of the 2016 Jubilee Year of Mercy, Pope Francis has enabled every priest across the world to absolve a person of the sin of abortion. Go to Confession; make a good, valid Confession; and all your sins will be forgiven.

But why does the Church stand so strongly against the evils of abortion, as well as other practices such as euthanasia? The Church draws a "hard line" on the life issues because lives (and souls) are at stake. The Second Vatican Council says:

> [W]hatever is opposed to life itself, such as any type of murder, genocide, abortion, euthanasia or willful self-destruction, whatever violates the integrity of the human person, such as mutilation, torments inflicted on body or mind, attempts to coerce the will itself; whatever insults human dignity, such as subhuman living conditions, arbitrary imprisonment, deportation, slavery, prostitution, the selling of women and children; as well as disgraceful working conditions, where men are treated as mere tools for profit, rather than as free and responsible persons; all these things and others of their like are infamies indeed. They poison human society, but they do more harm to those who practice them than those who suffer from the injury. Moreover, they are supreme dishonor to the Creator.[83]

Here you have a significant listing of the great sins and tragedies in human life. Aren't these the sorts of things that you would hope to hear the Church take a hard line against?

The Church condemns evil where she sees it, but she also offers forgiveness to all humans, no matter the sin. The depth and breadth of God's mercy can be shocking. People may consider it almost too broad, too encompassing. As Chesterton once laid out in a Father Brown mystery, the Church must go where no *merely human* compassion can reach:

> "[H]ang it all," cried Mallow, "you don't expect us to be able to pardon a vile thing like this?"
>
> "No," said the priest; "but we have to be able to pardon it."

He stood up abruptly and looked round at them.

"We have to touch such men, not with a barge-pole, but with a benediction," he said. "We have to say the word that will save them from hell. We alone are left to deliver them from despair when your human charity deserts them. Go on your own primrose path pardoning all your favourite vices and being generous to your fashionable crimes; and leave us in the darkness, vampires of the night, to console those who really need consolation; who do things really indefensible, things that neither the world nor they themselves can defend; and none but a priest will pardon. Leave us with the men who commit the mean and revolting and real crimes; mean as St. Peter when the cock crew, and yet the dawn came."[84]

The Church has mercy on the sinner, any sinner, all sinners. There is forgiveness waiting for anyone, everyone — for you, no matter what you've done. It's there for the asking. The *Catechism* explains:

In danger of death any priest, even if deprived of faculties for hearing confessions, can absolve from every sin and excommunication.[85]

You can receive absolution even if you have procured an abortion or assisted someone in procuring an abortion. *You can be forgiven!* The Church wants to forgive you.

There is mercy available, Divine Mercy in abundance, for people who perpetrate a sin, any sin. In fact, the one and only unforgivable sin is the sin against the Holy Spirit: refusing to acknowledge God's love and power to forgive, and despairing of His mercy. All else has been and will be forgiven to the repentant sinner. God loves all of us, every single person belonging to the human race. We are loved with a love surpassing understanding, so intense in its force that Scripture calls it a consuming fire (see 1 Jn 4:16; Heb 12:29). God loves you, no matter what you've done, no matter what background you have, no matter where you've come from. *God loves you!* He does not hate you. He has never hated you. He shall never hate you! He loves you, and me, and every other human being.

He waits for you to come home; to come to Him and confess; to let Him love you back to life, heal the aching inside, bring light to the darkness, and breathe His Holy Spirit into your heart. He wants to give you His strength to bear any burden and to lighten your loads. You've never had to carry your burdens alone — He has always been there, He and all the angels and all the saints, waiting to raise you up with their prayers and their strength, waiting to draw you into eternal communion, waiting for you to come home. God loves you, and all the saints and the angels love you, and all wait for you to come home.

Question 17:
How can you still be Catholic when the Church is so bureaucratic?

I can still be Catholic when the Church is so bureaucratic because, well, she has to be. Consider the Sacraments. We take them seriously, believing that Holy Orders make a man a deacon, a priest, or a bishop. We believe that Baptism really allows us to enter into a new and eternal life. We believe in the Church's teachings and the power of her Sacraments — and so it makes sense that the Church would work to keep track of those who have received the Sacraments. That means paperwork. And that means bureaucracy.

Consider also the need of the bishops to make sure their priests behave according to the office given to them. That requires paperwork, and performance reviews. And then there's the money donated to the Church: We want our donations spent well, and not squandered or spent on the wrong things. All of this means more paperwork, and more bureaucracy.

In short, stewardship and prudence will inevitably mean a Church that is, to some extent, bureaucratic. The Church can certainly become *too* bureaucratic, can be too focused on her call to govern and too little focused on her call to teach and to sanctify. But she sometimes neglects her governing role. The sex abuse crisis grew to a tragedy because of a failure of governance. Any number of problems within the Church have developed because of a failure to apply canon law to certain situations and a failure to properly manage the Church.

So bureaucracy is not necessarily something bad, some-thing that always gets in the way of the Church doing the work she is supposed to perform in the world. Rather, it is often necessary in order to get that work done. Just as any other human organization requires people to handle the paperwork that keeps track of its business and how it uses its resources, so, too, does the Church need to be a wise steward of the gifts of God.

Look at Jesus' Parable of the Talents (Mt 25:14-30), in which a master goes on a journey and entrusts his servants with the stewardship of varying amounts of wealth. He ex-pects a return on his investment. Or look at the Parable of the Wise and the Foolish Virgins (Mt 25:1-13). The wise virgins planned ahead, had enough oil left over to greet the bride-groom at his coming, and were able to go into the wedding celebration. Jesus expects His Church to be a wise and prudent steward of His wealth — that is, of the riches of His grace and the treasure of His people. Good stewardship requires keeping accounts — doing the books and tracking who has received which Sacraments, who has entered into marriage, and so on. In fact, all of us are called to be stewards of the talents God has given us. All Christians are called to wise use of their time, their talents, and their treasure, giving to the service of the kingdom of God, of the Church, and taking care of their fellow human beings.

So the Church, as a whole organization and in each and every Christian's life, is to be a prudent steward of resources.

Is bureaucracy always a good thing? No, of course not. It's a tool, and like any other tool, a bureaucracy is good when it is being used properly and bad when it gets in the way of the job to be done. If an excess of bureaucracy prevents a bishop from being a shepherd and a father to his people, then some-thing has gone terribly wrong.[86] If a priest is not available to truly be a father to his parish, and if a parishioner trying to get involved or get help has to run through a maze of discouraging paperwork and staffers, then something is wrong.

Using a tool well is a matter of balance. And when the balance is off, it's time for reform and renewal. The Church on earth, the "pilgrim people of God" as Vatican II says, has an ongoing need for renewal as she travels through time toward the end of all things, toward the new advent of Jesus Christ on earth.

We must always turn back again, and again, and again to God — allow Him to cut through the layers of red tape to reach us again, allow Him to transform our lives and our hearts. That's the real meaning of it all, not the properly filed forms, not the correct press releases. The Church is meant to be, like John the Baptist, a prophet crying in the wilderness announcing that the stone the builders rejected is here, has become the cornerstone, is standing — a martyr and prophet announcing a Lamb slain for the sins of the world.[87]

So I can still be Catholic even though we have canon law and lawyers, even though we have secretaries and filing cabinets and forms and committees, because we also have grace, and Sacraments, and disconcerting prophets, and shocking doctrines, and impossible faith and hope and love. I can still be Catholic in spite of the "organized religion" because the religion is true and the organization is organic. We are one Body in Jesus Christ — and there are few structures in the universe more complex, more organized, than the human body. And yet, life dwells in that ordered complexity, in that carefully crafted concatenation of cells, organs, and layers upon layers of intricate organization, permitting the Body to dance and sing before the tabernacle of our God.

Question 18:
How can you still be Catholic when priests are not holy?

I can still be Catholic in spite of priests who are not personally holy because, again, we are a Church of sinners on the way to becoming saints[88] — and also because there have been many, many holy priests in the Church throughout her history, and there are many, many holy priests today.

"Every saint has a past, every sinner has a future," Oscar Wilde said.[89] As I've been pointing out throughout this book, it should come as no surprise to Catholics that we sometimes have sinful priests serving sinful parishioners — look at the Scriptures! Take, for instance, the behavior of the earliest priest, Adam. He failed in his priestly paternal duty to tend and keep the Garden, and original sin was the result.[90] Consider Aaron and the Israelites in the desert. The people came to Aaron demanding he make a god for them while Moses was still on top of Mount Sinai and God was thundering in the cloud! And Aaron complied! Talk about a betrayal of one's priesthood. "As the ancient rabbis noted, what the forbidden fruit was for Adam, the golden calf was for Israel."[91] There are the sinful sons of Eli (1 Sam 2:12-25) as well — oh, the list could go on and on. We see bad priests throughout the Old Testament.

Look at the early Church! Many of the New Testament letters are prompted by problems of one sort or another surfacing in the local churches, demanding an apostolic response.

Look at the messages to the seven churches at the outset of the Book of Revelation — there's a litany of sins needing repentance and problems requiring solutions. And yet the presence of the bad with the good among the Lord's chosen does not mean that Israel is not the Chosen People of God or that the Church is not the household of God. In short, I'm still Catholic because I believe the Church to be that of Jesus Christ on earth, with the bread of life and the cup of eternal salvation to offer, as well as God's forgiveness and participation in His life and love. What else would I choose to be?

That Catholic priests are sinners like the rest of us simply means that we are in the field where the weeds grow alongside the wheat; we are in the net with good fish and bad; we are a Church of sheep and goats, and wolves in sheep's clothing. Why? Because goodness shall not be perfectly separated from badness until all are sorted into Heaven or hell, until the end of the present age and the Second Coming of Jesus Christ.

Servant of God Dorothy Day laid out this tension between the holiness that comes to the Church from Christ the Head and the behavior of far too many of the Church's hierarchy perfectly when she recounted her criticism of the apparent luxury in which far too many priests lived in her own day, even if they were personally humble and poor in spirit: "It is the scandal of our day in America." But she knew, and expressed in her famous memoir *The Long Loneliness*, that a person loves the Church for the sake of Christ, even though the Church is so often a source of scandal. She cited an insight of the great theologian Romano Guardini, that "the Church is the Cross on which Christ was crucified." Day said that you can't pick apart Christ from His Cross; "one must live in a state of perpetual dissatisfaction with the Church."[92]

The Church, then, does not always (or even often) present the grand witness of the purity and holiness of God that she could or should. She is not always a great city on the hill, drawing all the nations with her splendor. She sometimes appears to be a great ruin on a hill, driving the nations away with her squalor and her sin. But the Church in Heaven is ever resplendently pure, praying for the Church on earth, one Body with one head, no division, no separation. And on earth, we continue slogging our way toward the Promised Land, toward holiness, sustained by the grace and mercy of God.

We do get the consolation of people who reach that Promised Land, as well. Priests like St. Jean Vianney, Pope St. John Paul II, St. Anthony of Padua, St. Francis de Sales, and many, many more have shown the heights of sanctity that priests can achieve if they generously cooperate with the grace God gives them with their calling.

So we suffer through the sins and bad habits of some of our priests, loving them always and sometimes enduring them — because they must love us and forgive us in the name of the Triune God, even though we are sinners, even though we complain and are irritable, rousting them out of bed late at night or early in the morning for our sick calls, for our funerals, for our concerns and cares, for our souls and our salvation. We are all crosses for one another, one great mass of need and gift, of cost and charity. In other words, we are called to love one another as God has loved us, giving all and receiving all in return.

Must we always simply accept the sinfulness of our priests as a cross to bear and something that no one can fix? Of course not. Seminaries have screening processes to pick the best candidates for the priesthood and appoint spiritual directors to help candidates discern if the priesthood is truly their vocation (or calling). Bishops have oversight authority regarding their priests, and the Vatican can take certain actions if bishops are behaving badly. Laypeople have rights under canon law and can appeal to the bishop if a priest is breaking canon law, or call the police if the priest is breaking civil law. As the writer Mark Shea has pointed out repeatedly, the priest abuse scandal was not only the fault of the bishops who failed to apply canonical penalties to repeat offenders, or of diocesan officials who never called the police. It was also the fault of the laity who didn't call in the authorities when it was well past time to do so, and the fault of the authorities who had all the information they needed, but didn't act.

Further, laypeople have every reason to expect their priests to strive for holiness — just as priests have every reason to expect their parishioners to strive for holiness. We are not called to acknowledge our sinfulness, sigh, and say, "Well, there's no help for it!" We — priests and laity alike — are called to be perfect as our Father in Heaven is perfect. This requires a daily, dedicated effort to open ourselves to God's will and obey His commandments — that is, to love the Lord our God with all our heart, soul, strength, and mind, and to love our neighbor as Jesus loves us. Our priests are called to sanctity and to be sources of sanctification to the laity through the exercise of the ministry given to them by Jesus Christ.

The ordinary Christian life is the supernatural life, made possible only by God's grace. Bad priests are called to become not just good men, but holy men, perfect men, men who are living a life beyond any natural effort of human beings. And becoming holy priests, they are to take the laity with them to the highest heights of sanctity, to the heart of God.

So pray for them. Pray for them daily, asking for the intercession of such great priests as St. Jean Vianney, patron saint of parish priests; St. Padre Pio, the great confessor and wonder-worker; and St. John Paul II for their intercession for your spiritual fathers and mine, for all those men who stand *in persona Christi* at the altars of the world, bring God to us in the Eucharist, and absolve us of our sins.

Question 19:

How can you still be Catholic when so many of the Church's customs came from pagans?

Tell that to the Jewish converts to Catholicism who are stunned to see just how Jewish the Catholic faith and practice really are, or the recent tidal wave of Protestant converts who marvel at how biblical Catholicism is (see Appendix A: Recommended Reading). Watch conversion testimonies on Marcus Grodi's "The Journey Home" and listen to the reasons why people have returned to Catholicism or found their way into the Catholic Church for the first time. Attend a Catholic Mass and count the number of times Scriptures from the Old and New Testaments are read or incorporated into the prayers and ritual.[93] Read books like Dr. Brant Pitre's *Jesus and the Jewish Roots of the Eucharist*.

Now, this is not to deny that we've "baptized" some pagan customs and used them for our own, but it is to challenge the uncritical notion that Catholicism is essentially warmed-over paganism. The Church, like the New Testament, has its roots in the Old Testament. The Catholic faith emerges from Jewish roots, an early Church full of people who were convinced that Jesus was the Jewish Messiah, and that her Sacraments came about at Jesus' behest.

Further, to recognize that as Catholicism spread, it looked at some preexisting local practices and decided they could be turned from pagan use to Christian use isn't to say that Catholicism is simply paganism wearing different clothing. No — it's to recognize that there are a great many practices and acts in human life that aren't exclusively the property of any one religion. Certain gestures, for instance, such as bowing and kneeling, aren't simply Christian, Jewish, pagan, or Hindu. They are fairly universal gestures of respect. Certain practices such as making wreaths or decorating trees can be done by people of any faith or none at all. Certain symbols such as the sun, the moon, the stars, the human eye or hand, or certain colors aren't simply the property of pagans or Christians, but are rather symbols used across human cultures and eras.

The use of the symbols matters a great deal, as does the gesture. Catholics may certainly light candles as a way of symbolically asking a saint for his or her prayers, but Catholics went to their deaths rather than offer a pinch of incense to the Roman emperor. Why? The first action is a request for intercession, rather the same way that I "send up a flare" on Facebook when I ask friends for prayers for a particular intention. The second one is an act of worship of the Roman emperor as a god, one forbidden to Christians.

So yes, Catholicism has certainly adopted things from other peoples and lands, or permitted the faithful to partake of them, all while continuing to forbid the worship of idols, of false gods, or of anyone not the One, Triune God. The medieval Church embraced some of the philosophy of the ancient Greeks (see St. Thomas Aquinas' incorporation of Aristotle throughout his work, for example); the Renaissance-era Christians delighted in a rediscovery of the art and architecture of the Greeks and Romans; and the Church to this day preserves a host of pagan art treasures in the Vatican museum. The monks in their scriptoria carefully preserved many pagan works of literature and learning down through the centuries. But the Church has always professed that Jesus is Lord, and forbidden the worship of strange gods.

The Church has baptized pagan customs, but not pagan religions. She has drawn from the truths taught by pagan peoples, while sorting out and discarding those beliefs or teachings that are incompatible with the Gospel of Jesus Christ. She has adopted the habits of pagan peoples, but not their gods. Rather, she has come with Word and Sacrament, with the commission of God Incarnate, to bring all peoples to the worship of the One Triune God, the Creator at the back of all things. She has proclaimed Jesus Christ to all nations, and will continue to do so until the end of time, rejecting nothing that is good or true in the process, but rather claiming all things for Christ Jesus.

Question 20:
How can you still be Catholic when Church teachings seem so absolute?

I can still be Catholic because I believe those teachings to be true. If they are true, every other consideration is secondary — whether they are easy or hard; whether they are supposedly "liberal" or "conservative"; whether or not I have violated them in the past, struggle with them now, and will probably struggle with them in the future; whether they condemn or celebrate something I hold dear. Every other consideration is secondary to the question of truth. Why? Well, if the teachings are true, then in order to remain a sane human being, I must accept them.

Now, why is this an objection in the first place? What's the matter with absolute moral teaching that sets forward certain principles starkly, demandingly, with no shades of gray? I think many people would say that humans aren't simply good or evil, that any attempt to divide the human race into good guys and bad guys will always fail to judge the situation justly. So to be stark, to be black-and-white about morality, many say, is to condemn people whose situations you don't understand, whose lives you haven't lived. And it's true that most people are unable to read souls or see things through others' eyes. (Saints and prophets, of course, often break the boundaries of what's humanly possible!) But is the Catholic Church's teaching on morals so black-and-white?

Well, we do have some pretty clear teaching on morality. We do have the Ten Commandments (just like the Jews and all other Christians). Those are pretty bluntly stated. We've got the two great commandments that sum up the law and the prophets: "You shall love the Lord, your God, with all your heart, with all your soul, and with all your mind. This is the greatest and the first commandment. The second is like it: You shall love your neighbor as yourself" (Mt 22:37-40). We've got a number of moral teachings in the New Testament letters, and the *Catechism* speaks more extensively about the moral life of a Christian. So there's a fair amount of clear Catholic teaching on morality.[94]

Why does the Church care about morality? Saint John Paul II, in his encyclical *Veritatis Splendor* (*The Splendor of Truth*), lays it out: The reason is relationship.

What man is and what he must do becomes clear as soon as God reveals himself...[as] the One who despite man's sin remains the "model" for moral action, in accordance with his command, "You shall be holy; for I the Lord your God am holy" (Lev 19:2); as the One who, faithful to his love for man, gives him his Law (cf. Ex 19:9-24 and 20:18-21) in order to restore man's original and peaceful harmony with the Creator and with all creation, and, what is more, to draw him into his divine love: "I will walk among you, and will be your God, and you shall be my people" (Lev 26:12).

The moral life presents itself as the response due to the many gratuitous initiatives taken by God out of love for man. It is a response of love, according to the statement made in Deuteronomy about the fundamental commandment: "Hear, O Israel: The Lord our God is one Lord; and you shall love the Lord your God with all your heart, and with all your soul, and with all your might. And these words which I command you this day shall be upon your heart; and you shall teach them diligently to your children" (Dt 6:4-7). Thus the moral life, caught up in the gratuitousness of God's love, is called to reflect his glory: "For the one who loves God it is enough to be pleasing to the One whom he loves: for no greater reward should be sought than that love itself; charity in fact is of God in such a way that God himself is charity".[95]

The reason for the moral teachings of the Church is our love of God and God's love for us. We are called into a relationship with the All-Holy One, and so are called to be all-holy ourselves. Is this possible for human beings? Jesus answers that question: "For human beings it is impossible, but not for God. All things are possible for God" (Mk 10:27). So we are called to live a life animated by faith, by trust in God's love and mercy, because it is only by God's grace and constant presence in our lives that we will ever be able to live up to the law He gives us.

And what is the purpose of the law? The purpose of the law is to enter into a right relationship with God, with our neighbor, with ourselves, and with creation. The purpose of the law is to point us to righteous life and righteous love. That's why it's given to us with clarity and precision. It wouldn't be kind of God to make the law impossibly obscure and difficult so that the average human being couldn't know right from wrong.

Does that make it easy to live? I can tell you from personal experience — no! It can be really difficult to live, and I, for one, fail often. Why? Because God is cruel? No — because we fell a long, long time ago. As Chesterton said, "Certain new theologians dispute original sin, which is the only part of Christian theology which can really be proved."[96] We live in a world full of humans all struggling to deal with the consequences of broken relationships — with God, with their neighbors or families or friends, with their own bodies and minds, and with the created world around us, which is so often deadly and so often difficult.

The morality of Christianity is humanly impossible to live — but it is made a lighter yoke and an easier burden with God's grace. Still, He only gives us the grace we need to live the Christian life when we ask for that grace and accept it. God is tremendously respectful of human freedom. He empowers us to say "yes" to Him and then comes in and makes possible our complete self-gift to Him. When we give ourselves to Him completely, He elevates us to a new and supernatural height. We become His sons and daughters by grace, by divine adoption. It's saying "yes" to Him that can be so darn hard sometimes, because it demands that we trust Him absolutely, even if He asks that we suffer, even if He asks us to accept death. We must throw ourselves into the dark, believing that He will catch us, even as we feel ourselves start to fall.

In other words, we must trust Him as a child trusts that her father, who just tossed her into the air, will catch her — and even more. We must trust as Jesus trusted, taking up our crosses and following Him to Calvary and there dying — trusting in His Resurrection, which will mean ours, as well. That is the Christian life, made possible only by the Holy Spirit.

What reasons do we have for trusting? The saints; the graces we see come into people's lives through the Sacraments; the healing of lives lived according to the Word of God; the miracles present in the Church in all times, from her founding to the present age; and the wisdom we find in the teachings of the Church — all these are reasons for trust.[97]

So I believe it to be true teaching — and I know that, on those occasions when I fail to live up to it, God waits with the priest in the confessional to forgive.

Question 21:

How can you still be Catholic when the Church didn't stand up to the Nazis?

Did every single Catholic stand up to the Nazis? Nope. Did the Church simply stand down in the face of the rise of Nazism? Not on your life. The truth is somewhere in between, as indicated by Dr. Joseph L. Lichten, a former director of the International Affairs Department for the Anti-Defamation League of B'nai B'rith:

> What is the case against Pius XII [the pope throughout World War II]? In brief, that as head of one of the most powerful moral forces on earth he committed an unspeakable sin of omission by not issuing a formal statement condemning the Nazis' genocidal slaughter of the Jews, and that his silence was motivated by reasons considered in modern times as base: political exigency, economic interests, and personal ambition.
>
> What is the case for him? That in relation to the insane behavior of the Nazis, from overlords to self-styled cogs like Eichmann, he did everything humanly possible to save lives and alleviate suffering among the Jews; that a formal statement would have provoked the Nazis to brutal retaliation, and would substantially have thwarted further Catholic action on behalf of Jews.[98]

Lichten goes on to examine the two opposing sides in detail, but first, there's a huge, important historical point to make: The Catholic Church didn't have armies in the 1900s. The Church could not call a Crusade against Nazism. If that's what people wish she had done, then I'm afraid they'll never be satisfied, because that is not the role or *modus operandi* of the papacy in the modern age.

Now, what did the Catholic Church do in response to the rise of the Nazis and of Hitler? The Catholic Church in Germany did not simply welcome them with open arms, as shown by a German intelligence report from 1934 on the German Catholics and Protestants. The report "saw church antagonism to Nazism as the rule, acceptance as the very rare exception. A *Lagebricht* of the central security office for May/June 1934 reports on both churches and devotes almost eight times as much space to trouble with the Catholics as with the Protestants."[99]

According to the report, the Church regularly attacked "neo-paganism," understood by all concerned to be synonymous with Nazism. Catholic priests were mentioned for their strong disapproval of anti-Semitism. Pius XI was described as expressing himself in ways "tantamount to an appeal for resistance against the National Socialist state. ... The bishops were no better, and their statements had recently become increasingly sharper ... [these bishops included] Hugo of Mainz ... Erhenfried of Wurzburg, Bares of Berlin, Grober of Freiburg, Schulte of Cologne, Galen of Munster, and Faulhaber of Munich."[100]

The report goes on to detail examples of administrative anti-Nazism from the bishops, adding, "As for the lower clergy, their opposition was so widespread in all parts of the Reich that a recital of single cases was impossible and unnecessary ... Instruments of religious education were being used for political purposes ... Subsection 2, on 'clerical sympathizers' ... states that wholehearted sympathizers were exceedingly rare and were persecuted by their colleagues and superiors."[101]

So, according to the Nazis, the Church was quite hostile to their party and their program from the outset of their time in power. This did not change during the course of the 1930s, as shown by the publication and reception of Pope Pius XI's 1937 encyclical letter *Mit Brennender Sorge* (*With Burning Anxiety*). The letter was essentially an extended condemnation of Nazi racial theory and political doctrine, though it never mentions the Nazi party by name. The letter was smuggled into Germany on orders from the pope and read from every Catholic pulpit in Germany on Palm Sunday, a move taken by the Nazi party as a direct attack from the Catholic Church.[102]

The papal condemnation of Nazism continued when Pius XII issued the encyclical *Summi Pontificatus* (*On the Unity of Human Society*) in October 1939. The two pernicious errors the encyclical particularly targets are racism and the doctrine of the absolute nature of the state — two ideas at the very heart of Nazism.[103] In *Mit Brennender Sorge* and *Summi Pontificatus*, we have some very clear condemnations of foundational Nazi beliefs from the popes in place during the Nazis' rise and rule. Why no condemnation of Nazism by name? Simply because, as Dr. Lichten notes, Pius knew that any such condemnation would draw serious retaliation from the Nazis.

According to Lichten, Ernst von Weizsacker, the German ambassador to the Vatican during World War II, wrote in his memoirs about the silence of the Catholic Church alongside the silence of the Red Cross, saying it was "precisely because they wanted to help the Jews that these organizations refrained from making any general and public appeals; for they were afraid that they would injure rather than help the Jews thereby." Lichten points out that Pius did not publicly condemn persecutions of Catholics by the Nazis, either. Did he have reason to fear the consequences? Yes. Threats such as this message from the German foreign secretary Joachim von Ribbentrop to von Weizsacker on January 24, 1943, indicate that the dangers were real:

> Should the Vatican either politically or propagandistically oppose Germany, it should be made unmistakably clear that ... the German government would

have sufficient effective propaganda material as well as retaliatory measures at its disposal to counteract each attempted move by the Vatican. [104]

Dr. Lichten's monograph goes into extensive detail about the Vatican's humanitarian efforts to hide and protect the Jews and other targets of the Nazis' roundups. The Church poured forth a flood of fake baptismal certificates and other forged documents in order to protect as many lives as possible. The convents and monasteries of Rome were opened to Jewish refugees. Many Jews were hidden at the papal residence Castel Gandolfo and within Vatican City itself, all on the orders of Pius XII.

After the war, there was extensive Jewish testimony to the aid given by Pius XII and the Catholic Church. Dr. Lichten writes, "On June 4, 1944, when the Allies entered Rome, the Jewish News Bulletin of the British 8th Army said: 'To the everlasting credit of the people of Rome, and the Roman Catholic Church, the lot of the Jews has been made easier by their truly Christian offers of assistance and shelter. Even now, many still remain in places which opened their doors to hide them from the fate of deportation to certain death. ... The full story of the help given to our people by the Church cannot be told, for obvious reasons, until after the war.'"[105]

This is a story that's still being told by historians and researchers working today. Say what you will about Pius' choice not to publicly condemn the Nazis by name — the Catholic Church stood against Nazism.

Question 22:
How can you still be Catholic when the Church is so far behind the times on things like abortion?

"Behind the times"? When did being "behind the times" become a cardinal sin? The present moment is not, infallibly, a better moment than any in the past, and sometimes the future looks bleak. As Chesterton put it, "My attitude toward progress has passed from antagonism to boredom. I have long ceased to argue with people who prefer Thursday to Wednesday because it is Thursday."[106] Sometimes the Church needs to be "behind the times" on some issues because sometimes modern opinion is wrong. As Screwtape the demon says in C.S. Lewis' *Screwtape Letters*:

> Your man has been accustomed, ever since he was a boy, to having a dozen incompatible philosophies dancing about together inside his head. He doesn't think of doctrines as primarily "true" or "false," but as "academic" or "practical," "outworn" or "contemporary," "conventional" or "ruthless." Jargon, not argument, is your best ally in keeping him from the Church. Don't waste time trying to make him think that materialism is true! Make him think it is strong or stark or courageous — that it is the philosophy of the future. That's the sort of thing he cares about.[107]

So merely being "behind the times" is not necessarily a problem. Merely being "unfashionable" or "strange" or "out-of-date" shouldn't be embarrassing at all if the critics are objecting to what is true or good or beautiful.

Now, how can I still be Catholic when the Catholic Church is so starkly opposed to the "popular" or "progressive" view on abortion? Very easily: I believe the teaching to be true, and here's why.

One day I was walking between classes in high school. For some reason, the abortion issue was on my mind — either it had been in the news recently or it had come up in a discussion at school; I'm not sure which. But I realized that I didn't know whose side I supported on the issue and decided I needed to think it through. Yes, the Church opposed it, but did I agree? So I set myself to think about it and within about two seconds reached a conclusion. I realized, "I don't see any difference between killing a 6-week-old child in the womb and killing a 6-month-old out of the womb. I think killing a 6-month-old baby is absolutely wrong. So why would I support killing the child in the womb?" No matter how difficult the circumstances of the mother, I still wouldn't support the killing of a 6-month-old baby, so I wouldn't support ending the life of a child in the womb, either. Blinking for a moment, I realized I had finished thinking the thing through. There really wasn't much else to be said.

As time has gone by, I've never encountered a serious reason to doubt the conclusion I reached that day. In fact, the flow of bioethics seems to have confirmed my conclusion — namely, that if you support abortion, there is no clear reason to oppose infanticide. A 2011 paper in the *Journal of Medical Ethics* titled "After-Birth Abortion: Why Should the Baby Live?" took the notion to its logical conclusion, defending the claim that infanticide (termed by the authors of the paper "after-birth abortion") ought to be considered morally acceptable whenever abortion is accepted by society, including in cases of economic hardship.[108] On the one hand, I can understand the chorus of outrage with which this proposal was greeted when the paper was published; but on the other hand, I, too, base my reasoning about abortion on the fact that there's no essential difference between the child in the womb and the child out of the womb. I simply defend the pro-life conclusion, rather than attempting to justify either abortion or infanticide.

So I'm glad the Church has been so staunch on the issue of abortion. I believe her teaching to be true, and I hope that the logic of the position reaches as broad an audience as possible, because I believe that we have legalized the killing of innocent human beings, and it needs to stop.

A multitude of objections will be raised against my position, and a multitude of objections have been raised against the Church's position. Those have been answered by a number of people with far greater qualifications than I have.[109] But let's take a quick look at a few of those objections.

"Do you believe that abortion is forgivable?" Yes, absolutely. There's no such thing as an unforgivable sin, other than despairing of God's forgiveness. In other words, God can and will forgive you for every sin — unless you don't let Him forgive you. God loves every woman who has ever had an abortion, just as He loves every abortionist and clinic worker, just as He loves me and you, and every other human being for whom He died. God loves you absolutely.

"What about abortion in cases of rape and incest?" The child did not rape, and the child did not commit incest. Don't kill an innocent child for someone else's sin.

"Doesn't a woman have the right to control her own body?" Yes, but this right is not without accompanying responsibilities. A woman does not have the right to destroy herself by anorexia or bulimia. A woman does not have the right to commit suicide. A woman has an obligation to love herself as the person with dignity and value that she is. She has a responsibility to be a good steward of her body, and she has the responsibility to be a good mother to the children she conceives, even if that means putting the children up for adoption or letting them live with relatives. Further, a child in the womb is not simply "part of a woman's body." Look at the old phrases we continue to use to speak about pregnancy. A pregnant woman is "with child," "bearing a child," and "eating for two." We have never said, "The woman has four legs, now, and four eyes. Bet she'll be glad to be back to normal in a few months!" The child's body is in the woman's body — it is not indistinguishable from the woman's body.

"You're not a woman, so who are you to say anything about a woman's choice?" Essentially, this argument says that no human can justifiably decide whether someone else's action is right or wrong. That would be the end of law. Further, this argument would deny fathers any say whatsoever when it comes to the lives of their children. What if the father wants to keep the child and doesn't want the mother to have an abortion? Does he have absolutely no say in the matter? If not, why not?

"If you don't like abortion, don't have one." That's like saying, "If you don't like hiring hit men, don't hire one!" For the sake of society, we have to oppose the taking of innocent human life. Once such taking of life is accepted as normal, the effects on a society are wide-ranging and very dangerous. Mother Teresa made this plain in her acceptance speech when she was awarded the Nobel Peace Prize, saying, "I feel the greatest destroyer of peace today is abortion."[110]

Again, God can and will forgive someone who has procured an abortion or performed an abortion — a person can go to Confession and have all his or her sins forgiven. There are many mitigating circumstances that can reduce or remove a person's culpability for an abortion, but abortion remains wrong.

Question 23:
How can you still be Catholic
when progressive Catholics sometimes feel
unwelcome or unneeded in the Church?

That's a fairly political question. I may not have a political answer. I can still be Catholic because Jesus loves us all and calls us all to be one with Him in the Eucharist and Baptism, to bring His presence and His love to all nations, and to gather all humankind into one great assembly of praise. Catholicism calls us to be inclusive in ways that nobody else does.

Now, does this mean we are always successful at being inclusive and welcoming? No, of course not. In a hospital for sinners, sometimes the patients don't always take their medicine. Catholics are not always models of the lovingkindness of God, nor are we always models of the thanksgiving of a Eucharistic life. We don't always make all feel "welcome in this place." So sometimes different people will feel "unwelcome or unneeded," not because they are not welcome nor because they have nothing to bring, but because many other Catholics are still a long way from sanctity.

But let's take another look at one aspect of the question: "unneeded in the Church." Now, in a certain sense, every human being on earth is "unneeded" — because our very existence is a gift. We are gratuitous. We are extra. God did not need to create us, and He does not owe us our existence. Indeed, the very existence of the Church is a gift from God, because Jesus' coming and salvific acts were definitely not required of God by any obligation to us — except for the covenants that He entered into of His own free will. The whole cosmos is unneeded. It is a glorious gift, a wondrous extra created by God out of the overflowing abundance of His love and goodness. And in His love, we are all wanted, we are all desired, we are all intended from before the foundation of the earth.

When it comes to the life of an individual parish, of course, there are abundant needs, and God gives the parishioners the talents, time, and treasure to meet those needs, or at least the needs He expects them to address. So in that sense, all parishioners are, of course, needed. We are called to perform the works of mercy (see Appendix B), to go and preach the Gospel to the ends of the earth. We don't need to wait for our priest or our parish council to tell us to go do these things — we've already been called clearly by God and His Church! Look at the documents of Vatican II (especially *Apostolicam Actuositatem*, the *Decree on the Apostolate of the Laity*) or John Paul II's *Christifideles Laici* (*On the Vocation and the Mission of the Lay Faithful in the Church and in the World*) for more details on the call of the laity. We've all been given these missions, these tasks, by an ecumenical council and a great pope. So get going!

And the calls in these documents are universal for the laity, whether they would recognize themselves in the label "progressive," "conservative," "traditional," "liberal," "orthodox," or whatever. The Scriptures are normative for all of us. The documents from the Second Vatican Council are normative for all of us. The *Catechism* is normative for all of us. We are all called to be Catholic first, to be disciples of Jesus Christ and citizens of Heaven before we are political, before we are national, before we are local. This means that strongly political people are challenged not to simply pick and choose from the teachings of the Church what best fits their political affiliations.

Peter Maurin and the Servant of God Dorothy Day, who led lives of great fidelity to Christ and His Church in creating the Catholic Worker Movement and working for peace and justice wherever and however they could, proved that to be fully Catholic is to transcend merely national or political allegiances. Really, to be fully Catholic is to transcend one's own time, even as you live in it and are formed by it. We are not called to be modern, or to keep up with the times, or to embrace being a throwback to an earlier time. We are called to live in the light of the Second Coming of Jesus Christ, to bring about the end of history in our own lives and work. What does this mean? It means we are called to live in the light of eternity. We are to be conformed to the life and love of God, to be open to the Trinitarian life flowing through us into the world around us. All our works must be founded on prayer and sacrifice. All our efforts in the world must be rooted in our firm conviction that humans cannot build the kingdom of God; that God alone can build the kingdom of God; and that unless God builds the house, the builders labor in vain (see Ps 127:1).

We cannot embrace the false option of horizontal worship (worship focused on fostering the life of the Church on earth as community, first and foremost, rather than worship as a relationship between the Church and God) or vertical worship (worship whose first and perhaps only priority is adoring God, rather than taking any thought for the earthly experience of fellowship among believers), of having a high or low Christology. We are called to be Christians, marked by the sign of the Cross and realizing that this world and the divine life meet at the center, at Jesus Christ, and from His side flow blood and water, flow life and streams of living water. We are to be supernaturalized. We need to open the door between this world and the next in our own lives and communities.

This Christian call is not a political matter. The Christian call is transcendent. All are welcome to the supernatural life. All are welcome to the fullness of the faith and the pathway of Christian spirituality. And saints are needed in the parishes, in the kingdom of God.

So come, all you progressives, and progress in the interior life. Perform the works of mercy. Pass through the ways of purgation, illumination, and union with the living God. Walk the Catholic walk with all your brethren, and learn with them the full scope of the orthodoxy of the Church — social teaching and sacramental teaching, the call of peace and the call to spiritual combat, the ways of justice and the ways of supernatural faith. Seek to transform the structures of sin in light of Solzhenitsyn's great insight: that we can't simply seek out and destroy or incarcerate all the evil people, all "those" people, whoever they are, because "the line dividing good and evil cuts through the heart of every human being."[111] It's not a question of the enlightened versus the unenlightened, the paladins of progress and civilization against the retrograde forces of reaction and darkness; it's a question, fundamentally, of doing good and avoiding evil for all of us, every minute of every day.

The path to true justice and peace runs through the Heart of Jesus, through your own heart. The path to the transformation of the structures of this world runs along the path of the Christian spiritual life, the interior life.[112] We must seek our own transformation and offer Jesus to other people, for it is people who make up the structures and commit good or evil acts. You may change the party in power, but it is the people who make up the party who must be changed from the ground of their being by the grace of God before we will ever see justice again. And God alone has the competence for this. So be welcome in the parishes, come to the Sacraments, be brethren of all.

Question 24:

How can you still be Catholic when you see the Church treating women as second class?

Well, quite simply, I *don't* see the Church treating women as second class — any more than I see the Church treating married men as second class, or treating as second class any other group in the Church who are not priests and bishops.

Keep in mind that the foremost people in the eyes of the Church are the saints, not the popes, cardinals, bishops, or priests. Indeed, the supreme member of the Catholic Church, second only to Jesus, is His Mother, Mary. The greatest person in the Catholic Church is not a pope — it's a woman from the small towns of the Middle East. More than that — Mary is the supreme creature, the greatest of all created beings, the Queen of Heaven and earth.[113] Some of the saints held up by the Church as "Doctors" or wise teachers of the faith are women, as well: Teresa of Avila, Thérèse of Lisieux, Catherine of Siena, and Hildegard of Bingen. Some of the most influential people in the Church have been women, such as Mother Teresa of Calcutta, St. Faustina Kowalska, and St. Monica. All these, and many, many others.

What is the Catholic view of women? John Paul II laid it out in detail in a letter called *Mulieris Dignitatem* (*On the Dignity and Vocation of Women*):

> In God's eternal plan, woman is the one in whom the order of love in the created world of persons

takes first root. The order of love belongs to the intimate life of God himself, the life of the Trinity. In the intimate life of God, the Holy Spirit is the personal *hypostasis* of love. Through the Spirit, Uncreated Gift, love becomes a gift for created persons. Love, which is of God, communicates itself to creatures: "God's love has been poured into our hearts through the Holy Spirit who has been given to us" (Rom 5:5).

The calling of woman into existence at man's side as "a helper fit for him" (Gen 2:18) in the "unity of the two", provides the visible world of creatures with particular conditions so that "the love of God may be poured into the hearts" of the beings created in his image ... .[114]

In other words, woman is required for God's love to reach the created world. She stands as a sign of love and a means of love passing from Heaven to earth and from earth to Heaven — a role lived in a perfect way by the Blessed Virgin Mary. Women fulfill their roles as men are called to fulfill theirs — we are not interchangeable cogs in a machine. We are all members of the Body of Christ, and just as in a human body, there's a hierarchy of organs. It's almost an equality of differentiation. As St. Paul explains:

There are different kinds of spiritual gifts but the same Spirit; there are different forms of service but the same Lord; there are different workings but the same God who produces all of them in everyone. ...

As a body is one though it has many parts, and all the parts of the body, though many, are one body, so also Christ. For in one Spirit we were all baptized into one body, whether Jews or Greeks, slaves or free persons, and we were all given to drink of one Spirit.

Now the body is not a single part, but many. If a foot should say, "Because I am not a hand I do not belong to the body," it does not for this reason belong any less to the body. Or if an ear should say, "Because I am not an eye I do not belong to the body," it does not for this reason belong any less to the body. If the whole body were an eye, where would the hearing be? If the whole body were hearing, where would the sense of smell be? But as it is, God placed the parts, each one of them, in the body as he intended (1 Cor 12:4-6, 12-18).

The Church is not a body politic — she is a body *mystic*. The Church cannot be understood merely in terms of power politics and interest groups. She is most properly a family, the people of God, the sons and daughters of God.

In a family, there is a hierarchy of relationships. Different members have different rights and responsibilities — and there is no interchangeability. Each member is unique and irreplaceable. Different people can fill different roles to a certain extent, but all members are loved in their uniqueness, in their personal particularity. Further, the flourishing of the individual is tied to the flourishing of the group, and the flourishing of the group is tied up with the flourishing of the individual. The individual is not served by parents forfeiting parental authority; or by children failing to live out their lives and vocations as children at whatever stage of maturity; and so forth. In short, the Church is not democratic because families are not democratic.

Now, does this mean that women have full representation in positions of leadership in the Church? Nope, not yet. Is this something that can and should be fixed? Yes, absolutely — more women can become consultors to the different congregations and committees of the Vatican.[115] Let there be more female theologians. Let there be women religious with greater participation through the structure of the Church. Great! Why not?

As answered in Question 11 (see pg. 56), women will not be made priests, because priesthood is inextricable from fatherhood. But women can certainly take on a much larger role in the household of God than they currently exercise.

Question 25:
How can you still be Catholic
when you see what your being
Catholic is doing to your family?

Not having lived the conflict of being the first or the only
Catholic in a family that isn't friendly to the faith, I can only
give an answer uninformed by personal experience. The con-
flicts faced by converts or Catholics (and other Christians) in
the minority are those predicted by Jesus:

> Do not think that I have come to bring peace upon
> the earth. I have come to bring not peace but the
> sword. For I have come to set / a man "against his
> father, / a daughter against her mother, / and a
> daughter-in-law against her mother-in-law; / and
> one's enemies will be those of his household."
>
> Whoever loves father or mother more than
> me is not worthy of me, and whoever loves son or
> daughter more than me is not worthy of me; and
> whoever does not take up his cross and follow after
> me is not worthy of me. Whoever finds his life will
> lose it, and whoever loses his life for my sake will
> find it (Mt 10:34-39).

How can people be Catholic even if it causes family
strife, even if it costs them dearly? People do this because

they believe the faith to be true. They believe in Jesus Christ and His Church; in the Sacraments; in the power of prayer; and in the teachings on morality, the human person, and our final destiny. And since they believe the faith to be true — well, what else are they supposed to do? As Peter said to Jesus, "Master, to whom shall we go? You have the words of eternal life. We have come to believe and are convinced that you are the Holy One of God" (Jn 6:68).

Such a conviction has caused many people down through the centuries to convert, no matter the social stigma or concern from the family. From the earliest Roman martyrs to the many, many killed in the 20th century, even death has not deterred people from following Jesus and His Church. Most people, of course, don't face physical danger in order to be Catholic, but a fair number do face losing friends and communities, or at the least face misunderstanding, resistance, and hostility when they enter the Catholic Church.

There are many stories about this. To take just one, St. Monica, the mother of the great author and Doctor of the Church St. Augustine of Hippo, was for a long time the only Christian in her family. Her husband was a man of renowned temper. Her son had a mistress and was a learned Manichee — member of a gnostic sect — for many years. She persevered in prayer and patience for both the men in her family. Her husband converted toward the end of his life, and her son became one of the greatest bishops and teachers the Catholic Church has ever known.[116]

It can be hard to be a convert, so different groups of people who have already entered the Church have sprung up to assist those on the way. Protestants and other people considering Catholicism often find great solace and support through groups such as the Coming Home Network (chnetwork.org), run by former Protestant minister Marcus Grodi. CatholicsComeHome.org is another great resource for former Catholics.

Once in the Church, you should be able to find a network of friends to support you in walking the Catholic road and living the Gospel in the modern world. Join a parish Bible study (or start one!); enroll in the Knights of Columbus; join prayer groups, moms' groups, whatever groups the parish has that fit your needs and interests; or talk to the priest about starting such a group. Explore what your diocese or archdiocese offers in the way of faith formation and fellowship opportunities. We are called, not to walk the straight and narrow path on our own, but to go accompanied on the journey so that God, looking out of the gates of Heaven or the doors of the tabernacle, can say, "Here comes everybody!"[117]

Why does God permit His followers to suffer for their faith? Well, it is part of the package, really, and proposed as a blessing.

> Blessed are they who are persecuted for the sake of righteousness, / for theirs is the kingdom of heaven. / Blessed are you when they insult you and persecute you and utter every kind of evil against you [falsely] because of me. Rejoice and be glad, for your reward will be great in heaven. Thus they persecuted the prophets who were before you (Mt 5:10-12).

How can this be a blessing? Because by sharing in the Passion and death of Jesus, we come to share in His life with the Father, which is the total gift of self in love without end. Such total, divine self-gift is not natural for human beings — it is supernatural, and so it demands that we embrace the cross, that we embrace dying to self so as to enter into the divine relationship. Jesus has saved us by His suffering and death — now we must embrace the little deaths of giving up our free time so that we can be with a loved one, or giving up some money for the homeless man on the corner, or serving at a soup kitchen or youth group or parish social, or any of the million and one little things that call us to turn away from ourselves and turn toward another person, so that Christ's life may grow in us.

That said, if a Catholic needs help dealing with the re-action to their conversion, they should absolutely seek it out. Talk to your priest or someone else at the parish office for help processing the changes in your life. And make sure you plunge as deeply into the sacramental life as you can — regular Mass and Confession, regular prayer, regular reading of Scripture and other spiritual reading. Pray for your family and friends, especially those giving you the hardest time. Bring your suf-ferings to the foot of the Cross and ask Jesus to help you carry them. (And pray that your pain will be a source of grace for the conversion of the people giving you a hard time — a wonder-fully sneaky way to handle the problem!)

Most of all, drink deeply of the grace and beauty of your new Church. Explore her art, literature, and history. Read the philosophy and theology of the great minds of the Church. Go to the shrines and attend Mass on the feast days. Read the spiritual classics and learn how to grow in communion with the living God who loves us so much that He sent His only begotten Son, and sends the Son to us in every Mass, at every Eucharist, who pours out His Spirit on all flesh for the sanctifi-cation and transformation of the world.[118] Come to know your fellow Christians, and do not be surprised when you find other sinners in the pew next to you. Pray for us, and we'll pray for you. Welcome to the family.

Question 26:
How can you still be Catholic when the Church says masturbation will bring you eternal damnation?

No sin is damnable if it is properly confessed, first of all. That has to be absolutely clear. The Church is meant to be a highway to Heaven, not a swift slide to hell. The Church is here for our salvation, not our condemnation. And so we've been given the Sacrament of Confession.

But the question focused on masturbation, because many people find it ludicrous that such a relatively easy and common sin should be considered by the Church a mortal sin — that is, the sort of sin that can kill the divine life in a soul and send a person to hell.

Why on earth would masturbation be damnable under *any* circumstances?

Because going to Heaven isn't just about God making a decision and opening a door. Living in Heaven is taking part in the divine life, joining in the eternal dance of generosity, of self-gift between the Persons of the Trinity and all the other blessed people in Heaven. To be in Heaven, you have to be able to keep up. That's possible only through God's grace, and God's grace will not abide in an unwilling soul, to paraphrase a line from fantasy writer Diane Duane.

To be able to live happily in Heaven requires a soul filled with sanctifying grace, healed of its attachments to sin. The soul must have given up mistaking created things for God.

God must come first, not food, or pleasure, or even family or country. God must be treated as God in the soul, and the neighbor loved with the same love God has for the soul, and then the soul may share in the life of God in Heaven.

So a lot of sins that may seem unlikely can be damnable. The question isn't, "How many people does the sin visibly hurt on earth?" but rather, "Does it prevent you from loving? Does it prevent you from absolute generosity with God? Does it kill divine charity in your soul, leaving no room to love as God loves?"

God calls us to self-mastery and self-gift, not self-satisfaction. But masturbation is intrinsically a selfish act, training us in self-centeredness, not in self-donation. That's why it's a serious sin.

But the Church doesn't flat out say, "Masturbate, and you'll go to hell." Here's the *Catechism*:

> "Both the Magisterium of the Church, in the course of a constant tradition, and the moral sense of the faithful have been in no doubt and have firmly maintained that masturbation is an intrinsically and gravely disordered action." "The deliberate use of the sexual faculty, for whatever reason, outside of marriage is essentially contrary to its purpose."[119]

In plain English: masturbation is wrong, and shouldn't be done. However, to say it's wrong to do something isn't the same thing as saying a person is fully to blame for having done it. There are a number of factors that can lessen or nearly eliminate culpability for masturbation. The *Catechism* lists:

- Affective immaturity
- Force of acquired habit
- Conditions of anxiety
- Other psychological or social factors[120]

Here is one example of extenuating "social factors" that reduce the guilt of masturbation: If people are taught by their culture, their school, their parents, every authority that they know and trust that masturbation is all right … well, it's not really fair to hold them accountable for doing something wrong if everyone is insisting it's fine.

But why do masturbation and, indeed, all the other sexual sins matter so much?

Simply because sex matters so much, both because sex naturally leads to new life, but also because sex means so much more than simple desire. Sex says, "I love you." Sex naturally involves self-donation between two persons who shall endure forever, and leads to the formation of families. And more: When a married couple has sex, the spouses are imaging the love of God.

Look at the very structure of the Bible! Genesis begins with a husband and wife in a bridal bower of a garden (see Gen 1-3), and it ends with the Bride and the Bridegroom consummating history in the New Jerusalem in the presence of the tree of life (Rev 22). The centerpiece of Scripture is the Song of Songs, a great love poem between a lover and his beloved. Human sexuality mirrors divine self-gift. The relationship between a husband and a wife — a sexual, romantic relationship — is used by Sacred Scripture again and again as an image of the relationship between God and His creation; between God and Israel (see Hos 2, for example); and between God and His Church (see Eph 5:29-32). A great deal of Christian mystical literature compares the erotic love of a human couple to the love between God and the mystic's soul.[121] Now, we need to be clear — human love is like divine love, but divine love is not like human love. The lower is like the higher, but the higher is inexpressibly more than the lower.

Human sexuality, then, matters a great deal. Get it right, and it resembles divine love. Get it wrong, and the consequences can be catastrophic, as many, many stories told in novels, onstage, on film, and in songs make plain — stories about adultery, divorce, deception, betrayal, and loneliness.

So masturbation is wrong because it trains us away from self-donation and into self-satisfaction. It's a serious sin ("grave matter," in the theological language of the Church) because it involves a misuse of human sexuality, which is naturally ordered to the giving of new life and the formation of families, and which also serves as an icon of the love of Heaven. But those of us who masturbate are often not fully culpable for the act because of the mitigating circumstances laid out above.

Even after having gone through all of that, though, some people will, I suspect, still have problems with this particular Church teaching. Many people find the Church's moral code impossible, unthinkable, and incredibly harsh. Seemingly small things are treated as serious sins.

Why? Well, in part because the Church calls us to holiness, through God's grace, and holiness looks like dying to self. It looks like transcending our human nature and taking on divine nature through an unstinting, at times excruciating, generosity with God. It looks like the lives of the saints, in other words.

How can anyone live this way? It's possible through the grace of the Holy Spirit, through prayer, through the Sacraments, and through a love of God so powerful that everything else gives way before it. But it does require dying to self.

What happens if (when) we fail? Go to Confession. The Church preaches a morality of perfection to sinners, and so has the medicine of mercy ready for us when we fall and fail to live up to that morality. We trust that, by the grace of God, if we persist in trying to obey Him out of love, He will make it possible. We will be healed of our vices. We will be given clean hearts. Whether our perfection occurs in this life or in the life to come, it will happen by the grace of God and our openness to the will and the love of God.

But until our perfection comes, we will continue to acknowledge our sinfulness in the Our Father, the Hail Mary, and the *Confiteor* at Mass. We will continue to go to Confession and pray for a happy death — one where we die in the state of grace, our souls washed clean by the Sacraments and sped on the path to Heaven by the grace of God and the gift of the Church.

Question 27:

How can you still be Catholic
when the Church did such terrible things
during the Inquisition?

The brief answer is, "Because we've come a long way. Vatican II, an ecumenical council, enshrined religious freedom and the rights of the individual conscience in Catholic teaching in an indelible way.[122] Pope St. John Paul II was a tremendous defender of universal human rights and religious liberty all over the world,[123] reinforcing the precedent set by Pope St. John XXIII[124] and Blessed Pope Paul VI.[125] Pope Benedict XVI continued this tradition, currently maintained by Pope Francis, indicating that Catholic teaching on human rights and freedoms will continue."

The longer answer must start with a question: What was the Inquisition in the first place? The answer may be surprising. Historian Edward Peters sums up what it was not, explaining bluntly that the Inquisition of myth, "a single all-powerful, horrific tribunal, whose agents worked everywhere to thwart religious truth, intellectual freedom, and political liberty," simply never existed.[126]

He explains that "inquisition" is the name of a legal method, and it didn't start with the Catholic Church. It started in Roman law.[127] An inquisition was simply a particular method of inquiry or investigation that produced evidence relevant to the case. This method evolved over time.

Further, there were a number of regional inquisitions, as well as the supposedly universal Roman Inquisition. The most notorious, of course, was the Spanish Inquisition.

The Spanish Inquisition came into being after several centuries of war between native Spaniards and Islamic occupiers. The popes, after having authorized an Inquisition in Spain at the request of King Ferdinand and Queen Isabella of Spain, tried repeatedly to rein it in, but were prevented by the strength of the Spanish monarchs. Far from being a tyrannical imposition by the Church upon the state, it came about at the request of the monarchy. "The people as a whole gave support to its existence."[128]

Further, the Spanish Inquisition was far from being the totalitarian, omnipresent, omniscient body modern myth makes of it. Henry Kamen, a noted historian of the Inquisition, points out that the whole of Spain had 50 inquisitors. For them to exercise the control of myth, they would have needed a bigger organization as well as far more resources and power. In actual fact, for much of its existence, the Spanish Inquisition was irrelevant in large areas of Spain.[129]

Also, the Inquisition was criticized in Spain throughout its history.[130] The Spanish did not universally or uncritically accept its existence; some even made arguments for religious tolerance. The number of its victims is often grossly overstated — a good estimate would be around 3,000 to 5,000 executions over 350 years.[131] All executions were to be done by the civil authorities, since Church law forbade the clergy to kill or shed blood.[132] Further, the Inquisition had authority only over Christians.[133]

Does this mean the Spanish Inquisition was a perfectly fine institution? No. It was an organization entrusted with compelling orthodoxy and killing those who would not recant. Torture was used as part of its proceedings, though rarely.[134] Its activities had a nasty racial streak that often took the form of anti-Semitism. Though the "black legend" of the Spanish Inquisition, a horror story generated mainly by English-language propagandists, paints a far worse picture than the reality, the reality still looks bad enough from the perspective of an American raised in the land of liberty and the First Amendment. But let's be fair: The Spanish Inquisition came into existence at the tail end of about eight centuries of war between Christians and the Muslim invaders. It's not unthinkable that such a lengthy struggle would have left a mark and helped form the culture of *conquistadors* and inquisitors.

Does any of this justify the Inquisitions, the persecutions of heretics, the assault on apostates? No, not in light of what we've come to understand about religious liberty; the importance of the integrity of the individual conscience; and human rights, responsibilities, and freedoms. And St. John Paul II acknowledged this at the day of repentance in the year 2000. One of the confessions was a "confession of sins committed in the service of truth"[135] — because that is at the core of the whole process of the Inquisition. The point of the Inquisition was to compel people to believe and live according to the truth.

The problem with that is simple: Truth should be its own source of compulsion. Truth does not fail. Reality does not fail, as Msgr. Luigi Giusanni has said.[136] Forcing an individual to profess beliefs that he does not truly believe is a violation of his rights and dignity, and is a crime against the truth (for you compel that person to lie). Truth can compel only by force of reason or experience of reality. It can never legitimately compel someone's adherence by physical force.

Now, bringing people to the knowledge of the truth is a good thing. Violating their conscience and the integrity of their mind in order to force them to accept a truth is not a good thing. This was not clearly recognized for centuries of human history. Wrong was done in the service of a good cause. The Church was not simply out for power, or gain, or the suppression of dissent and opposition. She was pursuing the salvation of souls as best she knew how at the time. She has since learned better, of course. Vatican II has enshrined religious liberty in Catholic teaching in an enduring way.[137]

So I can be Catholic because the faith is better than the actions of Inquisitions past; and even in their acts of force, the

Inquisitions were hardly what the "black legend" would make them out to be. I can be Catholic with the Inquisition in the Church's past because it is in the past[138] — it has been faced and repudiated, and the Church has fully incorporated into her teaching the truths of universal human rights, religious liberty, and the responsibility of individuals to follow their rightly formed conscience.

Question 28:

How can you still be Catholic when praying to the saints and Mary contradicts Scripture, which says to pray to God alone?

We pray to the saints, asking for their intercession and their presence with us along the path to God. Why? Because they said yes to Jesus fully and completely. Their lives and hearts were completely open to the living God. When humans cooperate with His grace so completely, they become transparent to God's life and love, to His presence and power. The saints, then, become truly, fully temples of the Holy Spirit (see 1 Cor 6:19-20). Where they go, God goes.

The saints matter in Catholicism only because they have said "yes" to God, because they faithfully loved Jesus and are now in Heaven with Him. They have no strength apart from Jesus. All that they have and are comes from Him. So praying to the saints doesn't detract from the worship of and honor paid to Jesus, for the saints are the fruitful, fecund branches of the vine that is Jesus. To receive the help their prayers and presence can offer is to be surrounded by so great a cloud of witnesses, and to receive the fruits of Jesus. To love the saints is to love those whom Jesus loves. It's like getting married. When you marry, you don't refuse to get to know your spouse's family out of fear that you'll love him or her less. If you love your spouse, you love the people he or she loves. You love the family from which your spouse comes. You love people, places, and things that you might never otherwise have known or cared about, because your beloved loves them.

You talk to these people. You spend time with them. You do things with them. You may even ask them for help, or cooperate with them on a project for the family. None of this detracts from the love you have for your spouse; rather, all this fosters it.

But take a step back: I think the wording of the question needs work. The Bible is clear that God alone is to be *worshipped*. The whole of the Old Testament is a very long teaching on monotheism, in many ways, hammering away that the people of Israel shall have no gods before the God of Abraham, Isaac, and Jacob — they must be faithful to their covenants.

But prayer is not synonymous with worship (or adoration).[139] Further, take a look at the frequent Shakespearean use of "prithee," which expands to "I pray you." Prayer is a way to request or to communicate. It's speaking to someone.

Scripture doesn't condemn praying to the saints in order to ask their intercession. I think it condemns taking anyone as a god other than God.

"But wait a second — if a person is dead, isn't praying to him or her necromancy? And that's forbidden by Scripture!" Yes, necromancy is forbidden by Scripture — but according to Jesus, the saints aren't dead:

> ... [H]ave you not read what was said to you by God, "I am the God of Abraham, the God of Isaac, and the God of Jacob"? He is not the God of the dead but of the living (Mt 22:31-32; see Mk 12:26-27).

Why does He say this? Obviously, Abraham was long (physically) dead, as were Isaac and Jacob. Scripture elsewhere recounts their deaths (see Gen 25:7-11; 35:28-29; 49:29-33). So what was Jesus saying? The saints have entered into an eternal relationship with God through Jesus, and so they are not dead. They have eternal life.[140] Supreme Knight of the

Knights of Columbus Carl Anderson and Catholic University of America theology professor Fr. José Granados explain Jesus' words about Abraham, Isaac, and Jacob in terms of the covenant. God has sworn a covenant with these men using his own eternal name. The patriarchs, then, are in an eternal relationship with the source of life, with God. To be in communion with another is to be alive, so these men are alive for all eternity.[141]

Therefore, to speak to the saints is to communicate not with the dead, but with the living. Further, we are all members of the Mystical Body of Jesus Christ, all one in the new and everlasting covenant in the blood of Jesus Christ. Just as you ask your brothers and sisters in Christ to pray for you when something has come up, so do Catholics ask their brothers and sisters in Christ who are already in Heaven to pray for them to the Lord our God. Furthermore, as the Book of Revelation points out, the prayers of the saints matter in Heaven.

> When he broke open the fifth seal, I saw underneath the altar the souls of those who had been slaughtered because of the witness they bore to the word of God. They cried out in a loud voice, "How long will it be, holy and true master, before you sit in judgment and avenge our blood on the inhabitants of the earth?" Each of them was given a white robe, and they were told to be patient a little while longer until the number was filled of their fellow servants and brothers who were going to be killed as they had been (Rev 6:9-11).

> Another angel came and stood at the altar, holding a gold censer. He was given a great quantity of incense to offer, along with the prayers of all the holy ones, on the gold altar that was before the throne. The smoke of the incense along with the prayers of the holy ones went up before God from the hand of the angel. Then the angel took the censer, filled

it with burning coals from the altar, and hurled it down to the earth. There were peals of thunder, rumblings, flashes of lightning, and an earthquake (Rev 8:3-4).

So I can very easily be Catholic when it is Catholic practice in the Mass as well as in devotions to ask for the intercession of the saints (and the Orthodox can very easily be Orthodox, as well, when their churches use icons and pray to the saints almost more than Catholics do). The devotion to the saints comes from an intense awareness of the Communion of Saints and the meaning of the biblical covenants, which bring us into a living relationship with God, the Source of life everlasting.

Love Jesus? Love His family. Get to know these others who have loved Him for so long and so well. Talk to them. Have pictures of the family members of the household of God around. Come to know and love His Mother as Jesus loves her. Come to know and love the long litany of our forebears in the faith, those alive in God, who surround the Church on earth with love and care, with prayer and presence, so that more of us might make the journey home to Heaven. God requires us to love one another as He loves us. Why not talk to those who love us in God, those whom we are to love in God, and those with whom we shall, we hope, live in Heaven?

Question 29:
How can you still be Catholic when the Church has led so many organized acts of violence and oppression?

That's like asking, "How can you still be an American citizen after America has led so many organized acts of violence (the Civil War and other wars) and oppression (the Trail of Tears, internment of Japanese Americans, slavery and Jim Crow laws, etc.)?" The answer is essentially the same to both questions.

Why am I still an American? Because I see so much good in this country, good that outweighs the bad. We have some very dark moments in our history — shameful moments — but often, those dark moments came about through a failure to live up to our own ideals. America has values that are better than it is. That means we have higher levels of excellence for which to strive. We are set on an upward path, and I would like to walk with my country the whole way toward liberty and justice for all. I would like to see us achieve the full promise embodied in the statement, "We hold these truths to be self-evident, that all men are created equal, that they are endowed by their Creator with certain unalienable Rights, that among these are Life, Liberty and the pursuit of Happiness."[142]

Why am I still Catholic? Because I see infinite good in this Church and this faith, good that outweighs the bad. I believe in the Sacraments, and if you believe in the Sacraments, then you understand that the Church is the keeper of unfathomable treasures. I believe in grace, and God, and Jesus Christ, so I believe in the promises He made about His Church and its endurance. We have some very dark parts of our history, yes, but often those dark parts came from a failure to live up to the Church's own teaching.

The Church teaches that humans are to worship and seek the truth, to pursue justice in their dealings with their fellow human beings, to do good and avoid evil. We are forbidden from attacking the innocent and called to deal rightly with all people, loving them all, doing good for those who hate us. The faith is better than we are, and that is a wonderful thing.

Now, that having been said, it's worth asking, "Is the history of the Catholic Church as dark as commonly imagined?" And the answer to that is, "No, probably not." Sociologist Philip Jenkins wrote a book called *The New Anti-Catholicism: The Last Acceptable Prejudice* (Oxford University Press, 2003). In it, he pointed out that the Church has featured in a lot of horror stories, many of which tended to stretch the truth. Jenkins, a convert from Catholicism to the Episcopalian denomination, traced the history of anti-Catholic prejudice in America from the time of the founders to the new millennium and devotes an entire chapter to some of the "black legends" that surround Catholicism.[143] (We deal with specific incidents elsewhere in this book.) Jenkins points out that even though there is plenty of darkness in the true history of Catholicism, there's also what he calls "a whole alternative history, or historical mythology"[144] often cited by critics of the Church — a lot of stories and claims that simply aren't true. Yet they keep being repeated because so many people believe them and, in turn, pass them on.

My interest in reading about Catholic history began when I kept running into this historical mythology. It often surfaced at school: One textbook claimed the Church had persecuted witches because they challenged the Church's monopoly on magic, for instance.[145] We got a very basic sense of the Crusades and the Inquisition as acts of oppression and invasion, the Church as a force standing in the way of human progress, and, overall, better left in the dustbin of human history. It was sometimes difficult being a Catholic in public school. After all, everyone is basically getting the same version of history.

The storyline remained a constant as I grew up: *The Catholic Church tried to hold back human progress and individual liberty. The Church stood in the way of freedom of conscience until the Reformation broke her monopoly on religion in Europe and opened the way to true freedom. The Enlightenment firmly set the Church in her place by insisting on the rights of mankind and the independence of the state from religious oppression. The Church stood on the side of kings and royalty of all kinds until revolutions shook the people free from her tyrannical grasp throughout Europe. The Church was silent or colluded with the Nazis in the Holocaust because she's always been anti-Semitic.*

And on, and on, and on — always on the wrong side of history, always opposing everything we stand for as Americans, always with the forces of hidebound reaction and regression, always anti … .

I was interested in learning the truth, and if the truth was as bad as was being portrayed, then, well, that's all there was to it. Truth is truth. But I was skeptical. After all, my family went to church every Sunday at the local parish. My experience of Sunday Mass, the priests, and my fellow Catholics didn't come anywhere close to the dark, oppressive, power-hungry Catholic Church that was portrayed in textbooks, or that my classmates described in casual conversation.

So I began reading about the history of the Church and gradually began to discover books such as Jenkins' *The New Anti-Catholicism*, the works of Lutheran sociologist Rodney Stark, Thomas Woods' *How the Catholic Church Built Western Civilization*, and a bunch of others, discovering over time a very different portrait of the history of Catholicism. Yes, there were still very bad popes and clerics involved in cloak-and-dagger intrigue. Yes, bad men, sometimes ignorant men, did bad things in the name of Christ and His Church — bad things, ill-advised things, even evil things, like the slaughtering of innocents in the Crusades and violations of religious freedom during the Inquisition and under Charlemagne. But the dark times were almost never as dark as the textbooks implied or my classmates assumed.

And in the long lifetime of the Church there was a great deal of light that tended to be minimized or left unmentioned. Aside from the bad, there was also a wealth of saints, living and loving as Jesus Christ had done. There was also the creation of the universities, centers of free thought and perhaps the most rigorous use of human reason the world had ever known; and the invention of the hospital, source of more aid to the sick and dying than any other culture had ever invented. There were also the hundreds, if not thousands, of religious orders dedicated to the works of mercy. There was also the sponsorship of the cathedrals of Europe and the Renaissance, producing some of the most beautiful creations of human ingenuity in all of our history. There were also monasteries, some of the most effective engines of sanctification and international development the world has ever known, preserving so much of the best of antiquity and making major strides in agriculture, technology, medicine, and other scientific disciplines.[146] There was this, and so much more.[147]

Some of this is known by most people. *Some.* And yet it never seems to break through the dark cloud that hovers over the Church's past in so many minds. So until I've seen abundant evidence to the contrary, I have often been deeply skeptical of accusations directed at the Church. Not because I think the hierarchy can do no wrong — indeed, the average Catholic is well aware of the wrongs the hierarchy can do! Just as members of a family often know one another's faults all too well, Catholics know all too well the sins of our fathers. I'm often skeptical when someone says something bad about the Church because so much of what's said is simply untrue or, at the very least, incomplete. There is, as Paul Harvey used to say, "the rest of the story," and, whether mischievously or innocently, it gets left out — a lot.

Question 30:
How can you still be Catholic when they didn't immediately denounce slavery?

I can still be Catholic because Jesus did not come to condemn the institution of slavery. I think slavery is a great evil and should be eradicated from the world. But to be surprised that the Catholic Church did not get rid of it first thing is to work from the assumption that the Catholic Church is primarily dedicated to social activism.

She isn't. The Church is the Mystical Body of Christ, the pilgrim people of God, called into being by the covenants of God with humanity and the created order so as to extend the divine life and love throughout the cosmos by Word and Sacrament. We are to love God with all our being and to love our neighbor as ourselves. These are the first responsibilities. The responsibility to worship comes first, followed by the requirement to love our neighbor. The Church's first priority is to introduce people to God. When people are introduced to God, their lives change. Their priorities get rearranged. The world changes, and then the earthly societies change in which Christians dwell — which sometimes takes centuries.

So the apostles did not issue a prophetic denunciation of slavery in the first century. They did something even more radical, something with even farther-reaching consequences. They called all humanity to the universal brotherhood of the Church.

For through faith you are all children of God in Christ Jesus. For all of you who were baptized into Christ have clothed yourselves with Christ. There is neither Jew nor Greek, there is neither slave nor free person, there is not male and female; for you are all one in Christ Jesus (Gal 3:26-28; see Col 3:9-11).

As Christianity penetrated the world, it acted like leaven in a lump of dough, transforming the social structures around itself until slavery disappeared in the lands where Christianity predominated. Sociologist Rodney Stark explained that when the Church offered the Sacraments to all, both slave and free, and then achieved a ban on the enslavement of Christians and Jews, "that prohibition was effectively a rule of universal abolition."[148]

Stark points to a number of local condemnations of slavery from the first millennium of the Church, indicating that the abolitionist logic arising from the heart of the Gospel's teaching on humanity was at work throughout Christian history.[149]

Was that the end of slavery? Nope. Slavery continued on the borders of Christendom where Muslims and Christians warred against each other, enslaving their prisoners, though in at least one case, Venetian clergy did public penance for Christian involvement in the "Moorish slave trade."[150] Later, the New World slave trade was the target of explicit papal condemnations. For example, Pope Paul III, in the bull *Sublimus Dei*, issued May 29, 1537, said:

We ... noting that the Indians themselves indeed are true men ... by our Apostolic Authority decree and declare by these present letters that the same Indians and all other peoples — even though they are outside the faith ... should not be deprived of their liberty or their other possessions ... and are not to be reduced to slavery, and that whatever happens to the contrary is to be considered null and void.[151]

Now, obviously the bull was widely ignored. But it was used as the precedent for later Catholic rulings on slavery, such as Pope Urban VIII's bull of April 22, 1639, *Commissum nobis*, and the Roman Inquisition's response of March 20, 1686, to questions posed to it, as Stark recounts, in which the Holy Office flatly ruled against the enslavement of "Blacks and other natives who have harmed no one," holding that those who owned such persons were bound to set them free, and that the "captors, buyers and possessors" of such persons were bound to offer their freed slaves compensation.[152]

As Stark shows, the Church issued condemnations of New World slavery from the early days of exploration. Did Catholics listen as they should have? Nope. What happened? Original sin got in the way, with the same effects that humanity has been struggling against since the time of the Fall.

Stark also discusses how Catholics, both clergy and laity, owned and traded slaves at various times.[153] The Church's teaching on slavery, like her teaching on abortion, was widely ignored at the time it was promulgated for a host of reasons, including the fortunes to be made in the slave trade and the Church's waning political and military power from the end of the Middle Ages onward. But that teaching was, and is, clear. As Leo XIII taught in the 1890 encyclical *Catholicae Ecclesiae* (*On Slavery in the Missions*)[154] and the Church made clear at Vatican II, slavery is wrong.[155]

I can still be Catholic even though the Church did not immediately set out to end slavery because the Gospel doesn't usually transform an entire culture overnight. The implications of Jesus' message and the effects of God's grace work as a slow, oncoming tide, washing against human history with the tremendous, gradual force of the ocean. God doesn't always send tsunamis of change. It's taken a long time for the full force of the teaching of the New Testament on the equality of humans as brothers and sisters to really work its way into people's hearts and minds. We're still not done. I can still be Catholic because the Church, with her Sacraments and her teachings, is given by Jesus to the world as a gift. The fact that we failed in the past to fully live up to the gift is no surprise — we don't live up to the gift now. The faith is better than we are. Jesus, the Founder and Head of the Church, is better than all other Catholics combined — and He's worth following.

Question 31:
How can you still be Catholic
when the Church had corrupt popes?

I can still be Catholic even after corrupt popes because — well, heck, look at St. Peter himself, the very first pope, for Pete's sake! When Jesus was on his boat and caused the fishermen to pull in a huge catch, Peter's reaction was to fall flat on his face and explain just how completely sinful he was and how unworthy of having Jesus in his boat. In the Garden of Gethsemane, when Jesus asked Peter, James, and John to stay awake and watch with Him, Peter fell asleep. He abandoned Jesus when the soldiers came and denied three times that he knew Jesus.

The popes have not been perfect, no. They have followed the model of the first in their line, a mixed bag of goodness and vice, sometimes faithful, sometimes faulty. Peter was a changed man after Pentecost, preached a sermon that converted 3,000 people that day, and led the early Church through persecution and trouble of every sort. He went back and forth over how to treat Gentile Christians, but eventually, at the Council of Jerusalem, took a strong stance for equality. At the end of his life, Peter was martyred for Jesus in Rome. When he was crucified, he requested that he be placed on the cross upside down because he felt unworthy of dying in the same way as his Teacher.

What's the point? The point is this: Jesus Christ is perfect. His Mother is without sin. All other members of the Church

— sinners. All of us. Some are more egregious than others. Even the popes are sinners (see Question 13 on infallibility) in need of a Savior. But we all have the possibility and the promise of becoming saints, if only we say "yes" to the grace of God.

It is *men*, not angels, who are made popes. We hope our popes are men running the race and fighting the good fight, working out their salvation in fear and trembling so that one day they will be saints. But the Church elevates *men* to become vicars of Christ, His ambassadors, His prime ministers in this city on a hill, light to the nations, house built on a rock. Hence the reason the pope goes to Confession like the most ordinary Catholic in the pews: He's a sinner, just like the rest of us. Pope Francis has acknowledged this repeatedly in interviews and public statements,[156] as well as by going to Confession each year before he hears Confessions at the Vatican's 24 Hours for the Lord, a time of penance and prayer held each year during Lent.

We've recently been blessed with a long string of excellent popes, men of great courage and wisdom, of immense personal piety, often recognized as saintly men. It hasn't always been that way. And it probably will not always be that way. And sometimes, even the saintly pontiffs might not be the best administrators. Look at Pope St. Celestine V, a hermit elected as a compromise candidate. After a very short reign, he resigned. Saint Celestine is generally considered a holy man, and yet ineffectual as a pope. (By the way, his successor, Boniface VIII, wouldn't simply let him retire, but arrested him and held him in confinement until Celestine's death 10 months later.)[157]

The history of the popes is like the history of the human race — the good, the bad, and the ugly. But often the good ones do reach the heights of holiness, and often, the bad are not nearly as bad as we unquestioningly believe. Again, there's a lot of historical mythology that's been built up around the papacy, just as a lot of black legends and myths have been built up around the Inquisition and the Crusades. There are all sorts of villainy and vice in the history of the Church on earth, no question about that. We've had a number of sinful popes, a number of men whose legacy is not what we would have hoped. As the *Catechism* says:

> " ... The Church ... clasping sinners to her bosom, at once holy and always in need of purification, follows constantly the path of penance and renewal."[158] All members of the Church, including her ministers, must acknowledge that they are sinners.[159] In everyone, the weeds of sin will still be mixed with the good wheat of the Gospel until the end of time.[160]

Our faith is in Jesus Christ and His promises. He appointed Peter to be the rock on which the Church was built, a man who was not memorably steadfast before Pentecost, when the fire from Heaven changed his life. Peter's successors have been much the same, and are likely to be until the end of the world. The popes are called "Holy Father" because of their office, not because they must be holy or else the faith of Catholics will be shaken.

We pray for our pope at every Mass, asking God's help and protection for the man called to so huge a responsibility. We also pray for our bishops and priests, knowing how much they need it. For, after all, when the main criterion for entering the Catholic Church is being a sinner — being sick unto death with sin and in need of the resurrection promised through Jesus Christ — well, it should come as no surprise if we find weeds among the wheat.

So Catholics pray. We fast. We beg God's help and lean on the cross as our support, and walk haltingly along the way to Calvary, to our crucifixion and resurrection with Jesus, falling and getting up on the way. Grace is real. Transformation in Christ is real. But so is the spiritual combat. So we have had saints, and have saints now. We have had great sinners, and have great sinners now — saints and sinners among the popes, and among the laity. So it was in the days when Jesus walked the earth, and so it shall be again, and again, and again, until Jesus comes again.

Question 32:

How can you still be Catholic when the Church doesn't think gay people are still people who deserve their human rights?

I can be Catholic and believe that "gay people are still people who deserve their human rights" very easily — because what you've just said is the Catholic Church's teaching on gay people. Here's the *Catechism* on the subject (emphasis added):

> The number of men and women who have deep-seated homosexual tendencies is not negligible. This inclination, which is objectively disordered, constitutes for most of them a trial. *They must be accepted with respect, compassion, and sensitivity. Every sign of unjust discrimination in their regard should be avoided.* These *persons* are called to fulfill God's will in their lives and, if they are Christians, to unite to the sacrifice of the Lord's Cross the difficulties they may encounter from their condition.
>
> *Homosexual persons* are called to chastity. By the virtues of self-mastery that teach them inner freedom, at times by the support of disinterested friendship, by prayer and sacramental grace, they can and should gradually and resolutely approach Christian perfection.[161]

What does this teaching mean? First, the Church teaches that gay people are "people," that homosexuals have the same humanity and dignity that any other human being has. Second, the Church teaches that homosexuals are owed justice just as much as anyone else, that gay people have the same set of human rights as the rest of humanity, and that these rights must absolutely be respected, just as the human rights of everyone else must absolutely be respected.

"Yes," I imagine my friend saying, "but the Church teaches that gay people can't get married and shouldn't have sex, and that gay couples shouldn't adopt children. How is that treating them like everybody else?" As to marriage, the Church understands marriage to be:

> [t]he matrimonial covenant, by which a man and a woman establish between themselves a partnership of the whole of life, [which] is by its nature ordered toward the good of the spouses and the procreation and education of offspring; this covenant between baptized persons has been raised by Christ the Lord to the dignity of a sacrament ... .[162]

Gay persons are not forbidden by Church law from entering into such a relationship — provided it's a covenantal union *between a man and a woman*. In other words, there is no such thing as marriage between two men, or two women. Gay couples cannot be sacramentally married — not because the Church has decided to forbid it, but because it is simply, by the Church's understanding of the intrinsic nature of marriage, impossible.

And the Church has always taught that sex belongs in a marriage — and nowhere else. Further, the marital act must be the sort of act that is open to life. Under both counts, gay sex doesn't fit. The *Catechism* says:

> Homosexuality refers to relations between men or between women who experience an exclusive or

predominant sexual attraction toward persons of the same sex. It has taken a great variety of forms through the centuries and in different cultures. Its psychological genesis remains largely unexplained. Basing itself on Sacred Scripture, which presents homosexual acts as acts of grave depravity,[163] tradition has always declared that "homosexual acts are intrinsically disordered."[164] They are contrary to the natural law. They close the sexual act to the gift of life. They do not proceed from a genuine affective and sexual complementarity. Under no circumstances can they be approved.[165]

So the Church is not discriminating against gays. She is simply applying her sexual ethic uniformly to all people: Sex belongs inside marriage, which is a covenantal union between a man and a woman.

As to adoption, Catholicism sees the family as arising naturally from marriage and the marital act. Since this is the ideal family — a man and a woman joined as a biological unity and the children who spring from this union — the best place for children is such a family. Other family arrangements, though sometimes necessary (single-parent homes, for instance, or orphanages, or foster care), are not the ideal arrangement. Placing children with gay couples puts the children in a situation where they are missing a parent. Further, the model of life given in the household of a gay couple, according to the Catholic understanding of human nature and what we are called to by God, is not the model for children to be formed by.

Does this sound harsh? I'm sure to many people it does. But the Church believes it to be true and, as true, binding. After all, when you have come to the conclusion that something is true about the world in which we live, you cannot wish it away because you find it unpleasant.

Do many people agree with the Church today? Not nearly as many as used to — but then that doesn't really matter. Is Church teaching true or a cause just? If so, it doesn't matter who agreed or stood alongside to fight for the same cause — it's where we all should have taken our stand.

If the Church is right about human nature and sexuality, about the structure of the family and the role of the parents, about God's plan for our lives and the love He holds for all of us which is meant to be transmitted in a chain anchored in Him and reaching down through the generations of families to the end of the world, then by God, I'd better stand with the Church. And I believe the Church to be right in her teaching on marriage and sexuality.

Does that make it an easy walk? No — chastity is something many of us struggle with, even though it's something every Christian is called to, in or out of marriage. Chastity is not the same thing as celibacy. Celibacy means you never have sex. Chastity means that you never have sex outside marriage and that you are pure in mind and heart, as well. We are called to this hard virtue of chastity because other people are worth it. People are more than their physical attractiveness, far more than their youth and beauty, and everyone should be treated as a person rather than a mere object of desire. Use things, not people. Lust is far from a victimless sin.

And yet we live in a culture that, to this day, is deeply marked by the sexual revolution, a movement that never recognized the consequences of original sin in human nature. Our passions are disordered. "If it feels good, do it" is a livable slogan only for angels and unfallen humanity. Fallen humanity is the inheritor of the consequences of the choices of Adam and Eve. We are all, in some way, wounded.

Which answers another key aspect of this question. "How can the Church teach this about homosexuality when people are born this way?" We all must wrestle with our fallen nature, our disordered desires and weakened will. We must all (save those exempted by a special grace from God, a quirk of biology, disease, or age) struggle to be chaste.

Question 33:
How can you still be Catholic
when your Church has closed Communion
to everyone other than Catholics?

Very easily — people who are not in communion with the
Catholic Church should not eat Catholic Communion. If you
do not share the Catholic faith or morals, then don't eat the
Eucharist. Why does this seem scandalous to people today?
Why do people find it offensive? I think because it seems exclusive. It says that not all people are absolutely equal, that
there are some permitted to take full part in the banquet and
others who are not. And, after all, don't we believe that God
welcomes all humanity into His Church?

Everyone is welcome to come to Mass, yes, and everyone
is free to become a Catholic. But not even Catholics are always
welcome at the table of the Lord. It's a very simple principle
that has a clear Scriptural foundation. Saint Paul teaches:

> Therefore whoever eats the bread or drinks the cup
> of the Lord unworthily will have to answer for the
> body and blood of the Lord. A person should exam-
> ine himself, and so eat the bread and drink the cup.
> For anyone who eats and drinks without discern-
> ing the body, eats and drinks judgment on himself.
> That is why many among you are ill and infirm, and
> a considerable number are dying (1 Cor 11:27-30).

Why are Catholics sometimes not supposed to receive Catholic Communion? Because we sometimes fail to meet Paul's criteria. Sometimes, we are not capable of "eating the bread or drinking the cup" worthily. We need to go to Confession. Anyone in the state of mortal sin (that is, we've broken one or more of the Ten Commandments, for instance, with full knowledge and complete consent; see *Catechism*, 1855-1861 for more) is not supposed to go up and receive Communion. Why? Because we are not alive in Jesus Christ when we are in a state of mortal sin. The Trinity is not dwelling within us. We are not prepared to receive the Son into ourselves.

The life of God comes into the soul at Baptism and can be renewed and restored by Confession: People wash themselves in the Blood of the Lamb when they confess their sins, receive a penance to do, make an act of contrition, and are absolved by someone empowered by Jesus to forgive sins, an empowerment given in John 20:23. People who are not baptized or are not in the state of grace aren't in any shape to welcome Jesus in, to eat the bread and drink the cup worthily. I've had to abstain from receiving Communion repeatedly. Having fallen in one way or another, I am sometimes absolutely unprepared to receive Jesus properly. So I go to Mass, I step aside to let others go up to receive, and I wait until I've been to Confession to receive again.

Also, when it comes to respecting the law of the Church on Communion, I've had the example of my Protestant father. Mom is Catholic, but Dad is Protestant. For years, he's been very respectful of the teachings of the Church. He's assisted Mom to raise my sister and me as Catholics. He's gone to Mass every Sunday with us. Heck, he regularly gets invited to join the Knights of Columbus because they see him being such a faithful attendee at Mass. But he has always observed the Church's rules on Communion. He doesn't believe the Church's teaching on Transubstantiation; therefore, he knows and abides by the requirement that he should not receive the Eucharist. My whole life, I've seen him do this. It's quite a witness of love and fidelity to my mother, to his kids, and even to the Catholic Church. He honors the teaching. He honors the institution. He loves God.

But why does the Eucharist matter so much? Again, look at Paul's words. "For anyone who eats and drinks without discerning the body, eats and drinks judgment on himself." The Eucharist is the Body and Blood, Soul and Divinity of Jesus Christ. The Eucharist is Jesus. The Mass is in part a community meal. It is in part a supper. But it is also a re-presentation of the sacrifice of Calvary. As Dr. Brant Pitre lays out in great detail in *Jesus and the Jewish Roots of the Eucharist*, the Eucharist is the Passover of the new People of God, where we eat the "Lamb of God, who takes away the sin of the world" (Jn 1:29). The Eucharist is the new manna, the bread that comes down from Heaven for life eternal (see Jn 6:32-35), the new bread of the presence (see Ex 25:30; see also Lev 24:1-9) that shows God's love and presence in the world.

Further, Jesus says, "This cup is the new covenant in my blood" (Lk 22:20), indicating that the meal to be eaten in remembrance of Jesus is a covenantal meal, a meal that signifies the relationship established between God and those entering into the new and everlasting covenant. As Jesus said, those who eat and drink this meal worthily eat

> the bread of God ... that which comes down from heaven and gives life to the world.
>
> ... everyone who sees the Son and believes in him may have eternal life, and I shall raise him [on] the last day.
>
> Amen, amen, I say to you, whoever believes has eternal life. I am the bread of life. Your ancestors ate the manna in the desert, but they died; this is the bread that comes down from heaven so that one may eat it and not die. I am the living bread that came down from heaven; whoever eats this bread will live forever; and the bread that I will give is my flesh for the life of the world (Jn 6:33, 40, 47-51).

So belief and participating in the meal are inextricably bound together. A person who sees the Son and believes in Him may have eternal life in the eating of the bread and drinking from the cup. But a person who does not discern the body and blood of Jesus in the bread and cup, or a person who receives unworthily, "eats and drinks judgment on himself," according to St. Paul.

Now, does this mean that only people who are practically perfect in every way may receive the Eucharist? No, of course not. Jesus is the Divine Physician — He's here to heal the sick, not hang out with the healthy. He is the Redeemer — He's here to help the sinners, not merely spend time with the saints. Make sure you go to Confession when you are aware that you've committed a serious sin (like breaking one of the Ten Commandments or committing one of the Seven Deadly Sins, all of which are listed in Appendix B), but don't be afraid to receive the Eucharist if you're a baptized Catholic and you've done your best to go to Confession when you know you need it. Jesus is here to help and to heal you.

The saints have often pointed to Eucharistic Adoration and regularly going to Mass as the greatest ways of becoming a saint. For instance, in her *Diary,* St. Faustina Kowalska wrote: "All the good that is in me is due to Holy Communion" (1392). "Herein lies the whole secret of my sanctity" (1489). "One thing alone sustains me and that is Holy Communion. From it I draw all my strength; in it is all my comfort. ... Jesus concealed in the Host is everything to me. ... I would not know how to give glory to God if I did not have the Eucharist in my heart" (1037).[166] And there is more where those declarations of love for the Eucharist came from in the writings of St. Faustina and of saints as varied as St. Francis of Assisi, Mother Teresa of Calcutta, Pier Giorgio Frassatti, and others.

Love Jesus? Love Him in the Eucharist. Even if you are not Catholic, or for whatever reason can't receive Communion, go to spend time and read the Bible before the tabernacle where He waits. Pray before Him at Eucharistic Adoration. Come to the Lord of love.

Question 34:
How can you still be Catholic when the Church tries to control every aspect of your personal life?

I can still be Catholic because the Church doesn't try to control every aspect of my life — rather, it offers Jesus Christ as the new center of my life and helps me discern the implications of that choice.

He reshapes everything. Everything becomes part of that relationship with Him. The morals of Catholicism are all about following His two commandments: "You shall love the Lord, your God, with all your heart, with all your soul, and with all your mind. This is the greatest and the first commandment. The second is like it: You shall love your neighbor as yourself. The whole law and the prophets depend on these two commandments" (Mt 22:37-40). We're supposed to love God with everything we have.

What does it mean to love God? Jesus explained, "If you love me, you will keep my commandments" (Jn 14:15). He gave us a number of commandments throughout the Gospels, commandments elaborated on in the New Testament letters. The teachings of the New Testament extend to matters of sexual morality; to honoring and loving spouses as Christ and His Church honor and love each other; to telling the truth; to not getting drunk; to a whole range of "personal" or "private" aspects of life. There's no part of life that's off-limits. We are to live the love of God and of neighbor in every part of our lives. At the same time, we do not have an extensive set of little laws governing every thought or deed. We have one law — Jesus. "What would Jesus do?" is a great summary of the law of Christian life. Even better: "If I love Jesus fully, what will I do in this situation?"

Love is supposed to govern our life, all of it, every moment of every day. We're supposed to give it all to him, everything, right down to the little details of our personal life. And what do we get out of that? We get God, who is worth everything, who is the source of everything. We give Him every aspect of our passing lives in exchange for Him who is eternal life, who is eternal love, who made us for Himself. As St. Augustine said at the start of his *Confessions*, "You have made us for yourself, O Lord, and our heart is restless until it rests in you." Our whole being is oriented toward God, our highest good.

Why is it so hard to live some parts of the moral life? Because of the Fall. Our relationships with God, with our neighbor, with ourselves, and with the created order are all disrupted to a certain extent from the first moment of our life. We are all out of order. You can see this every time you're speaking with others and somehow they don't get what you're saying, even if it should be perfectly clear; or when you feel lonely or alienated, even in a crowd. You can see this when you know what is right and it's hard to do, or you know something is wrong and it seems so easy, so tempting (see Rom 7:15, 22-24). We live with the effects of original sin every day.

So how can anyone live the Christian life if original sin affects us? The apostles wondered the same thing, asking, "Who then can be saved?" Jesus looked at them and said, "For human beings this is impossible, but for God all things are possible" (Mt 19:25-26). We are called to live life in the Holy Spirit of God. Prayer is powerful, fueled by the Sacraments, which come to us as a gift of Jesus to permit us to become adopted sons and daughters of God. When we are in that relationship with God, we get to live lives suffused with His life, strengthened with His strength, loving Him and the world with the love of God.

It's still really hard. The way to enter fully into the relationship with God is to take up your cross and follow Jesus to Calvary — that is, to accept utter self-sacrifice and a fair amount of suffering in order to follow Him and love as totally as He loves. It may sound harsh, but really, in a religion whose morality is all inspired by love, the element of suffering is unavoidable. Pope Benedict XVI explains:

> Pain is part of being human. Anyone who really wanted to get rid of suffering would have to get rid of love before anything else, because there can be no love without suffering, because it always demands an element of self-sacrifice, because, given temperamental differences, it will always bring with it renunciation and pain. When we know that the way of love — this exodus, this going out of oneself — is the true way by which we become human, then we also understand that suffering is the process through which we mature. Anyone who has inwardly accepted suffering becomes more mature and more understanding of others. Anyone who consistently avoids suffering does not understand other people; he becomes hard and selfish ... . If we say that suffering is the inner side of love, we then also understand why it is so important to learn how to suffer — and why, conversely, the avoidance of suffering renders someone unfit to cope with life. [167]

So how can I still be Catholic even when I am called to suffer into love? I am convinced that the faith is true and that I would rather suffer meaningfully within the Church than suffer during my life without meaning outside the Church. I would rather be next to my suffering Savior on the Cross than walk away from what I know to be true. I am very bad at both suffering and following Jesus, and yet where else can I go? To whom else should I go? I echo Peter: I believe Jesus has the words of eternal life. I believe that the teachings are true, no matter how hard they are, how demanding. (And oh, can they be hard and demanding at times!)

I believe them to be true, and to be the pathway toward true freedom, toward life and love in God. So even though I often forget, and fall, and must turn back to Jesus to be saved, I have not the slightest intention of giving up the fight or the faith. Remember, "Every saint has a past, and every sinner has a future."[168] Everyone must walk that road to Calvary as part of their spiritual journey in order to arrive at the tomb, and resurrection. Everyone must welcome the struggle for prayer, and the offering up of the suffering that comes with fighting the effects of original sin to return to spiritual health and to a relationship with God.

When people criticize the Church for "controlling" the faithful, oftentimes it's the issue of contraception that irks them most. See Question 8 (page 46) for a discussion of the Church's prohibition of contraception, a prohibition that goes straight back to the earliest days of the Christian community. Heck, it's not as though Christianity is the only religion with laws about sexual morality. And it's not as though Christian laws are the most punitive or the most restrictive. Also, our expectations of marital fidelity, fecundity, and chastity match up pretty darn well with the way the human psyche works, with people's need to give and receive steadfast, reliable love. So the teaching of the Church on "personal" matters, though hard to live, is well worth hearing and obeying.

Question 35:
How can you still be Catholic
when the Church is not biblical;
rather, it draws on "Sacred Tradition"?

Very easily, because really, the Bible is part of "Sacred Tradition." It's the part of it that's written down. The Church is quite biblical. In fact, we get the Bible from the People of God (both the Jews and the Church). Christianity would have no Bible at all if it were not for the Church.

You can see this clearly when you pay attention to the titles of Paul's letters. Which came first, the letters or the communities to which he was sending them? Obviously, the Christian communities, the local churches in communion with the apostles that Paul had visited or was going to visit. We have the New Testament, in fact, because the Church needed it. The early Church lived and flourished on the teaching of the Apostles, the breaking of the bread and the prayers, and the Scriptures of the Jews. Gradually, as the decades rolled on, Paul wrote his letters, the evangelists wrote their Gospels, and so forth. But the Bible emerges in the Church. The Church was not founded on the Bible.

Indeed, Jesus is quite clear regarding on what — or rather, on whom — He founds His Church:

Jesus said to him in reply, "Blessed are you, Simon son of Jonah. For flesh and blood has not revealed this to you, but my heavenly Father. And so I say to you, you are Peter, and upon this rock I will build my church, and the gates of the netherworld shall not prevail against it. I will give you the keys to the kingdom of heaven. Whatever you bind on earth shall be bound in heaven; and whatever you loose on earth shall be loosed in heaven" (Mt 16:17-19).

As we see from the Gospel of John, "Peter" is a synonym for "Cephas," which means "rock": "Then he brought him to Jesus. Jesus looked at him and said, 'You are Simon the son of John; you will be called Cephas' (which is translated Peter)" (Jn 1:42).

It is on Simon Peter, on Cephas, the Rock, that the Church is founded. Paul later expands on this:

So then you are no longer strangers and sojourners, but you are fellow citizens with the holy ones and members of the household of God, built upon the foundation of the apostles and prophets, with Christ Jesus himself as the capstone. Through him the whole structure is held together and grows into a temple sacred in the Lord; in him you also are being built together into a dwelling place of God in the Spirit (Eph 2:19-22).

The Church is founded on those who preach Christ, whether they be the Apostles who walked with Jesus and knew Him in His earthly ministry or they be the prophets who foretold Christ's coming. And what is the Church? 1 Timothy 3:15 reiterates: "the household of God, which is the church of the living God, the pillar and foundation of truth."

If the Church is the pillar and foundation of truth, then what she teaches is solid and true. We can see at the Council of Jerusalem that the early Church accepted that Christ had given this teaching authority, when the apostles and elders gathered together to authoritatively teach that Christians are not bound to follow all the tenets of the Jewish Law:

> It is the decision of the holy Spirit and of us not to place on you any burden beyond these necessities, namely, to abstain from meat sacrificed to idols, from blood, from meats of strangled animals, and from unlawful marriage. If you keep free of these, you will be doing what is right. Farewell (Acts 15:28-29).

This teaching depended, not on Scripture (though James cited Amos 9:11-12 in support of it), but on the "decision of the holy Spirit and of us." The apostles and the presbyters, gathered in council, taught authoritatively on a disputed matter, one which cut to the very heart of Christianity's Jewish heritage: They ruled that Christians were free of many of the Scriptural obligations of the Jewish Law. Their ruling preceded the acceptance of Paul's letters as Scripture, and obviously came before the Book of Acts was accepted — before the teaching on Gentiles and the Mosaic Law was recognized as a Scriptural teaching. The Church's ability to teach authoritatively has been recognized from the beginning.

And what does she teach authoritatively? She preaches the Gospel to all nations. The apostles went out and taught, for the most part entirely orally. We know from the New Testament that there was a lot of preaching and teaching going on that didn't take place in writing — preaching and teaching that were authoritatively delivered, considered by the Christians of the day to be coming from the Church, the pillar and foundation of the truth. Paul references this:

> Therefore, brothers, stand firm and hold fast to the traditions that you were taught, either by an oral statement or by a letter of ours (2 Thess 2:15).

> I praise you because you remember me in everything and hold fast to the traditions, just as I handed them on to you (1 Cor 11:2).

Further, there are the fourfold aspects of the life of the early Church:

> They devoted themselves to the teaching of the apostles and to the communal life, to the breaking of the bread and to the prayers (Acts 2:42).

So there's a liturgical life in the early Church, a life of ritual worship that re-presents the Lord's Supper as He had commanded. We don't get a whole lot of clear liturgical instruction in Scripture. We do see some in the *Didache*, one of the earliest, non-Scriptural writings in existence today. We also get Paul's clear teaching on the Eucharist (see 1 Cor 11:17-34), which ends with. "The other matters I shall set in order when I come." The proper celebration of the Lord's Supper mattered and was the subject of individual instruction from the Apostles to those they ordained for priestly duties.

There's much more to be said, but I'll have to let the Recommended Reading for this question (see Appendix A) take care of it. Let me end by mentioning the tradition of the authority of the "See of Peter," the seat or chair of Peter in Rome. We're not talking about a literal chair in which the pope must sit in order to exercise his teaching authority. It's like talking about the "office" of the president of the United States. He doesn't need to be sitting in the Oval Office to exercise his power. The "office" of the president includes the rights and responsibilities of the presidency, the powers of his position. Peter's power has a precedent in Scripture:

> The scribes and the Pharisees have taken their seat on the chair of Moses. Therefore, do and observe all things whatsoever they tell you, but do not follow their example. For they preach but they do not practice (Mt 23:2-3).

Though some Catholic bishops and some popes have been corrupt at times, though the hierarchy of the Church sometimes gives scandal, Scripture does not leave us an out from obeying their teaching authority, from giving assent to the Sacred Tradition handed on from the apostles — for the Church is the pillar and foundation of truth.

Question 36:

How can you still be Catholic when they made belief in Mary's Immaculate Conception required a full 1,800-plus years after Christ's death?

I can still be Catholic because I think it's not hard to find Scriptural evidence for the Immaculate Conception and because the notion of the development of doctrine makes perfect sense to me.

But first, let's define our terms. What is the Immaculate Conception?

When we proclaim our belief in the Immaculate Conception, we are saying that the Blessed Virgin Mary, by a special, unique grace of God "given by virtue of the merits of Jesus Christ," was conceived entirely free from the stain and the effects of original sin on her soul.[169] This means that she always had sanctifying grace in her soul; she always welcomed the indwelling of the Blessed Trinity in her soul from the moment of her conception; and at no point did she suffer from concupiscence — the darkened intellect, weakened will, and disordered passions that most human beings have had to struggle with because of the Fall of man.

Why did she receive such great gifts? Well, I tend to think that if she hadn't been immaculate, "full of grace" (see Lk 1:28), then I'm not sure she could have withstood the Incarnation. Think of it! God taking on human flesh is like dropping

fire into a paper bag — and yet with proper preparation, that
paper bag can be a paper lantern, and cast light on the whole
world. Just so with the Son of God, and the Mother of God.

Mary housed the All Holy One within her womb for nine
months, sharing blood, breath, and flesh, bearing within her
the One whose body was called the new Temple (see Jn 2:19).
The earthly Temple was constructed by the finest craftsmen
using the best of materials (see 1 Kgs 6; 2 Chr 3). Mary has
been compared throughout Christian history to the Ark of the
Covenant, on which was the mercy seat. God descended upon
the Ark, "overshadowing" it (see Ex 40:34-38), just as the
Holy Spirit does to Mary at the Annunciation (see Lk 1:35).
Kept within the Ark were the stone tablets of the Law; some
of the manna or bread from Heaven given to the Jews by God;
and Aaron's rod, the sign of his priesthood (see Heb 9:4).
Within her womb, Mary bore the Bread of Heaven (see Jn 6);
the eternal High Priest in the order of Melchizedek (see Heb
7:13-17); and the Word of God, the Son (see Jn 1).

Mary is like the Ark of the Covenant — and the Ark of
the Covenant was crafted according to extensive design spec-
ifications from imperishable metals and durable woods (see
Ex 25:1-22). The Ark was — well, immaculately conceived
and crafted. And that Ark was merely God's seat among the
people. Mary was His Mother! If God took such care over the
stone Temple and the earthly Ark, wouldn't He take all the
more care over His Mother, the woman from whom He takes
His humanity, His flesh and blood?

That's why I find the Immaculate Conception completely
credible, even though it wasn't defined as a dogma to be held
by all Catholics until December 8, 1854. Yes, there were theological disputes over it, sometimes even between saints and
Doctors of the Church (for more on that, see Mark Shea's
chapter on the Immaculate Conception in *Mary, Mother of
the Son*). The Immaculate Conception was more controversial
than some truths, being the result of a centuries-long discussion about the precise nature of Mary's unique sanctity, even
though everyone agreed from the earliest days of the faith that

Mary was a uniquely holy woman — blessed among women, in fact (see Lk 1:42). But the notion that Mary was uniquely sinless, uniquely pure even from the first moment of her existence, has deep roots in Christianity.

If that's the case, why did it take so long for the Church to say so definitively? Simply because we're still coming to understand the full implications of the example, teaching, and gifts given to us by God through divine revelation. To say that doctrine develops is not to say that doctrine can change any way we want it to. Rather, it means that our understanding of the revelation given by Jesus deepens through the years. You can see that process taking place over the course of the first ecumenical councils, at which a lot of brilliant, saintly theologians and philosophers thrashed out the ways in which we can talk about Christ's divinity and humanity, His relationship with His Mother, and the relationship among the three Persons of the Trinity. The Nicene Creed is not in Scripture, and yet most Christians accept it as authoritative and true.

Why? Because the councils and the creeds express fundamental choices about how to interpret Scripture. How do we understand the teaching that Jesus is the Son of God and the Son of Mary? Mainline Christians owe to the early Church and the ecumenical councils the basics of the faith that we all profess today.

How can the Church make this sort of decision? Because the Church has always made this sort of decision, going back at least as far as the Council of Jerusalem (see Acts 15), declaring in the name of the gathered successors to the apostles and the Holy Spirit what is and is not to be definitively held by the Christian faithful as truths of the faith, and determining the disciplines or the practices for the Church.

The same process of discernment occurred with the truth of the dogma of the Immaculate Conception, a discernment that lasted until the teaching was crystallized by Pius IX's dogmatic definition of it in *Ineffabilis Deus* in 1854.

I need to be clear: The Blessed Virgin Mary's Immaculate Conception depends upon the grace that comes through the

Incarnation, all of it, from Annunciation to Ascension into Heaven. She needed a savior just like the rest of us. For her, though, the grace of redemption and sanctification all kicked in from the first moment of her existence.[170] She received grace from the Incarnation even though the Incarnation hadn't occurred yet. How? The same way any of the people who lived before the time of Christ ever received grace from God: through Jesus Christ. All grace comes through Jesus. No grace passes into creation except through Jesus. So every time the Spirit of God acts in the Old Testament, every time grace operates — every time, it's all through Jesus and the Incarnation.

How? God is eternal; He has a very different relationship with time. It isn't native to Him. He enters time through the Incarnation and weds creation, coming as a Bridegroom to His Bride — but all that's far more than we need to discuss here.

The cause and effect involved in Mary's Immaculate Conception are ultimately no stranger than the cause and effect involved in God's grace passing to Abraham, Isaac, and Jacob; to Moses and Aaron; to David and the prophets, through the Incarnation of Jesus.

There's plenty more to be said about the Immaculate Conception. For that, I point you to the Recommended Reading for this question (Appendix A).

Question 37:
How can you still be Catholic if loved ones can go to hell?

I can still be Catholic because God wants us all to be saved; because in all probability more people go to Purgatory than to hell; and because we can pray, fast, and cooperate with God to help bring people into full communion with Him. Also, realistically, you could focus on the possibility that I might go to hell, as well. Being Catholic is not necessarily an inoculation against damnation — heck, I've heard it said that Catholics who go to hell will go deeper into hell than anyone else because we knew better, we had the Sacraments, we had all sorts of protections and help, and we still ended up there somehow.

How can I still be Catholic when the Church teaches that hell exists and it's a real possibility for me and for my loved ones? Well, it's the sort of teaching you pay attention to only if you believe it's true. If the Church is just making up a place to scare us, then she's engaging in the worst sort of manipulation and fearmongering. Also, she would be lying to us, and an institution that lies is not exactly going to be the "pillar and foundation of truth" (1 Tim 3:15), is it?

But if the teaching is true, then what else can the Church say? She is bound to warn of a real danger where it exists, especially something as permanent and as painful as damnation. And warn she does in the *Catechism*:

> The teaching of the Church affirms the existence of hell and its eternity. Immediately after death the souls of those who die in a state of mortal sin descend into hell, where they suffer the punishments of hell, "eternal fire."[171] The chief punishment of hell is eternal separation from God, in whom alone man can possess the life and happiness for which he was created and for which he longs.[172]

Where does the Church get this teaching?

> Jesus often speaks of "Gehenna" of "the unquenchable fire" reserved for those who to the end of their lives refuse to believe and be converted, where both soul and body can be lost.[173] Jesus solemnly proclaims that he "will send his angels, and they will gather ... all evil doers, and throw them into the furnace of fire,"[174] and that he will pronounce the condemnation: "Depart from me, you cursed, into the eternal fire!"[175]

So the Church receives this teaching from Jesus. He teaches this very firmly. Further, there are people who have seen hell. The Fatima visionaries received a vision of hell, for instance,[176] as did St. Faustina Kowalska[177] and St. Teresa of Avila,[178] among others. Also, we do not know who is in hell, so we pray for the dead in the hope that they may pass through Purgatory into Heaven.

But how can a good and merciful God condemn people to everlasting hell? The answer comes at the intersection of God's justice and mercy, God's respect for our freedom, and His longing for us to be united with Him in Heaven forever.

> We cannot be united with God unless we freely choose to love him. But we cannot love God if we sin gravely against him, against our neighbor or against ourselves: "He who does not love remains in death. Anyone who hates his brother is a murder-

er, and you know that no murderer has eternal life abiding in him."[179] Our Lord warns us that we shall be separated from him if we fail to meet the serious needs of the poor and the little ones who are his brethren.[180] To die in mortal sin without repenting and accepting God's merciful love means remaining separated from him forever by our own free choice. This state of definitive self-exclusion from communion with God and the blessed is called "hell."[181]

Putting it another way, C.S. Lewis once said, "The gates of hell are locked from the inside."[182] He went on to explain that even though people in hell may wish to be elsewhere, he doubted they could even for a moment contemplate the sort of self-abandonment it would require to live in the other option — Heaven. Heaven is partaking in the divine life, sharing in the eternal dance of life and love at the heart of the Trinity. The Trinitarian life is revealed most fully at the Crucifixion, when Jesus is lifted high on the Cross and pours out His life for the life of the world. The life of God is absolute self-sacrificial love.

The life (or, rather, unending death) of hell is utter inversion, utter turning toward the self or toward the idol that has taken the place of God. Lewis elsewhere explains:

There are only two kinds of people in the end: those who say to God, "Thy will be done," and those to whom God says, in the end, "*Thy* will be done." All that are in Hell, choose it. Without that self-choice there could be no Hell. No soul that seriously and constantly desires joy will ever miss it. Those who seek find. To those who knock it is opened.[183]

We can enter into Heaven only when we accept the divine adoption, when we consent to become adopted sons and daughters of God. And that adoption extends, by God's grace, to our partaking in the divine nature (see 2 Pet 1:4), being elevated by grace to divine sonship, divine daughterhood. But in order for that to happen, we must repent. We must say to God, "Thy will be done, on earth as it is in Heaven." Thy will — no matter how hard, no matter how terrifying. *Thy* will, not *my* will, until God's will becomes our will, until our "yes" is identical to His "yes," not because He has been conformed to us, but because we have become conformed to Him.

Why should we say yes to His will so absolutely? Because God is the Way, the Truth, and the Life. God alone is good. To say "yes" to God is to say "yes" to absolute life, love, truth, goodness, and beauty. To be conformed to God is to be conformed to the best of all things. So obeying God's commandments is not an imposition of His will on our autonomous, independent will — it's following the inner logic of our own natures and the structure of the universe to allow God to raise us to utter joy.

Does that make it easy? Nope. I struggle a lot with following His will and conforming my will to His. I fail a lot. I go to Confession a lot. It can be very disheartening. And yet I know that it's worth it. How? By looking at the saints and seeing human lives that were lived as they should be lived, seeing the radiation of God's goodness, life, and love coming through human beings into the world, healing and strengthening whatever they touch, casting out evil, and raising us all closer to God's heavenly light.

But how can the saints in Heaven be happy when others are suffering in hell? I think C.S. Lewis's answer is pretty good:

> "...What some people say on earth is that the final loss of one soul gives the lie to all the joy of those who are saved ... ."
>
> "That sounds very merciful, but see what lurks behind it ... The demand of the loveless and the self-imprisoned that they should be allowed to blackmail the universe: that till they consent to be happy (on their own terms) no one else shall taste joy: that theirs should be the final power; that Hell

should be able to *veto* Heaven ... Either the day must come when joy prevails and all the makers of misery are no longer able to infect it: or else for ever and ever the makers of misery can destroy in others the happiness they reject for themselves."[184]

Question 38:

How can you still be Catholic when there are contradictions in Scripture?

I can still be Catholic because of our understanding of the nature of the Bible. To put it briefly: The Bible is not the Qur'an.

The Qur'an, according to traditional Islam, is the perfect copy of an eternal book written on gold tablets that remains with Allah. The whole thing was revealed through Muhammad in one lifetime. It is, to a certain extent, held to be ahistorical.[185]

The Bible, on the other hand, is a collection of books, written by a number of human authors from different times and places; these books were gathered together first by the learned teachers of the Jews and then by the Church. Some books are intended as history or, at least, as the story of a nation or a tribe, but others are collections of proverbs, songs, prayers, and prophecy — there are a number of different genres in the Bible. Further, we are to read the Scriptures in the context of all the other books in the Bible, in light of the fullness of God's revelation. For instance, the New Testament teaches that a great many aspects of the Law of Judaism are not binding on Christians (see Acts 10:1-11:18; 15:1-31), something that is crucial to a proper Christian understanding of the teachings of the Scriptures. The Bible is an organic whole. It has many individual parts, each with its own particular function and rules. But all those parts work together to convey the inspired and inerrant Word of God.

So when you find things in Scripture that seem contradictory (the different accounts of certain scenes from Jesus' life in the Gospels, for example, or the apparently stark contrasts between the morality of the Old and New Testaments, and between the wrath of Yahweh and the mercy of Jesus), take into account all the many, many reasons: different human authors, different historical circumstances, different genres, different levels of scientific and natural knowledge, etc. Given all that, what ties the Scriptures together into a coherent whole? Why do we care what these books say? Simply, Catholics and other Christians believe that "[a]ll scripture is inspired by God and is useful for teaching, for refutation, for correction, and for training in righteousness, so that one who belongs to God may be competent, equipped for every good work" (2 Tim 3:16). The whole of the Bible is inspired by God.

What does that mean? The Second Vatican Council's Constitution on Divine Revelation *Dei Verbum* explains (emphasis added):

> [S]ince everything asserted by the inspired authors
> or sacred writers must be held to be asserted by the
> Holy Spirit, it follows that the books of Scripture
> must be acknowledged as teaching solidly, faithfully
> and without error *that truth which God wanted put
> into sacred writings for the sake of salvation*".[186]

So the Scriptures teach reliably the truth that is necessary for salvation. Is a detailed overview of Darwin's theory of evolution necessary for salvation? Nope — and so the creation accounts of Genesis are written in a way appropriate to liturgically introduce the teaching of God's creative work, rather than as scientific accounts. Some parts of the Old Testament aim to present history while others aim to convey wisdom. Some things are written according to styles and genres that have fallen out of fashion or are particular to a certain place and time, and so seem incomprehensible, deceptive, or wrong to those of us brought up on modern journalism, biography, and historical writing. The Bible must be read according to the styles in which it was written in order for the reader to fully receive its intended message according to the intentions of the human and divine authors.

And that message is the truth necessary for our salvation, not the truth needed for a comprehensive scientific description of reality. The purpose of God's revelation is to open our way to relationship with Him.

> In His goodness and wisdom God chose to reveal Himself and to make known to us the hidden purpose of His will (Eph 1:9) by which through Christ, the Word made flesh, man might in the Holy Spirit have access to the Father and come to share in the divine nature (Eph 2:18; 2 Peter 1:4). Through this revelation, therefore, the invisible God (Col 1:15, 1 Tim 1:17) out of the abundance of His love speaks to men as friends (Ex 33:11; John 15:14-15) and lives among them (Bar 3:38), so that He may invite and take them into fellowship with Himself.
>
> This plan of revelation is realized by deeds and words having [a]n inner unity: the deeds wrought by God in the history of salvation manifest and confirm the teaching and realities signified by the words, while the words proclaim the deeds and clarify the mystery contained in them. By this revelation then, the deepest truth about God and the salvation of man shines out for our sake in Christ, who is both the mediator and the fullness of all revelation.[187]

God reveals Himself throughout the Scriptures, as well as through His words and deeds in history, so that humanity might come into eternal communion with the life and love of God. In order to read the Bible in the language it was written in, a person needs to read the text with the eyes of faith. The Bible was written by people who believed in God, who believed they were telling of true revelations given by God to them and to their forebears. A person needs to understand that faith in order to understanding the Scriptures.

Further, the Bible is a word spoken to us, a message with infinite latent possibility, as shown by the ancient Christian practice of *lectio divina*, divine reading, which involved praying one's way through Scripture. Consistently throughout the life of the Church, *lectio divina* has given rise to great saints and mystics, transforming them and bringing them into a depth of sympathy, of connaturality (or "likeness"), with the divine realities conveyed by the text that transformed their lives and their prayer. [188] They used their minds and hearts to ponder the things of God, to allow the realities presented through the Word of God to touch and change them, obeying Paul's instruction: "[B]e transformed by the renewal of your mind, that you may discern what is the will of God, what is good and pleasing and perfect" (Rom 12:2).

A Catholic reading Scripture, therefore, should always approach the Bible with an acknowledgement of its incarnational nature, of its dual authorship by humans and by God, leading us to use the full range of methods appropriate when trying to read ancient texts accurately and to study the works of excellent biblical scholars. We'll also use the sources of grace available through the Christian faith, such as personal prayer, reception of the Sacraments, and listening to magisterial teaching to help us accurately read and understand the teachings of Scripture. We are to come to Scripture with our minds and hearts awake, called to ponder the sacred page, discover its human context, and allow ourselves to be transformed by the sacred realities mediated by the incarnational text.

Question 39:

How can you still be Catholic when the world's so screwed up, it seems like God doesn't care, and so many people are in need of practical help, not prayer?

I can still be Catholic because of people like Mother Teresa.

Contrary to what a lot of people might think, her primary mission in life was not to change the living conditions of the world, or even to go out to the poor and help them. Her primary mission was to love God with her whole being. That relationship with God flowed through her Eucharistic Adoration and attendance at Mass, her prayer and reading of Scripture, her devotion to the Rosary and the Mother of God. Her love of her neighbor, reaching into the depths of poverty and extending out into the whole world, was fueled and formed by her prayer life. That prayer life was the rocket fuel that launched the Missionaries of Charity into orbit around the world, shining like the sun, bringing hope to the hopeless and all the works of mercy to people who are abandoned by the world. She began her work with the poorest of the poor because Jesus called her to leave the school where she was serving as a consecrated religious. She began her efforts on her own, with only God as a helper, but that radiant sanctity, that radiant Christian life, quickly attracted others to help and support her work. And the ministry flowed from there.

How did she do so much? Because she was deeply united

to God, so deeply united that even though she experienced decades of spiritual dryness and desolation, she loved God in and through it all. Even though she often felt a deep spiritual darkness, feeling as though God didn't exist, as though God didn't care, she loved Him and so continued her service.[189] From her faithful bearing of the cross, from her fidelity in prayer and the sacramental life, flowed the grace and transformational presence of God in her life that attracted so many to be Missionaries of Charity and raised up so many other collaborators around the world.

I can still be Catholic even though the world is so screwed up because God does care, and the Church, the Body of Christ in the world, is His face turned lovingly toward all those in need, all those suffering. We are meant to be His response! The piece of verse attributed to St. Teresa of Avila, beginning, "Christ has no body but yours, no hands, no feet on earth but yours," explains it very well. We are the Mystical Body of Christ, we believers, we Christians, we baptized. We are meant to be sources of God's mercy in this fallen, suffering, screwed-up world. The Church has traditionally called us to perform the "works of mercy." The list includes both the "corporal works of mercy," meaning the more physical, bodily acts, and the "spiritual works of mercy," which answer the needs of the human mind, heart, and soul.

The corporal works of mercy are:
- Feed the hungry.
- Give drink to the thirsty.
- Clothe the naked.
- Shelter the homeless.
- Visit the prisoners.
- Comfort the sick.
- Bury the dead.

The spiritual works of mercy are:
- Teach the ignorant.
- Pray for the living and dead.

- Correct sinners.
- Counsel those in doubt.
- Console the sorrowful.
- Bear wrongs patiently.
- Forgive wrongs willingly.

For full explanations of the works of mercy, see 'You Did It to Me' by Fr. Michael Gaitley, MIC; The Work of Mercy: Being the Hands and Heart of Christ by Mark Shea; and What to Do When Jesus is Hungry: A Practical Guide to the Works of Mercy by Fr. Andrew Apostoli, CFR. For now, though, I want to come back to the issue of prayer.

Yes, it can seem like people are wasting their time on their knees when all around us there are so many others in so much need. But remember Mother Teresa! What fueled her ministry? What made all her work possible? Her prayer life! Why? Because prayer is the way we enter and remain in communion with God, the extension of the divine life and love imparted to us in the Sacraments throughout the rest of our life. Prayer is our conversation and relationship with the divine. When we pray, our lives are transformed into eternal life. Our love is transformed into divinized love. We are then able to give eternally, to love infinitely, in ways that are impossible for the simply human. The saints were not merely extraordinary human beings — they were human beings living the life of Heaven on earth, of total self-gift and endless love. Because of that, miracles abounded. Many lives were touched; many people healed; many starving fed; and many thirsty given drink. Where saints go, God goes. Where God goes, the source of all life and sustenance and healing and goodness and truth goes.

The world is starving for saints! The Second Vatican Council recognized this and devoted an entire chapter of Lumen Gentium, the Dogmatic Constitution on the Church, to the "Universal Call to Holiness." Every Catholic is called to be a saint, to be holy, to live a life animated completely by the love of God, which leads to love of neighbor and right love of self.

We are meant to be the visible sign of God's care in the

world, and many thousands, many millions of Christians have been that sign through the millennia — the consecrated religious with their hospitals, schools, orphanages, and charitable institutions of all kinds; the laity with their lived witness to Christ in the world wherever they are, through the St. Vincent de Paul Society, the Knights of Columbus, and many other organizations for charity; on and on the flood of Christian charity has flowed. We are a hospital for sinners, yes, and many Christians have failed to live up to the great call of Christ, but a great many have answered that call, as well. Many answer that call today. God cares. God so loved the world that He gave His only begotten Son, that He gives these adopted children to the world for the life, the healing, the renewing of the world.

Question 40:
How can you still be Catholic when politics dictate papal policy?

I can still be Catholic when politics are taken into consideration in determining papal policy because, well, policy is a matter of politics. The question seems to imply that everything the pope does is a matter of politics, or that all the teaching that comes from Rome is really a matter of political expediency, the exercise of power, or an attempt to maintain the pope's influence.

But not everything in the Church is a matter of "policy" or politics. Regardless of what happens politically, there are doctrines and practices that we shall not give up. This is proved by the tradition of the Christian martyrs, including such distinguished names as St. Peter and St. Paul, St. Agnes and St. Felicity, St. Thomas More, St. Lucy, St. Thomas Becket, and many, many others (more, in fact, in the 20th century than ever before).[190] From the times when the martyrs refused to give a pinch of incense to worship the emperor and were killed for it to the times when popes were seized by Napoleon and taken from Rome, there are times and places where it might have been brilliant politics for the popes to bend or break on key points — but they didn't.

Does this mean that the Church is never involved in politics? Of course not. The Church was a major political player for many years, and retains a strong diplomatic profile to this day. We have a checkered past when it comes to the exercise of political influence — but is it always a problem if the pope and his assistants play a role in politics? I think many people would say no.

It's not a problem, for instance, that the Vatican takes positions on matters of justice and peace, serving as a strong voice for human rights the world over. It's not a problem when the pope is elected by the College of Cardinals, even though there will inevitably be politicking among them. Jesus is the Lord of history, and the Holy Spirit can work through the deliberations of men and women, even if the men and women are powerful and playing politics. Consider the evidence of the Scriptures. Jesus is the Savior of the world, the Passover Lamb offered for the sins of the world, because the Sanhedrin found Him guilty of blasphemy in a politically motivated trial:

> So the chief priests and the Pharisees convened the Sanhedrin and said, "What are we going to do? This man is performing many signs. If we leave him alone, all will believe in him, and the Romans will come and take away both our land and our nation." But one of them, Caiaphas, who was high priest that year, said to them, "You know nothing, nor do you consider that it is better for you that one man should die instead of the people, so that the whole nation may not perish." He did not say this on his own, but since he was high priest for that year, he prophesied that Jesus was going to die for the nation, and not only for the nation, but also to gather into one the dispersed children of God. So from that day on they planned to kill him (Jn 11:47-53).

Politically motivated decisions, taken by the religious leaders of the Chosen People, ended up securing the salvation of the entire world. Our God is mighty to save, even though our leaders are sometimes venal and corrupt. And our leaders are to be listened to, even when they are sinners themselves. Look at the witness of Jesus:

> The scribes and the Pharisees have taken their seat on the chair of Moses. Therefore, do and observe all things whatsoever they tell you, but do not follow their example. For they preach but they do not practice. They tie up heavy burdens [hard to carry] and lay them on people's shoulders, but they will not lift a finger to move them (Mt 23:2-4).

Further, look back to the witness of the Old Testament. Throughout, we find the leaders of the people making good or bad decisions, sending out armies and enacting laws for the land. The Scriptures bear witness that God's ends are achieved, either because Israel has good rulers who do God's will and rule justly according to wisdom, or because God sends mighty nations to disperse the Jews among the nations as a means of drawing them back to fidelity. "We know that all things work for good for those who love God, who are called according to his purpose" (Rom 8:28).

So to me, the fact that politics has played a role in the life and history of the papacy is not a matter of scandal. Rather, it's only to be expected. Perhaps the wisest thing Malachi Martin ever said was that the chair of Peter is an enduring source of power in this world, and so it shall always be a player in the world of politics and money. The papacy shall endure. It has endured for 2,000 years, and it shall last till the end of the world. It shall remain a source of teaching and Sacrament for the human race, and so shall ever have a voice in the lives and choices of billions of people throughout human history. This shall occur by the very nature of the office of Peter. So politics — well, we are doomed to it.

Perhaps there shall come a day when the pope has a voice only within the Church, when the Catholic community shall become very small and only a few members survive. Perhaps we shall become again the Church of the earliest days, a small enough Church to all fit into an upper room. Then, maybe, Peter will have no obvious voice in worldly affairs. But the pope shall always be a leader of men and women until Christ comes again. And so, of course, politics go with the job.

Question 41:

How can you still be Catholic when the story of a virgin birth is found in many cultures predating Christianity?

The simple, immediate answer is that the question gets the chronology of events backward. Christianity exists, not because of a story, but because of an event. The reason the apostles believed in Jesus was not the virgin birth; rather, they believed in the virgin birth because they believed in Jesus.

Consider: The disciples met Jesus walking around, a man of about 30. They followed Him because He was different, compelling. He taught with authority (see Mt 7:29); He worked miracles (see Mt 4:23-25); He knew things no one else could have known. Jesus met Simon and renamed him Peter (see Jn 1:42); Jesus walked along the shores of the Sea of Galilee and called fishermen from their nets (see Mt 4:18-22); Jesus changed lives with a word, a touch, a glance, a miracle. The apostles believed in Him first as an adult man, a wonder-worker, a teacher of great wisdom and power.

Only later, probably after Jesus had ascended into Heaven, did they ask His Mother to tell them stories, to share with them what He meant to her, what she remembered. What was His childhood like? What did He do? And of whatever stories of hers they heard, they recorded very few. One of those stories was that she had not known man; that an angel from Heaven had come and spoken with her, calling her "full of grace," saying that the Lord had chosen her; had loved her; and wanted her to be His bride, His spouse, His Mother (see Lk 1). She would have been the one to tell them that she had given birth as a virgin and remained a virgin ever after.

Because they believed in Him, they would have believed in her. Because they believed Jesus and Mary, we have the story in the Gospels of a woman being visited by an angel; we have the story of the virgin birth. The Church came first, not the Bible; the faith, not the Christian Scriptures. The earliest Christians didn't read the Gospels and then decide to follow Jesus. No — they heard the preaching of the apostles and disciples. They saw the miracles or experienced the power of the Holy Spirit themselves. Several decades into the whole Christian project, the Scriptures were written.[191]

And no, the virgin birth isn't likely to have been a simple artifact of paganism borrowed and brought into Christianity. Why? Because the first Christians were Jews, and the early Christian Church had to wrestle over the question of whether the Gentiles, the surrounding pagan peoples, could be brought into the Church. See the debates, the signs and wonders, the final decision recorded in the Book of the Acts of the Apostles — it was a question decided by a Jewish Christian Church. A Church that was so cautious about receiving pagan converts was hardly likely to bring in pagan myths. Indeed, the early Christians were martyred for refusing to accept paganism's fundamental premise — that it really doesn't matter which god you want to worship, so long as you're open to the worship of all the gods. It seems hardly likely that people who would go to their deaths because they refused to compromise their monotheistic Christianity would gladly adopt pagan myths into the taproot of the religion.[192]

It's also worth asking: How prevalent, exactly, are these pagan myths of a virgin birth?

The answer: They're not, really.[193]

And I say this as someone who's loved myths and fairy tales since early elementary school. There are a few things about Christianity that differ from the ordinary expectations of paganism. For one, Christianity privileges celibacy far beyond what any of the surrounding peoples, including the Jewish people of the time, would have tended to do. The idea that a virgin birth matters especially would not have been the first thing to come to the minds of your average pagans, or to seem important to them. Indeed, Christian sexual morality stood out during the early days of Christianity in much the same way that it stands out today. .

There's not really any extensive tradition, then, of virgin births in pagan mythology for Christianity to have drawn from. In classical mythology, the gods tend to have sex, just as mere mortals do — and sometimes the gods are having sex *with* the mere mortals.

The Greek gods and goddesses have offspring all over the place, and sometimes give birth rather oddly (Athena springs from Zeus' head; Dionysius, from Zeus' leg), but these aren't presented as virgin births.

The Egyptian god Horus, we are told, was the child of Isis and Osiris. Horus' conception was miraculous, certainly (Isis magically restored life to the dead Osiris for a time; the two made love; and Horus was the result), but not the same thing as a virgin birth.[194]

The god Mithras became popular in Rome around the second century AD, a little late for Christianity to have been borrowing much of anything from him — indeed, one might wonder to what extent the worshippers of Mithras were borrowing from Christianity.[195] Further, it's far from clear that his worshippers or anyone else from the time of the Roman Empire ever thought that Mithras had had a "virgin birth."

We could go on, but the number of religious systems that Christianity could realistically have borrowed from is limited. And again: Early Christians went to their deaths rather than deny Christ for paganism. Is it really likely that they would have embroidered on the life of Christ with pagan myths?

But some people would argue that the life of Christ is entirely mythic, entirely made up, and so it would have been constructed from whole cloth, anyway.

Even if I were to grant that Jesus didn't exist (which I don't — there's plenty of good evidence for His existence as a historical figure),[196] it's hardly likely that a new religion emerging from the heart of first-century Judaism would have drawn many adherents if it was deeply rooted in pagan myth. Why? Because the pagans were the oppressors, the occupying force, and the Jewish religion, in response, was ever more focused on purity, orthodoxy, and self-sacrifice. It was the time of the Zealots and riots because of pagan worship in the land of Israel, not a time of religious accommodation and laxity.

Further, there is every reason to believe that Jesus existed, that He is the reason for the existence of Christianity; and, I believe, there is every reason to believe He was God Incarnate — not one of a thousand gods, but the Son of the Father, the Second Person of the Blessed Trinity. The reasons for believing this include the witness of 2,000 years of lives supernaturally transformed, of saints and scholars, of signs and wonders. And if there is every reason to believe Him God, then there's no reason to find the virgin birth impossible or even improbable.

Question 42:

How can you still be Catholic when the Bible is a collection of oral history written down 300 years after the fact and then has been (mis)translated not once but three times and is still taken literally?

OK, let's take this question one step at a time.

First, what is the Bible? The Bible is a collection of books, written by a number of human authors from different times and places; these books were gathered together first by the learned teachers of the Jews and then by the Church. The whole Bible was not written down "300 years after the fact" because, again, it contains *many* books written at *various* times. Not all of it is oral history. Some books are intended as history, or at least, as the story of a nation or a tribe, but others are collections of proverbs, songs and prayers, or prophecy. Indeed, there are many genres represented in the Bible.

This means that to flatly ask, "Is the Bible accurate?" is to ask an unanswerable question. Here's why: Tell me, if you are able to, whether T.S. Eliot's poetry is accurate, or if the songs of the Beatles are accurate, or if the classified ads in today's newspaper accurately recount the day's news. These are nonsense questions because they fail to take genre into account. You don't often look to limericks for historical accuracy, to T.S. Eliot's poetry for a straightforward recounting of prosaic fact, to the songs of the Beatles for facts and figures on anything, or to the classified ads for the headlines. Similarly, to attempt to read Psalms (a book of hymns or prayers) as though they are the Gospels (four literary accounts of the life of Christ) is doomed to failure; to expect of the Old Testament histories the same methods of writing history as modern academics bring to bear on their subjects is to invite serious confusion; and to demand of Genesis a scientific account of the creation of the cosmos is simply not a good idea.

To best understand a given book of the Bible, we should learn the literary conventions that governed its writing. What is its genre? Is it intended as narrative? Poetry? Wisdom? Prophesy? The reality of genre influences our understanding of each book of Scripture individually, and at times it will guide our approach to individual passages of Scripture. Jesus' parables, for instance, must be read differently from the recounting of the calling of the 12 apostles or the Crucifixion. If you demand of me the specific names and places of origin of the prodigal son, his father, and his elder brother before you begin to take the story seriously, I will be strongly tempted to laugh because they're all entirely beside the point of the parable.

All that having been said, yes, we take the historicity of the Gospels seriously, and there are good reasons to do so.[197] For more, see the Recommended Reading (Appendix A).

Second, has the Bible been translated? Yes — and a lot more often than three times — into a host of languages all over the world. How do we know the translations we have today are reliable? Because we have ancient copies of the texts, most notably the Dead Sea Scrolls, which substantially confirmed the accuracy of the Old Testament as handed on through the centuries. According to one Hebrew scholar, "It is a matter of wonder that through something like one thousand years the text underwent so little alteration.'"[198] For the New Testament, we have thousands of manuscripts, some dating back to the 100s AD, to provide a consistent witness to the accuracy of the transmitted text.[199]

Third, are we supposed to read this collection literally? Well, yes. That is, we are to read what's on the page as literally what the author of that particular book, writing in that particular genre from the standpoint of that particular time, cultural milieu, level of scientific knowledge, and a host of other factors meant to say. That's a long way from trying to treat the Book of Genesis as a science textbook, or the Book of Revelation as a sort of documentary "preview of coming attractions." Further, we are to read the Scriptures in the context of all the other books in the Bible, in light of the fullness of God's revelation. The Bible is an organic whole — it has many individual parts, each with its own particular function and rules, all gathered by the People of God (Israel first, and then the Church) into one collection. But all those parts work together to convey the inspired and inerrant Word of God.

When we read the Bible in the same way as the authors of the New Testament read it, we find the same thing Jesus revealed to the disciples on the road to Emmaus: "beginning with Moses and all the prophets, he interpreted to them what referred to him in all the scriptures" (Lk 24:27). To paraphrase St. Augustine, "In the Old Testament the New Testament is concealed; in the New Testament the Old Testament is revealed."

What does that mean? It means we are to acknowledge the full range of the "senses" of Scripture. The *Catechism* (115-118) explains those senses in detail. But in brief, all of Scripture has both a literal sense and a spiritual sense, and to understand the full meaning of the text, the reader would need to plumb the depths of both senses. The *Catechism* explains, "The *literal sense* is the meaning conveyed by the words of Scripture and discovered by exegesis, following the rules of sound interpretation: 'All other senses of Sacred Scripture are based on the literal.'"[200]

You find the *spiritual sense* of the text by reading not just the words on the page, but "also the realities and events about which it speaks."[201] The spiritual sense can be subdivided into the *allegorical sense* (often, how the events of the

Old Testament foreshadow the coming of Christ in the New Testament), the *moral sense* (the morals taught by Scripture), and the *anagogical sense* (the ways in which the text foreshadows the second coming of Christ, or the meaning of human existence). All the senses are summed up by the *Catechism* in a medieval poem:

> The Letter speaks of deeds; Allegory to faith; The Moral how to act; Anagogy our destiny.[202]

These senses are clearly explained by Mark Shea in *Making Senses Out of Scripture*. Along the way, he notes, "[O]ne of the standing temptations of the biblical student is to oversimplify by seizing on one truth and using it to discount other, equally important truths." Shea describes how some scholars seize upon the literal and dismiss the spiritual senses of Scripture as indefensible "eisegesis" or the reading into Scripture of meanings that the original human author never intended.[203]

But the spiritual senses are absolutely necessary for a right understanding of the text. As Jesus pointed out on the road to Emmaus, the whole of Scripture speaks of Him. How? Not always explicitly, nor always by the intention of the human author. But His coming is the definitive revelation of God in the world until the end of time, when God shall be all in all (see 1 Cor 15:28). So He is the Word of God that is mediated to us through Scripture. Reading prayerfully, we shall encounter the Trinitarian persons waiting to commune with us, speaking through the sacred page. The Bible is a great gift of God to the Church and the world, but like all of God's gifts, it can be misused.

That's why it's so important to read the Scriptures in the light of the long reflection and prayer done by the saints and great teachers of the Church in order to come to the fullest understanding possible of the teaching of the sacred page. And what is that teaching? At its heart, the Bible tells us that God, the Creator of all things, loves us and calls us into a relationship with Him. The Bible and *lectio divina* (divine reading) have been among the treasures at the center of Christian spirituality for these past 2,000 years.[204] The Bible is essentially a long love letter, or a series of love letters, telling us of God's justice and mercy, of His power and weakness (see 1 Cor 1:25), of His life and His love, and of who we are and how we are to come into a right relationship with Him.

Question 43:

How can you still be Catholic when until very recently the Masses were conducted in another language on purpose so the common man would be totally mystified as to the whole point?

I can still be Catholic because that question gets the whole issue backward. Latin used to be the only language in the Roman rite of the liturgy so that anywhere a person went in the world, he or she would know what was going on. With one common language for the liturgy, everyone, all over the world, would be able to participate in any Mass anywhere. A Catholic would not be mystified at Mass anywhere in the world because it would be the same as the Mass celebrated at home. The original motive for using Latin for the Mass stemmed from the early Church evangelizing in the context of the Roman Empire. Latin was a universal language, as was Greek, the language of the worship of the Eastern churches.

Does that mean every Catholic has always been able to speak and read Latin fluently? No, of course not. That's why, over the years, there were side-by-side translations of the words of the Mass made for Catholics the world over, so that they would be able to follow along with what was being said and done by the priest on the altar. One of the most influential was Fr. Joseph Stedman's 1932 English translation, produced under the title *My Sunday Missal*. Stedman's translation was a huge success. Many other translations were made of *My*

Sunday Missal and distributed around the world.[205]

Further, when one has been praying the same prayers and singing the same songs for years, one comes to know their meaning. Also, the Church has long placed a high priority on catechesis (instruction in the faith). Catholic schoolchildren were taught their prayers and what they meant. They were taught the meaning of the Creed, how to live good Christian lives, and what happens at Mass. You have only to look back at the *Baltimore Catechism* (a local guide to the faith in use in America after the Third Plenary Council of Baltimore)[206] or the *Roman Catechism* (drafted after the Council of Trent) to get some sense of the extent to which average Catholics could answer questions about their faith and the Mass. Catholics were carefully instructed on "the point" of the whole thing.

The Catholic use of Latin in the liturgy is very much like the Jewish use of Hebrew in synagogues. In both religions, part of the instruction of children in the faith has traditionally included worship, the language of worship, and the meaning of the rituals of worship. It's part of the heritage of both religions, part of their patrimony, and as such, not to be dispensed with lightly. Latin remains important to this day for deep scholarly study of the history and patrimony of the Church and the civilizations she inspired, since Latin was for so long the language of literacy in the West.

Is it a good thing for Catholics to be able to pray the Mass in their local languages now? Yes, I think so, though some disagree. I think that it makes worshipping God a lot easier when the average person is responding in their own language. But I do think we've lost something with a vernacular Mass for every group. There's something to be said for the unity that the universal use of Latin gave to Catholic worship, transcending local cultures. There are parishes where real tension arises over the Spanish Mass, or the Vietnamese Mass, or the Tagalog Mass, or the Pick-Your-Language Mass. If the Mass was universally celebrated in Latin, then all cultures and ethnicities could gather around this one common worship — a great achievement for bringing diversity into unity. Even if every parish had at least one Latin *Novus Ordo* Mass each Sunday, it could go a long way toward helping Catholic worshippers encounter a universal liturgy.

But as I said, I like being able to pray in my own language. I like hearing the Scriptures read in my native tongue, and the deepest mysteries of the faith celebrated in English. I think it's immensely valuable in making the Word of God available to all, no matter their level of education. When Jesus walked the earth, He spoke to the people who listened to Him in their own languages, after all. The Apostles at Pentecost spoke, and everyone could hear them in his or her own tongue. As I've mentioned above, in the earliest years of the Church, Latin was a universal language throughout the Roman empire, and so the original reason for using Latin was to worship in a language everyone could understand.

Circumstances changed, of course. But it's worth remembering that Latin was an ordinary part of education in many high schools and colleges until shortly before Vatican II. It's not as though Latin was the language of an elite group or as though the ordinary person had no chance to learn it.

So, no, the point was not to mystify the common man, but to make universal a certain way of praying Mass. The goal was not to preserve power for the few, but to enable all the world to worship together in spirit and in truth, according to the Roman Missal. The Church sought to bring all of humanity together to pray the awesome mystery of the Mass, where Jesus comes and is present on the altar under the appearance of bread and wine, where angels and saints pray and the barrier between time and eternity is sundered, where the end of all things meets the beginning in one timeless place, where God and creation join in the closest of unions.

That was, is, and will always be the point of it all: the communion of God and His Church. Language didn't necessarily get in the way of that communion and sanctification — we had many saints in the days when the Mass was celebrated in Latin. But sometimes language did become an impediment, which is why the Church changed her practice.

Question 44:
How can you still be Catholic when Jesus came to set us free from ritual, tradition, and law?

Actually, Jesus came to set us free from sin, death, and hell. Rather than repudiating ritual, tradition, and law, He brought new rituals, a fullness of tradition, and a new law written on the hearts of Christians.

First, let us be clear on one thing: the Law of Israel *was* not and *is* not an evil. It was, and is, genuinely a God-given Law. There is no dispute about this in the New Testament. Jesus Himself said, "Do not think that I have come to abolish the law or the prophets. I have come not to abolish but to fulfill" (Mt 5:17; see also 18-20).[207]

Does this mean that Christians must also be observant Jews? No. That was decided at the Council of Jerusalem in 50 A.D. (see Acts 15). Paul's theology of grace in the Letter to the Romans is plain: We are saved not by faithful adherence to the prescriptions of the Law of Moses but by the grace given through Jesus Christ. Nothing else suffices. We must be saved through Jesus, or we shall not be saved at all.

But although portions of the Law of Moses do not bind Christians, this does not mean Christians are not bound by the Law at all.[208] Indeed, Jesus reveals Himself throughout the Gospels to be the Lawgiver, the Lord, the God of Israel, the Son of the Father. Jesus also said, "If you love me, you will keep my commandments" (Jn 14:15). Jesus' words on the Law and prophets mean that Christians must behave according to the Law given through the religion of the people Israel — that is, we must obey the two great commandments: "You shall love the Lord, your God, with all your heart, with all your soul, and with all your mind. This is the greatest and the first commandment. The second is like it: You shall love your neighbor as yourself. The whole law and the prophets depend on these two commandments" (Mt 22: 36-40; see also Mt 7:12).

When asked by the rich young man what he must do to inherit eternal life, Jesus answered, "If you wish to enter into life, keep the commandments ... 'You shall not kill; you shall not commit adultery; you shall not steal; you shall not bear false witness; honor your father and your mother'; and 'you shall love your neighbor as yourself'" (Mt 19:16-21), indicating the enduring validity of the Ten Commandments.[209]

Another commandment, given very specifically, is, "I give you a new commandment: love one another. As I have loved you, so you also should love one another. This is how all will know that you are my disciples, if you have love for one another" (Jn 13:34-35).

His disciples are commanded to love one another. This love will be the mark of a Christian — the mark of those who believe in Jesus. What else does Jesus say will identify the believers? "Amen, amen, I say to you, whoever believes in me will do the works that I do, and will do greater ones than these, because I am going to the Father" (Jn 14:12).

So we shall know the believers in Jesus by their works, following another principle of Jesus: judging a tree by its fruits (see Lk 6:43-45). Christians shall be marked by their belief in Jesus, their love of God, and the works that flow from this faith and love. Make no mistake, we are given a law by Jesus Christ,.

It is a law that encompasses traditional rituals. Those who love Jesus will follow His commandments, which include the commandment to "do this in memory of me" (Lk 22:19), to ritually reenact the Last Supper, which is the great Passover of the Christians. We are to gather and eat the flesh of the Lamb of God who takes away the sins of the world, drink the blood poured out for us that washes away our sins, and remember how our salvation was accomplished:

> Jesus said to them, "Amen, amen, I say to you, unless you eat the flesh of the Son of Man and drink his blood, you do not have life within you. Whoever eats my flesh and drinks my blood has eternal life, and I will raise him on the last day. For my flesh is true food, and my blood is true drink. Whoever eats my flesh and drinks my blood remains in me and I in him" (Jn 6:53-56).

He also gives a very specific command about baptizing according to a ritual formula, saying:

> Go, therefore, and make disciples of all nations, baptizing them in the name of the Father, and of the Son, and of the holy Spirit, teaching them to observe all that I have commanded you (Mt 28:19-20).

In this short section, of course, we're certainly not going to get into a complete description of the theology of Baptism and the Lord's Supper, or Christian morality, or how Jesus fulfills and transcends the Old Testament, or all the teachings of Jesus. Make sure to check out the Recommended Reading (Appendix A) for more.

But I hope a few things have become clear — that Jesus gives us a law, and tradition, and ritual. He is the new Moses, not the enemy of Moses. He is the prophet whom Moses foretold (see Dt 18:18), the liberator who comes out of the land of Egypt to bring a new law and a new and everlasting covenant in the blood of the Passover Lamb (see Mk 14:24). He comes with fire from Heaven, and life, and love, all for the sake of our salvation and sanctification. He comes to bring us home to the Father. And along with words of teaching and His own life and witness, He gives us things to do if we have faith. If we believe in Him and love Him, we will follow His commandments; we will do the works He commanded us to perform.

We cannot have our sins forgiven through the animal sacrifices of the Temple, but we are certainly washed clean in the blood of the Lamb of God, of Jesus Christ, and in the Baptism that He orders for us, a Baptism for the forgiveness of sins (see Acts 2:38). Man cannot forgive sin — only God can do that, and those bishops and priests to whom God grants the power (see Jn 20:23). We are called upon to adhere to the traditions of the Body of Christ (see 2 Thess 2:15), of the Church, which is the pillar and foundation of truth (see 1 Tim 3:15). We are called to ritual accuracy and obedience when it comes to the celebration of the Lord's Supper, handed on to us as it was to St. Paul:

> I praise you because you remember me in everything and hold fast to the traditions, just as I handed them on to you (1 Cor 11:2; see also 20-30).

Question 45:
How can you still be Catholic when they branded Galileo a heretic?

I can still be Catholic after the Galileo affair because, to put it bluntly, that whole debacle wasn't about religion versus science but rather had to do with two ornery Italians getting mad at each other. Suffice it to say here that the affair largely came down to the wounded feelings and pride of Galileo and the pope at the time, Urban VIII; Galileo was not tortured; he was not thrown in prison; and he died at home.[210] Further, Copernicus, a Catholic priest, was never persecuted for the theory that later caused Galileo so much trouble.[211] In the 20th century, Pope St. John Paul II commissioned a study of the Galileo affair quite early in his pontificate; this study led the sainted pope and the Vatican to acknowledge that a mistake had been made in Galileo's case.[212]

No, the Galileo affair is not proof of an eternal war between Catholicism and science. How can I say that? Simple. Name five scientists who were ever arrested or convicted at the behest of the Church because of their scientifically sound conclusions.

I could argue that we should exclude Galileo from that list because, though he was right that the earth moves around the sun, his science was not flawless. Some may name 16th century Dominican Giordano Bruno, but he's far from being a straightforward example — indeed, he was rather more likely put to death for his theology than for his theories about the infinity of the universe and multiple worlds.[213]

And after that, the well runs dry. I'm open to correction, of course, but in my experience, that's about as far as the list of scientific martyrs goes.

On the other hand, the list of Catholics who've made major contributions to science is quite long and continues to grow. A small sampling:

- Roger Bacon (1214-1294), one of the first great proponents of experimental science
- Copernicus (1473-1543) and Galileo (1564-1642)
- Blaise Pascal (1623-1662), the mathematician and physicist
- Gregor Mendel (1822-1884), Catholic priest and father of genetics
- Georges Lemaitre (1894-1966), who first published the Big Bang theory

The list could be longer, including the vast array of priests in religious orders who have taught at the various Catholic universities down through the years (see Appendix A: Recommended Reading for this question to learn more).

No, Catholicism isn't opposed to science; rather, the Church has often poured resources into science through the ages, an effort continuing in the present day. Consider the Catholic universities; the Catholic healthcare systems; and institutions such as the Vatican Observatory, the Pontifical Academy of Sciences, and the Pontifical Academy of Social Sciences.

Now, it's quite true that the Church does not uncritically cheer on every experiment or new scientific endeavor. We do oppose embryonic stem-cell research, just as we oppose experimentation on unwilling human subjects or treating human beings as objects that scientists can manufacture to order, as in cloning or eugenic breeding programs. The Church does believe that technology has moral implications, and that the use of the knowledge we gain needs to be considered in light of the dignity of the human person. In other words, the Church does care about the consequences of scientific progress, and she's not alone. Mary Shelley was no Catholic, and yet she wrote *Frankenstein*, about as powerful a morality tale warning of the consequences of unchecked, unfettered technological experimentation with human beings as has ever been written. And what about Robert Louis Stevenson's *The Strange Case of Dr. Jekyll and Mr. Hyde*? Or Aldous Huxley's *Brave New World*? These authors created classics of literature based on the notion that science could indeed overstep the boundaries of what is right or just, and they weren't motivated by Catholic faith.

No, the Catholic Church is not the only institution or body of people expressing concerns about the pace or direction of modern science. As has been expressed by several popes and a number of other observers in various ways, our technological development has dramatically outstripped our moral or cultural development. Today, our leaders have the powers of the gods of myth and legend, the power to smite from the skies, to poison fields and streams so that nothing shall grow for a hundred generations, to fly across the world in a single night and speak instantly from faraway places. We live in an age of wonders, made possible by science and technology, an age of achievements that would have seemed miraculous or magical in other ages.

But do we use these things well? Do we take better care of our neighbors than previous generations did, in ways that are commensurate with our resources? Do we protect the weak, support the needy, love the elderly? Or do we make laws to drive the homeless away, abort the unborn, euthanize the old and the sick?

Science is a tool. It can be used for good or for evil. It's good to seek out truth, good to wonder at and seek to understand the world. It's also good to recognize the limits on what we can do without harming our neighbors or ourselves; good to recognize when a particular experiment would be meddling with the very foundations of what it means to be human; and good to be able to discern when certain things should be stopped, such as the Tuskegee syphilis experiments on unknowing African-Americans, the Nazi experiments on prisoners in concentration camps, or the eugenics drive in Virginia, Oregon, and other American states to sterilize the "unfit" in mental institutions and prisons during the 1900s.

So Catholicism is fundamentally open to science, and yet is not uncritical of it. I think that's a perfectly reasonable stance. I'm glad of my fellows Catholics' contributions to science, both past and present, and I enjoy modern conveniences as much as the next person does. I am grateful for modern medicine. I like the information age. And I hope that both ethics and science — informing each other, not pitted against each other — can continue to improve the lot of the human race, not endanger it through their innovations and new discoveries.

Question 46:

How can you still be Catholic when divorce can sometimes (sadly) be the end result of a marriage — and sometimes the only reasonable path?

I can still be Catholic even when I see divorce happening all around me because love stories make sense only if marriage is intended to be forever. The human experience of being in love leads to all sorts of declarations of total fidelity, of lifelong love, of forever and ever, of anything and everything. Are we willing to throw all of that out the window, to give up on it, when there are still stories of elderly couples whose marriage has lasted their entire lives dying within minutes of each other, loving each other to the very end? Will we allow ourselves to despair of such fidelity when 50th and 60th anniversaries are still being celebrated and honored in our churches, in our families (my maternal grandparents had 50 years of marriage before Grandpa died, and my paternal grandparents are still going at 65 years of marriage), and in our communities? However hard lifelong love has become in our modern culture, it is still an attainable goal, and it is a good one, a worthwhile one — indeed, it is the reality that has been expressed through sex from the beginning.

As St. John Paul II taught with his theology of the body, sex conveys through body language, "I give you everything I am, everything I have, the very deepest and most secret parts of me. I hold back nothing." To make that true, to prevent sexual body language from being a lie, marriage must be meant to be permanent. A lover is worth absolute self-gift, for better or worse, for richer or poorer, in sickness and in health. Marriage is worth it. A lifelong covenant is worth it. A beloved other is worth it. In other words, I believe that the Church's teaching on the permanence of marriage makes sense, since marriage inherently involves a total gift of self.

Here's the Church's understanding of marriage:

> The matrimonial covenant, by which a man and a woman establish between themselves a partnership of the whole of life, is by its nature ordered toward the good of the spouses and the procreation and education of offspring; this covenant between baptized persons has been raised by Christ the Lord to the dignity of a sacrament.[214]

Marriage is an exchange of persons. The husband gives himself to the wife, and the wife gives herself to her husband. And each person is totally worth the complete gift of self that marriage entails. A life is worth a life. The marriage vows are a total self-gift, not partial, not holding back. One version runs:

> I promise to be faithful to you, in good times and in bad, in sickness and in health, to love you and to honor you all the days of my life.[215]

This is the commitment involved in marriage in the Church. This is the level of commitment that has historically been expected of people when it comes to marriage. The *Catechism* explains the teaching on the unbreakable character of marriage like this:

> This unequivocal insistence on the indissolubility of the marriage bond may have left some perplexed and could seem to be a demand impossible to realize. However, Jesus has not placed on spouses a

burden impossible to bear, or too heavy — heavier than the Law of Moses.[216] By coming to restore the original order of creation disturbed by sin, he himself gives the strength and grace to live marriage in the new dimension of the Reign of God. It is by following Christ, renouncing themselves, and taking up their crosses that spouses will be able to "receive" the original meaning of marriage and live it with the help of Christ.[217]

Now, does this mean that all marriages will be ideal? No, of course not. There's a reason why the *Catechism* talks about the couples "taking up their crosses" in the context of marriage. You really do have to give yourself away, to die to yourself, in order to get married. That doesn't mean you give up your personality or your individuality when you get married. After all, your spouse fell in love with *you*, as you are. But in every relationship, there come times when you need to make sacrifices for the other person.

For some people, those sacrifices are substantial, as in the case of a loved one's illness, or when a family is struggling financially. Being a caregiver or working extra hard to make ends meet is difficult. But we are called to love as Jesus loved, and so dying to self is part of the package. Yes, it's hard. I for one am very bad at dying to self. But it's part and parcel of the joys and glory of the Christian life. "If anyone wishes to come after me, he must deny himself and take up his cross daily and follow me. For whoever wishes to save his life will lose it, but whoever loses his life for my sake will save it" (Lk 9:23-24).

Is spousal abuse a reality? Yes, and it makes sense for the spouses to live apart from each other in such a case. The Church does not prohibit such separation. Further, in cases where people entered into marriage without informed consent or under a number of other circumstances, the Church may look at the marriage and declare it null and void — that a true, sacramental marriage never took place. The Church may make this finding of nullity when, for instance, at least one of the spouses was pressured into marriage; when the spouses were not properly prepared for marriage; when at least one of the spouses didn't intend to remain faithful; or when at least one of the spouses didn't enter the marriage with an openness to having children. This decree of nullity is called an "annulment," and it is not the same as divorce, which would be breaking an intact marriage. There is no such thing as a "Catholic divorce."[218]

Civil "divorce" — the legal recognition of a couple as no longer married — happens all the time, of course, even among Catholic couples. That's undeniable. Why is this distinction important? Because the Church's understanding of marriage as a sacramental union, an institution that came before the state and that will be around long after states have crumbled into dust, means that the state can't determine whether a marriage has, in truth, ended. The state can recognize its dissolution only in civil law.

It is worse than sad when many marriages end in divorce. It is tragic. There is often a high personal,[219] social,[220] and cultural cost[221] when married couples break apart. And when divorce is normalized, the bonds that held couples together past the age of peak sexual attraction, past the time when the kids were at home, past the career and into the time of greatest dependence on the spouse, are gone.

I think the Church's teaching on divorce takes into account the true nature of marriage very well. When marriage is no longer "till death do us part," couples often part, leaving all sorts of wounds and brokenness in their wake.

Question 47:
How can you still be Catholic when they seem so intent on complicating a very simple message?

That's like asking, "How can someone believe in biology when it complicates a very simple natural world?"

You see, reality is both very simple and very complex at the same time. Take a daisy, for instance. A 4-year-old can look at the flower, smell the flower, pluck the flower, take it home, and put it in a vase of water. And a scientist could spend a lifetime studying the flower, breaking it down to its component parts, then further down to its molecular structures, and further down to its atomic and subatomic structures. In that one flower is in some sense all the complexity of the cosmos, as well as a simplicity that a small child can grasp.

That's Catholicism, as well. You can teach the faith to children — and spend an entire lifetime studying it. Why? Because of needless overcomplication? No. Because reality is both simple and complex; because the least intellectual of human beings can live full, happy lives, just as the brightest minds can spend their whole lives figuring out how the universe works.

"God is love," Catholics proclaim, and everyone has some idea of what that entails. "God is love," Pope Benedict XVI proclaims, and writes an entire encyclical (*Deus Caritas Est*) exploring that one line. Indeed, that line has launched books and lifetimes over the years. It's a truth of infinite depth, once you really start grappling with its implications, as well as the fact that it appears in the context of the rest of the Bible, and of the lived experience of thousands of years of Judaism, as well as thousands of years of Catholicism.

God is love. Jesus is Lord. There's the Catholic faith.

And then there are the Apostles' Creed and the Nicene Creed — longer, more detailed, but still relatively simple. They still fit on one page. The Church didn't come up with those in a vacuum, though. They arose because serious questions were being asked by people honestly seeking truth, questions like, "Is Jesus really the Lord God? How does that work? And the Father — who *is* He exactly in relation to the Son? And the Holy Spirit - what can we say truthfully about Him?"

And there's the extensive theological work of saints and scholars throughout Catholic history, people who were seeking truth, not working to obscure it. These are people who, on the one hand, know that the truths of the faith can be grasped on one level by the simplest of minds, and yet, on the other hand, realize that the implications and subtleties of these truths reach into depths and heights of mystery beyond human comprehension in this life.

Take the following questions, for example:

- How does Divine Providence still allow room for free will?
- How does the eternal God relate to events in time, especially through the Incarnation?
- How do the body and the soul interact?

These will plague philosophers until the end of the world — or perhaps I should say intrigue, or entice, or interest philosophers.

Because there is delight in the pursuit of truth. There can also be headaches and annoyances, grumbling at needless complexity or obscurity, and so on. But the pursuit of truth has inspired generations of people to become scientists or journalists, theologians and philosophers, spies and saints. Indeed, "our hearts are restless until they rest in thee," wrote

St. Augustine of the longing of the human heart for God, and Jesus made plain that God is truth, the fullness of truth, truth in itself.

Now, all that presumes the question is asked out of a natural frustration with needless overcomplication of something simple. But sometimes this sort of question may be motivated because someone wishes for a simpler Gospel for personal reasons — that is to say, they'd like to dispense with certain hard truths, seemingly impossible demands, or supernatural teachings of the Gospel.

I understand the impulse. It would be nice if Jesus simply affirmed me in my okayness, to borrow a phrase from Mark Shea, and said that I in my present state am perfectly all right, or even heroically virtuous.

But the Gospels don't do that. The New Testament lays out before our feet a challenging road of self-sacrifice out of love, a way of learning to live a divine life now in which we are pouring ourselves out into God, and God is pouring Himself out into us. Our former selves, the old man of sin and simple satisfaction with the world, are to be crucified with Christ; we are to take up the cross of dying to self, of self-discipline and virtue (see Rom 6:6). It's hard. All of us at times rebel against it, for we are all afflicted with the effects of original sin — darkened intellect, weakened will, and disordered desires — save, of course, Jesus and Mary.

The whole burden can be made sweet and light through grace, through love. And yet how often do we remain perfectly in love? How often do we say an unhesitating "yes" to God's grace? All too often, of course, we choose our own way and learn once again that we multiply cross on cross, problem on problem when we refuse to be generous with God, trust, and obey. For those times, there's Confession, penance, and renewed strength through the Eucharist.

The Gospel is what it is. No attempt to "simplify" it to make it fit our desires, our demands, our times, or the opinion of those we admire will help anyone. Rather, that's a great way to cause a great deal of harm.

Of course we must present it simply. Of course we must stick to the limits of the Gospel, and not add our own demands or preferences to it. But of course we must not reduce it to fit our own preferences, as well. Of course we may not remove key elements in the name of simplicity.

Question 48:
How can you still be Catholic when they are more focused on the Crucifixion of Jesus than the life of Jesus?

Quite easily, because we merely follow in the footsteps of St. Paul: "We proclaim Christ crucified, a stumbling block to Jews and foolishness to Gentiles ... When I came to you, brothers, proclaiming the mystery of God, I did not come with sublimity of words or of wisdom. For I resolved to know nothing while I was with you except Jesus Christ, and him crucified" (1 Cor 1:23; 2:1-2).

We imitate the Gospel writers, who spend much more time on the Passion than they do on any other single incident in the life of Christ.

Why so much focus on the Crucifixion? Simply because this is the supreme revelation of the love of God, as St. John Paul II taught. How so? Well, God is love, and not just any sort of love, but utter, absolute self-gift. Nowhere in the life of Christ is that absolute and utter self-gift made more plain than on the Cross, where He literally pours Himself out to the last drop in order to win the salvation of sinners and the redemption of the world.

The Cross makes Divine Mercy plain. The Cross shows Jesus for who He is most clearly and reveals the face of the Father through the self-gift of the Son. The Cross is the throne of the Son of David, and He enters His Kingdom outside the walls of Jerusalem, speaking the first words of a psalm (see Ps 22; see also Mt 27:46) and dancing on the Cross (as the great hymn "Lord of the Dance" describes) before His Mother, the Ark of the New and Everlasting Covenant, just as his forebear, David the King, had danced outside the walls of Jerusalem before the Ark of the Covenant, entering into his kingdom (see 2 Sam 6). The Cross is the hinge of history, the turning point, the moment when Heaven was reopened to us, when the covenant in Christ's blood was enacted, when all our sins were washed away.

And everything that happened throughout Christ's life on earth is in some sense eternal, as Fr. Michael Gaitley, MIC, explains so well in his book *The 'One Thing' is Three*. It wasn't just 2,000 years ago that Calvary happened — Calvary took place for an eternal person, the Son of God. Calvary is an eternal event, and every single Mass is a participation in that once-for-all sacrifice. Each celebration of the Eucharist is a re-presentation of Christ's self gift to the Father, a way of bringing the event out of the past and into the present again, and again, and again. Just as each Passover of the Jews is in some way each generation of the Jewish people reliving the events of their escape from Egypt, so, too, is the Mass the Passover of the Christians, both remembering and making present again to each generation until the end of the world what happened through Jesus at Jerusalem.

And the Cross was the destination of Christ's life. A long time before Good Friday, He started telling His disciples what would happen to Him — what *had* to happen to Him — a long time before Good Friday.

Further, as a colleague recently reminded me, the Cross is the reality of our lives here below. Oh, there are joyful and luminous times in our lives, as well, just as there were in Christ's earthly life. But in all the little pains and big tragedies of life, all the ways in which even ordinary days bring us some measure of suffering and self-sacrifice, we know that our lives are touched by the Sorrowful Mysteries, by the Cross. We are pilgrims on the way to our heavenly home. This fallen world isn't the final destination (thank God!), nor is the present life the only life, to be grasped at desperately.

No — we are citizens of Heaven, and strangers and sojourners in this world below.

All this does not mean that we do not ever remember or focus on the rest of the life of Christ, of course. Look at the liturgical calendar of the Church, the cycle of feasts and fasts, of different seasons dedicated to different portions of the life of Christ. We have Advent and Christmas as well as Lent and Holy Week, and of course our commemoration of Christ's self-gift culminates in Easter and Divine Mercy Sunday. We're hearing readings at Mass from across the Gospels throughout the year, living with and hearing homilies on the whole life of Christ. In the Rosary, one of the most commonly recited of Catholic prayers, there are four sets of mysteries, and only one set is sorrowful.

No, the Catholic Church does not neglect the rest of the Incarnation for the sake of the Crucifixion. But Christ on the Cross is the great symbol of the triumph of love and mercy, of the forgiveness of our enemies and the great lengths Christians are called to go to in order to help heal the world. The crucifix is the symbol of God's own inner life of self-gift, showing God on His throne ruling His kingdom through utter self-dona-tion, through humility, through emptying Himself and taking on the form of a slave (see Phil 2:7).

The Cross is the source, center, and pattern of the Christian life — self-gift to God and neighbor, dying to self, leading into Resurrection and eternal life. Of course we often focus on it.

Question 49:
How can you still be Catholic when the music for liturgy is so awful?

You know, I was once asked a very similar question by an ex-Catholic. He wanted to know if I thought the Mass was boring. After all, it's the same thing every week, the routine doesn't vary much, and honestly, wouldn't it be much better to worship God in a more free-flowing, changeable sort of way?

I said, "Boredom is a really bad reason not to worship God."

That said, yes, sometimes I don't like the music at Mass. But in this, Catholics do not suffer alone. C.S. Lewis had a similar opinion of the hymns at Anglican services. He said:

> I disliked very much their hymns, which I considered to be fifth-rate poems set to sixth-rate music. But as I went on I saw the great merit of it. I came up against different people of quite different outlooks and different education, and then gradually my conceit just began peeling off. I realized that the hymns (which were just sixth-rate music) were, nevertheless, being sung with devotion and benefit by an old saint in elastic-side boots in the opposite pew, and then you realize that you aren't fit to clean those boots. It gets you out of your solitary conceit.[222]

Not to say that all objections to Mass music involve "solitary conceit," of course. There are standards for sacred music that Catholic musicians playing at Mass should adhere to. Vatican II dedicated an entire chapter of *Sacrosanctum Concilium* (*Constitution on the Sacred Liturgy*) to the question of sacred music.[223] The Council Fathers clearly placed a high importance on the music traditionally used in the liturgy of the Church, saying, "The musical tradition of the universal Church is a treasure of inestimable value, greater even than that of any other art. The main reason for this pre-eminence is that, as sacred song united to the words, it forms a necessary or integral part of the solemn liturgy … ."[224]

Why is the liturgy so important? Because it is in the Mass that we worship in spirit and in truth, in the fullness of communion with the heavenly host of saints and angels adoring around the throne of God throughout all eternity.[225] So when we sing at Mass, we enter into the endless song of Heaven. The priest even explicitly acknowledges this during the Mass, right before the assembly sings the "Holy, Holy, Holy":

> … with the Angels and all the Saints we declare your glory, as with one voice we acclaim …[226]

So the music at Mass matters:

> The treasure of sacred music is to be preserved and fostered with great care. Choirs must be diligently promoted, especially in cathedral churches; but bishops and other pastors of souls must be at pains to ensure that, whenever the sacred action is to be celebrated with song, the whole body of the faithful may be able to contribute that active participation which is rightly theirs.[227]

We are all supposed to sing at Mass, not just the choir. We are all supposed to join our voices to the endless praise and thanksgiving offered to God in the heavenly worship. And what does the Church recommend we sing?

The Church acknowledges Gregorian chant as specially suited to the Roman liturgy: therefore, other
things being equal, it should be given pride of place
in liturgical services. But other kinds of sacred music, especially polyphony, are by no means excluded
from liturgical celebrations, so long as they accord
with the spirit of the liturgical action ...[228]

So the Second Vatican Council calls for Gregorian chant to
normally have pride of place in the Roman liturgy (that means
the Mass celebrated according to the Roman rite — there are
a number of different rites within Catholicism). Other styles
of music are permitted as long as they are appropriate for the
Mass — especially if other styles of music are part of the traditions of different parts of the world:

In certain parts of the world, especially mission
lands, there are peoples who have their own musical
traditions, and these play a great part in their religious and social life. For this reason due importance
is to be attached to their music, and a suitable place
is to be given to it, not only in forming their attitude toward religion, but also in adapting worship
to their native genius ... [229]

The Council recommends the pipe organ as a particularly
suitable instrument for use at Mass, though the document
permits the use of other instruments if they are "suitable, or
can be made suitable, for sacred use, accord with the dignity
of the temple, and truly contribute to the edification of the
faithful ..."[230] People are invited to compose new pieces of
music for the Mass, so long as the music produced is appropriate for use in worship. Also, "[t]he texts intended to be sung
must always be in conformity with Catholic doctrine; indeed
they should be drawn chiefly from holy scripture and from
liturgical sources."[231]

So there are objective rules for the music sung at Mass.
There's an artistic standard — the music should be beautiful

and appropriate for use at Mass — but there is also a lot of room for people to write new music and for traditional styles of music from all over the world to be incorporated into use in the liturgy. I leave it to the liturgists and musicians to discuss whether what's current practice throughout America is the most faithful implementation of the letter and spirit of Vatican II, but even if the music at a particular parish is awful, remember that the point of the Mass is not the music. The point of the Mass is Jesus Christ, present in Word and Sacrament to the Mystical Body of Christ. We are to seek to present a more beautiful liturgy, yes — because it's appropriate that we offer our very best efforts to God when we gather to worship Him. But that growth in beauty should remain faithful to the norms and teaching of the Church.

So bad music is a problem where it exists, and it should be corrected if possible. But it's certainly not worth ceasing to be Catholic because of bad music. And remember — we are asked to give what we can to God, even if it is the widow's mite. Oftentimes, the people who volunteer to serve as musicians at Mass are not professionals. They are good-hearted people trying to serve the Church. That's a contribution that we shouldn't scorn. Sometimes, charity demands that aestheticism sit down and be quiet, because God loves us even when we offer Him smudgy finger paintings and tone-deaf performances of poorly written, badly orchestrated songs. We are not to be more finicky than God. We are to follow the Master, not second-guess His charity.

Yes, I can sympathize with the complaint. Yes, we should aim for beauty and excellence in all our works as Catholics, for our God is the God of order, reason, and harmony. But the whole point of making the Mass more beautiful is to show more clearly what's already there, not to make up for something lacking. God is the fullness of beauty. So long as He is at Mass, nothing is lacking.

Question 50:
How can you still be Catholic when you're such a sinner?

Good question. My answer is the same as that given by the man who denied Jesus, who was called "Satan" by Jesus, and who went on to become the Rock on which the Church was founded. That is, my answer is the same as St. Peter's: "Master, to whom shall we go? You have the words of eternal life. We have come to believe and are convinced that you are the Holy One of God" (Jn 6:68-69).

Where else shall I go? I believe the creeds and the codes of Catholicism to be true. I believe in the Church's Sacraments, in her prayers, in her practices. I believe in the Catholic faith, in Jesus Christ and His revelation and promises. I believe. So where else am I supposed to go?

I also echo Chesterton's answer:

When people ask me, or indeed anybody else, "Why did you join the Church of Rome?" the first essential answer, if it is partly an elliptical answer, is, "To get rid of my sins." For there is no other religious system that does really profess to get rid of people's sins. It is confirmed by the logic, which to many seems startling, by which the Church deduces that sin confessed and adequately repented is actually abolished; and that the sinner does really begin again as if he had never sinned.[232]

Lest anyone be deceived by the existence and nature of this book, let you now know the truth: I am a sinner, and know that I am a sinner.

Am I a good Catholic? Nope.

I'm a bad Catholic. And thus, I gotta go to Confession.

It's a Chestertonian paradox at the heart of the Church. The Catholic who frequents the Sacraments is a Catholic who regularly confesses their sins and prays the *Confiteor* at the start of Mass. The supposedly "good Catholic" is the one who knows he or she is a bad Catholic.[233]

Hence, Cardinal Timothy Dolan blogged in 2012 about the experience of going to Confession at St. Peter's in Rome, talking about how he usually goes to Confession every two weeks or so in New York City (his archdiocese) because he needs it, but that the Sacrament took on a "special urgency and meaning" in the Eternal City. He writes, "Adjacent to his burial place, I even admit that, like Peter, I have, in my thoughts, words, and actions, denied Jesus."[234]

That's a cardinal speaking, ladies and gentlemen, acknowledging that he *needs* to go to Confession, that he falls, that he's a sinner. And so he goes to Confession, trusting in the promises of Jesus that the apostles and those to whom they delegate the authority can forgive sins (see Jn 20:21-23; Jas 5:16). Listen to the man — he knows of what he speaks. So pray for me — I need it. And pray for all the other bad Catholics out there — we need it. Because that's what's in the *Confiteor* we pray at the start of Mass:

> I confess to almighty God and to you, my brothers and sisters, that I have greatly sinned in my thoughts and in my words, in what I have done and in what I have failed to do, through my fault, through my fault, through my most grievous fault; therefore I ask blessed Mary ever-Virgin, all the Angels and Saints, and you, my brothers and sisters, to pray for me to the Lord our God.

In a certain sense, I am a Catholic because of my sins, not in spite of them. I need to be a Catholic — compelled by conscience and by intellectual recognition of the truth of the Church's teaching, called to resist all the times when disordered desire and unruly passion would say chuck the whole thing, strengthened by the Sacraments and illuminated by Catholic teaching, I need to be a Catholic. I need the grace and strength. I need the fellowship on the journey, the sheltering bulk of the Church. I need to be surrounded by the heavenly host, that great cloud of witnesses cheering all of us on in the race for Christ. I need the angels on my side!

I need God, and He comes in the Eucharist. I need forgiveness, and He gives me that in the confessional. I need help knowing the true and the good, and the teaching magisterium of the Church gives me the Scriptures and acts as a sure guide along the straight and narrow path to Heaven. I need my Lady, my Queen, St. Mary, Mother of the Church, and her most chaste spouse, St. Joseph, to guide and guard me, to pray me home and introduce me to their beloved Son, Jesus. I need the devotions to anchor me, to guide my prayer, and to draw me daily into the divine life, the relationship with God.

I am one great bundle of need, and God is giving infinitely through the channel of His Church. Will there come a day when I complete my repentance, my turning back to God, and I go and sin no more? By God's grace, yes, there can be, and I hope there will be. There does come a day in the life of a Christian when they have walked the whole spiritual path. They have been purged, illuminated, and united by God to the Trinitarian life in such a fashion as to make it permanent, so that a person walks the earth as a great saint. The spiritual writers and mystics have described the path — the three ages of the interior life, the great transformation worked in the life of a sinner by the Holy Spirit, and the full flowering of the Christian life have all been laid out and described.

That path has been walked to completion by the likes of St. John of the Cross, St. Anthony of Egypt, St. Thérèse of Lisieux, St. Teresa of Avila, St. Jean Vianney, St. Faustina

Kowalska, and many more. It is a path of grace and glory, as well as suffering and death. It is the way of life, and so it is the way of Calvary. Why is it so hard? The path demands everything — Jesus demands everything from you, so that you have room in your heart for Him and His family. It is the process that makes a human heart the heavenly home. It is death. It is life.

We are called to be perfect as the heavenly Father is perfect, which means we are to love and live as God loves and lives — perfect self-gift and total receptivity to the other, something possible only in a person on fire with the Holy Spirit, the love of God and neighbor. I am a pile of wet wood, and God is slowly setting me aflame. Again — pray for me. I'll pray for you.

How can I be Catholic? God's calling me. He's calling you, as well, and your family, your friends, your neighbors, your enemies, to come enter the household of the living God. "For God so loved the world that he gave his only Son, so that everyone who believes in him might not perish but might have eternal life" (Jn 3:16).

Recommended Reading

Question 1: How can you still be Catholic when the Church overall has so much dirty laundry?

- Philip Jenkins, *The New Anti-Catholicism: The Last Acceptable Prejudice*
- Rodney Stark, *Bearing False Witness: Debunking Centuries of Anti-Catholic History*
- Dr. Alan Schreck, *Catholic and Christian: An Explanation of Commonly Misunderstood Catholic Beliefs*
- Bishop Robert Barron, *Catholicism*
- Father Michael Gaitley, MIC, *The 'One Thing' is Three: How the Most Holy Trinity Explains Everything*

Question 2: How can you still be Catholic when they arrogantly think they are the one true religion?

- G.K. Chesterton, *Orthodoxy*
- Frank Sheed, *Theology for Beginners*
- C.S. Lewis, *Mere Christianity*
- Congregation for the Doctrine of the Faith, *Dominus Iesus*
- Vatican II, *Lumen Gentium*; see also *Gaudium et Spes*

Question 3: How can you still be Catholic when the Crusades happened?

- Andrew Bostom, *The Legacy of Jihad*
- Rodney Stark, *God's Battalions: The Case for the Crusades*
- Efraim Karsh, *Islamic Imperialism: A History*
- Thomas Madden, *The New Concise History of the Crusades*

- Jonathan Riley-Smith, *What Were The Crusades?*

Question 4: How can you still be Catholic when they just want you to suffer and feel guilty about everything?

- Father Michael Gaitley, MIC, *'You Did It to Me': A Practical Guide to Mercy in Action*
- Archbishop Fulton Sheen, *Peace of Soul*
- Ralph Martin, *The Fulfillment of All Desire*
- C.S. Lewis, *The Problem of Pain*; see also *A Grief Observed*
- Pope Benedict XVI, *Deus Caritas Est*
- Pope John Paul II, *Salvifici Doloris*

Question 5: How can you still be Catholic when they believe sex has only one objective: to procreate?

- Helen Alvare (ed.), *Breaking Through: Catholic Women Speak for Themselves*
- Jennifer Fulwiler, *Something Other Than God: How I Passionately Sought Happiness and Accidentally Found It*
- Kimberly Hahn, *Life-Giving Love: Embracing God's Beautiful Design for Marriage*
- Simcha Fisher, *The Sinner's Guide to Natural Family Planning*
- Carl Anderson and Jose Granados, *Called to Love: Approaching John Paul II's Theology of the Body*

Question 6: How can you still be Catholic when priests have abused little boys?

- Paul Thigpen (ed.), *Shaken by Scandals: Catholics Speak Out About Priests' Sexual Abuse*
- George Weigel, *The Courage to Be Catholic*
- Philip Jenkins, *Pedophiles and Priests*; see also *The New Anti-Catholicism: The Last Acceptable Prejudice*
- Phil Lawler, *The Faithful Departed: The Collapse of Boston's Catholic Culture*
- Mary Eberstadt, *Adam and Eve After the Pill*

Question 7: How can you still be Catholic when homosexuality is clearly genetic?

- Melinda Selmys, *Sexual Authenticity: An Intimate Reflection on Homosexuality and Catholicism*
- Janet E. Smith and Fr. Paul Check (eds.), *Living the Truth in Love*
- Carl Anderson and Jose Granados, *Called to Love: Approaching John Paul II's Theology of the Body*
- Dr. Scott Hahn, *Lord, Have Mercy: The Healing Power of Confession*
- Ralph Martin, *The Fulfillment of All Desire: A Guidebook to God Based on the Wisdom of the Saints*

Question 8: How can you still be Catholic when the Church continues to forbid birth control?

- Jennifer Fulwiler, *Something Other Than God: How I Passionately Sought Happiness and Accidentally Found It*
- Kimberly Hahn, *Life-Giving Love: Embracing God's Beautiful Design for Marriage*
- Dr. Janet Smith, *Humanae Vitae: A Generation Later*; see also *Why Humanae Vitae Was Right: A Reader*, with Dr. Christopher Kaczor, *Life Issues, Medical Choices: Questions and Answers for Catholics*
- Dr. Christopher Kaczor, *The Seven Big Myths About the Catholic Church: Distinguishing Fact from Fiction About Catholicism*
- Pope Paul VI, *Humanae Vitae*

Question 9: How can you still be Catholic when they want you to have so many babies in a world that's already overcrowded?

- Simcha Fisher, *The Sinner's Guide to Natural Family Planning*
- Helen Alvare (ed.), *Breaking Through: Catholic Women Speak for Themselves*
- Brandon Vogt, *Saints and Social Justice: A Guide to Changing the World*
- Pope Francis, *Laudato Si'*, Encyclical Letter on Care for Our Common Home
- *Compendium of the Social Doctrine of the Church*

Question 10: How can you still be Catholic when Mary is elevated above God?

- Dr. Robert Stackpole, *Mary: Who She Is and Why She Matters*

- Dr. Scott Hahn, *Hail, Holy Queen: The Mother of God in the Word of God*
- Mark Shea, *Mary, Mother of the Son*
- Pope John Paul II, *Redemptoris Mater*
- Vatican II, *Lumen Gentium*, Chapter 8

Question 11: How can you still be Catholic when there is no reason a woman cannot be just as good of a priest as a man?

- Dr. Scott Hahn, *Many Are Called: Rediscovering the Glory of the Priesthood*
- Archbishop Fulton Sheen, *The Priest Is Not His Own*
- John Paul II, Apostolic Letter *Ordinatio Sacerdotalis*; see also *Mulieris Dignitatem: On the Dignity and Vocation of Women*
- Vatican II, *Presbyterorum Ordinis*

Question 12: How can you still be Catholic when Christ says to take care of the poor and yet the pope lives in a mansion?

- Bishop Robert Barron, *Heaven in Stone and Glass: Experiencing the Spirituality of the Great Cathedrals*
- Thomas Woods, *How the Catholic Church Built Western Civilization*
- Father Michael Gaitley, MIC, *'You Did It to Me': A Practical Guide to Mercy in Action*
- Mark Shea, *The Work of Mercy: Being the Hands and Heart of Christ*

Question 13: How can you still be Catholic when you have to believe that everything the pope says and does is "infallible"?

- Mark Shea, *By What Authority? An Evangelical Discovers Catholic Tradition*
- Dr. Robert Stackpole, *The Papacy: God's Gift for All Christians*
- Steve Ray, *Upon This Rock: St. Peter and the Primacy of Rome in Scripture and the Early Church*
- Vatican I, *Pastor Aeternus* (First dogmatic constitution on the Church of Christ, July 18, 1870)

Question 14: How can you still be Catholic when God doesn't exist?

- Rebecca V. Cherico (ed.), *Atheist to Catholic: 11 Stories of Conversion*
- C.S. Lewis, *Miracles*; see also *Mere Christianity*; *Surprised by Joy*
- Matthew Bunson, Margaret Bunson, and Stephen Bunson, *Our Sunday Visitor's Encyclopedia of Saints*
- G.K. Chesterton, *The Everlasting Man*
- Father Robert Spitzer, SJ, *New Proofs for the Existence of God: Contributions of Contemporary Physics and Philosophy*

Question 15: How can you still be Catholic when Catholics behave in such un-Christian ways?

- C.S. Lewis, *The Screwtape Letters*; see also *The Great Divorce*
- Dr. Scott Hahn, *Lord, Have Mercy: The Healing Power of Confession*
- Dr. Alan Schreck, *Rebuild My Church*
- Father Benedict Groeschel, CFR, *Reform and Renewal*
- Pope John Paul II, *Dives in Misericordia* (*Rich in Mercy*, November 30, 1980); see also the post-synodal exhortation *Reconciliation and Penance* (December 2, 1984)

Question 16: How can you still be Catholic when the Church draws such a hard line on life issues (abortion, for example) with no room for mercy?

- Theresa Bonopartis, *A Journey to Healing Through Divine Mercy: Mercy After Abortion*
- Abby Johnson, *Unplanned: The Dramatic True Story of a Former Planned Parenthood Leader's Eye-Opening Journey Across the Life Line*; see also *The Walls Are Talking: Former Abortion Clinic Workers Tell Their Stories*
- Dr. Bernard Nathanson, *The Hand of God: A Journey from Death to Life by the Abortion Doctor Who Changed His Mind*
- Dr. Scott Hahn, *Lord, Have Mercy: The Healing Power of Confession*
- Father Robert Spitzer, *Healing the Culture: A Commonsense Philosophy of Happiness, Freedom, and the Life Issues*

- Pope John Paul II, *Evangelium Vitae*
- Pope Francis, *Misericordia et Misera*

Question 17: How can you still be Catholic when, despite the simplicity of Jesus' teachings, the Church itself is so bureaucratic?

- Pete Vere and Michael Trueman, *Surprised by Canon Law: 150 Questions Laypeople Ask About Canon Law*
- Vatican II, *Lumen Gentium*

Question 18: How can you still be Catholic when priests are not holy?

- Dr. Scott Hahn, *Many Are Called: Rediscovering the Glory of the Priesthood*
- Pope John Paul II, *Gift and Mystery: On the 50th Anniversary of My Priestly Ordination*
- Vatican II, *Presbyterorum Ordinis*

Question 19: How can you still be Catholic when so many of the Church's customs came from pagans?

- Roy Schoeman, *Honey from the Rock: Sixteen Jews Find the Sweetness of Christ*
- Dr. Scott Hahn, *Signs of Life: 40 Catholic Customs and Their Biblical Roots*; see also *Rome, Sweet Home: Our Journey to Catholicism*, with Kimberly Hahn
- David Currie, *Born Fundamentalist, Born Again Catholic*
- Mark Shea, *Mary, Mother of the Son*
- Rod Bennett, *Four Witnesses: The Early Church in Her Own Words*
- Jimmy Akin, *The Fathers Know Best: Your Essential Guide to the Teachings of the Early Church*

Question 20: How can you still be Catholic when Church teachings seem so absolute?

- Father Donald Calloway, MIC, *No Turning Back: A Witness to Mercy*
- Father Servais Pinckaers, *Morality: The Catholic View*

- C.S. Lewis, *Mere Christianity*; see also *The Abolition of Man*
- Pope John Paul II, *Veritatis Splendor*

Question 21: How can you still be Catholic when the Church didn't stand up to the Nazis?

- Ronald Rychlak, *Hitler, the War, and the Pope*; see also *Righteous Gentiles: How Pius XII and the Catholic Church Saved Half a Million Jews from the Nazis*
- Rabbi David Dalin, *The Pius War: Responses to Critics of Pius XII*
- Mark Riebling, *Church of Spies: The Pope's Secret War Against Hitler*
- Eugenio Zolli, *Before the Dawn: Autobiographical Reflections by Eugenio Zolli, Former Chief Rabbi of Rome*
- Pope Pius XI, Encyclical Letter *Mit Brennender Sorge*
- Pope Pius XII, Encyclical Letter *Summi Pontificatus*

Question 22: How can you still be Catholic when the Church is so far behind the times on things like abortion?

- Abby Johnson, *Unplanned: The Dramatic True Story of a Former Planned Parenthood Leader's Eye-Opening Journey Across the Life Line*
- Dr. Bernard Nathanson, *The Hand of God: A Journey from Death to Life by the Abortion Doctor Who Changed His Mind*
- Jennifer Fulwiler, *Something Other Than God: How I Passionately Sought Happiness and Accidentally Found It*
- Father Robert Spitzer, SJ, *Healing the Culture: A Commonsense Philosophy of Happiness, Freedom, and the Life Issues*
- Pope John Paul II, *Evangelium Vitae*

Question 23: How can you still be Catholic when progressive Catholics sometimes feel unwelcome or unneeded in the Church?

- Brandon Vogt, *Saints and Social Justice: A Guide to Changing the World*
- Mike Aquilina and David Scott, *Weapons of the Spirit: Selected Writings of Father John Hugo*
- C.S. Lewis, *The Screwtape Letters*

- Vatican II, *Apostolicam Actuositatem*
- Pope John Paul II, *Christifideles Laici*

Question 24: How can you still be Catholic when you see the Church treating women as second class?

- Helen M. Alvare, *Breaking Through: Catholic Women Speak for Themselves*
- Colleen Carroll Campbell, *My Sisters the Saints: A Spiritual Memoir*
- Donna Steichen, *Prodigal Daughters: Catholic Women Come Home to the Church*
- John Paul II, *Mulieris Dignitatem*; see also *Redemptoris Mater*
- Vatican II, *Lumen Gentium*, Chapter 8

Question 25: How can you still be Catholic when you see what your being Catholic is doing to your family?

- Dr. Scott Hahn and Kimberly Hahn, *Rome, Sweet Home: Our Journey to Catholicism*
- Patrick Madrid, *Surprised by Truth* series
- Marcus Grodi, *Journeys Home*; see also *Thoughts for the Journey Home*
- Roy Schoeman (ed.), *Honey from the Rock: Sixteen Jews Find the Sweetness of Christ*
- Donna Steichen, *Chosen: How Christ Sent Twenty-Three Surprised Converts to Replant His Vineyard*

Question 26: How can you still be Catholic when the Church says masturbation will bring you eternal damnation?

- Christopher West, *Theology of the Body for Beginners: A Basic Introduction to Pope John Paul II's Sexual Revolution*, Revised Edition
- Vinny Flynn, *7 Secrets of Confession*
- Dr. Scott Hahn, *Lord, Have Mercy: The Healing Power of Confession*
- Carl Anderson and Jose Granados, *Called to Love: Approaching John Paul II's Theology of the Body*
- Ralph Martin, *The Fulfillment of All Desire*

Question 27: How can you still be Catholic when the Church did such terrible things during the Inquisition?

- Rodney Stark, *For the Glory of God: How Monotheism Led to Reformations, Science, Witch-Hunts, and the End of Slavery* (especially Chapters 1 and 3)
- Henry Kamen, *The Spanish Inquisition: A Historical Revision*
- Edward Peters, *Inquisition*
- Vatican II, *Dignitatis Humanae: Declaration on Religious Freedom*; see also *Nostra Aetate: Declaration on the Relation of the Church to Non-Christian Religions*
- Cardinal Joseph Ratzinger, *Truth and Tolerance*

Question 28: How can you still be Catholic when praying to the saints and Mary contradicts Scripture, which says pray to God alone?

- Dave Armstrong, *A Biblical Defense of Catholicism*
- Patrick Madrid, *Where Is That in the Bible?* See also *Why Is That in Tradition?* and *Answer Me This!*
- Mark Shea, *Mary, Mother of the Son*; see also *The Heart of Catholic Prayer: Rediscovering the Our Father and the Hail Mary*
- Dr. Scott Hahn, *Hail, Holy Queen: The Mother of God in the Word of God*
- Louis de Wohl's historical novelizations of the lives of the saints are remarkably good. Some of my favorites are *Citadel of God* (St. Benedict of Nursia); *The Glorious Folly* (St. Paul the Apostle); *The Joyful Beggar* (St. Francis of Assisi); *Lay Siege to Heaven* (St. Catherine of Siena); *The Quiet Light* (St. Thomas Aquinas); *The Restless Flame* (on St. Augustine of Hippo); *The Golden Thread* (St. Ignatius of Loyola); *Set All Afire* (St. Francis Xavier); *The Spear* (St. Longinus).

Question 29: How can you still be Catholic when the Church has led so many organized acts of violence and oppression?

- Thomas Woods Jr., *How the Catholic Church Built Western Civilization*
- Brandon Vogt, *Saints and Social Justice: A Guide to Changing the World*

- Dorothy Day, *The Long Loneliness*
- George Weigel, *The Final Revolution: The Resistance Church and the Collapse of Communism*
- *Compendium of the Social Doctrine of the Church*

Question 30: How can you still be Catholic when they didn't immediately denounce slavery?

- Rodney Stark, *The Victory of Reason: How Christianity Led to Freedom, Capitalism, and Western Success*
- Father Joel Panzer, *The Popes and Slavery*
- Pope Paul III, *Sublimus Dei*
- Leo XIII, *Catholicae Ecclesiae*
- Vatican II, *Gaudium et Spes*

Question 31: How can you still be Catholic when the Church had corrupt popes?

- Dr. Robert Stackpole, *The Papacy: God's Gift for All Christians*
- Patrick Madrid, *Pope Fiction: Answers to 30 Myths and Misconceptions About the Papacy*
- Steve Ray, *Upon This Rock: St. Peter and the Primacy of Rome in Scripture and the Early Church*
- Pope Benedict XVI, *The Apostles: The Origin of the Church and Their Co-Workers*

Question 32: How can you still be Catholic when the Church doesn't think gay people are still people who deserve their human rights?

- Melinda Selmys, *Sexual Authenticity: An Intimate Reflection on Homosexuality and Catholicism*
- Jennifer Fulwiler, *Something Other Than God: How I Passionately Sought Happiness and Accidentally Found It*
- George Weigel, *The Truth of Catholicism: Inside the Essential Teachings and Controversies of the Church Today*
- Carl Anderson and Jose Granados, *Called to Love: Approaching John Paul II's Theology of the Body*

- Congregation of the Doctrine of the Faith, *Letter to the Bishops of the Catholic Church on the Pastoral Care of Homosexual Persons*; see also *Considerations Regarding Proposals to Give Legal Recognition to Unions Between Homosexual Persons*

Question 33: How can you still be Catholic when your Church has closed Communion to everyone other than Catholics?

- Mark Shea, *This Is My Body: An Evangelical Discovers the Real Presence*
- Dr. Scott Hahn, *The Lamb's Supper: The Mass as Heaven on Earth*; see also *Swear to God: The Promise and Power of the Sacraments*; *A Father Who Keeps His Promises*; *Covenant and Communion*
- Cardinal Joseph Ratzinger, *The Spirit of the Liturgy*; see also *God Is Near Us: The Eucharist, the Heart of Life*
- Pope John Paul II, *Mane Nobiscum Domine*; see also *Ecclesia de Eucharista*

Question 34: How can you still be Catholic when the Church tries to control every aspect of your personal life?

- Matthew Leonard, *Louder Than Words: The Art of Living as a Catholic*
- C.S. Lewis, *The Screwtape Letters*; see also *Mere Christianity*
- Mary Eberstadt, *Adam and Eve After the Pill*
- Bishop Robert Barron, *The Strangest Way: Walking the Christian Path*
- Cardinal Joseph Ratzinger, *What It Means to Be a Christian*

Question 35: How can you still be Catholic when the Church is not biblical; rather, it draws on "Sacred Tradition"?

- Mark Shea, *By What Authority? An Evangelical Discovers Catholic Tradition*
- Patrick Madrid, *Why Is That in Tradition?* See also *Where Is That in the Bible?*
- Dr. Scott Hahn and Kimberly Hahn, *Rome, Sweet Home: Our Journey to Catholicism*; see also *Signs of Life: 40 Catholic Customs and Their Biblical Roots*

- David Currie, *Born Fundamentalist, Born Again Catholic*
- Vatican II, *Dei Verbum*

Question 36: How can you still be Catholic when they made belief in Mary's Immaculate Conception required a full 1,800-plus years after Christ's death?

- Mark Shea, *Mary Mother of the Son*; see also *By What Authority? An Evangelical Discovers Catholic Tradition*
- Dr. Robert Stackpole, *Mary: Who She Is and Why She Matters*
- Dr. Scott Hahn, *Hail, Holy Queen: The Mother of God in the Word of God*
- David Currie, *Born Fundamentalist, Born Again Catholic*
- John Henry Cardinal Newman, *Apologia Pro Vita Sua*; see also *An Essay on the Development of Christian Doctrine*

Question 37: How can you still be Catholic if loved ones can go to hell?

- C.S. Lewis, *The Great Divorce*; see also *Mere Christianity* and *The Screwtape Letters*
- Matt Baglio, *The Rite*
- Father Andrew Apostoli, CFR, *Fatima for Today: The Marian Message of Hope*
- *Diary of Saint Maria Faustina Kowalska: Divine Mercy in My Soul*
- Cardinal Joseph Ratzinger, *Eschatology: Death and Eternal Life*

Question 38 How can you still be Catholic when there are contradictions in Scripture?

- Mark Shea, *Making Senses Out of Scripture*
- Dr. Edward Sri, *The Bible Compass: A Catholic's Guide to Navigating the Scriptures*
- Dr. Scott Hahn, *A Father Who Keeps His Promises: God's Covenant Love in Scripture*; see also *Letter and Spirit*, Volume 6, *For the Sake of Our Salvation: The Truth and Humility of God's Word*
- Dr. Tim Gray, *Praying Scripture for a Change: An Introduction to Lectio Divina*; see also (with Jeff Cavins) *Walking with God: A Journey Through the Bible*

Question 39 How can you still be Catholic when the world's so screwed up, it seems like God doesn't care, and so many people are in need of practical help, not prayer?

- Father Michael Gaitley, MIC, *'You Did It to Me': A Practical Guide to Mercy in Action*
- Mark Shea, *The Work of Mercy*
- Brandon Vogt, *Saints and Social Justice: A Guide to Changing the World*
- Mike Aquilina and David Scott, *Weapons of the Spirit: Selected Writings of Father John Hugo*
- Susan Conroy, *Praying with Mother Teresa: Prayers, Insights, and Wisdom of Saint Teresa of Calcutta*
- Vatican II, *Apostolicam Actuositatem*; *Lumen Gentium* (especially Chapter 5); *Gaudium et Spes*

Question 40: How can you still be Catholic when politics dictate papal policy?

- John Allen, *The Global War on Christians: Dispatches from the Front Lines of Anti-Christian Persecution*
- George Weigel, *Witness to Hope: The Biography of Pope John Paul II*; see also *The End and the Beginning: Pope John Paul II — The Victory of Freedom, the Last Years, the Legacy*; *God's Choice: Pope Benedict XVI and the Future of the Catholic Church*; *The Cube and the Cathedral: Europe, America, and Politics Without God*
- Pope John Paul II, *Redemptor Hominis: The Redeemer of Man*
- G.K. Chesterton, *The Everlasting Man*
- Jacques Maritain, *Christianity and Democracy*

Question 41: How can you still be Catholic when the story of a virgin birth is found in many cultures predating Christianity?

- Mark Shea, *Mary Mother of the Son*
- Rod Bennett, *Four Witnesses*
- Dr. Robert Stackpole, *Mary: Who She Is and Why She Matters*
- Dr. Brant Pitre, *The Case for Jesus: The Biblical and Historical Evidence for Christ*

Question 42: How can you still be Catholic when the Bible is a collection of oral history written down 300 years after the fact and then has been (mis)translated not once but three times and is still taken literally?

- Dr. Brant Pitre, *The Case for Jesus: The Biblical and Historical Evidence for Christ*
- Mark Shea, *Making Senses Out of Scripture*
- Dr. Scott Hahn, *Letter and Spirit: From Written Text to Living Word in the Liturgy*, see also *Letter and Spirit*, Vol. 6, *For the Sake of Our Salvation: The Truth and Humility of God's Word*; *Covenant and Communion: The Biblical Theology of Pope Benedict XVI*
- Vatican II, *Dei Verbum*
- Pope Benedict XVI, *Verbum Domini*

Question 43: How can you still be Catholic when, until very recently, Masses were conducted in another language on purpose so the common man would be totally mystified as to the whole point?

- Dr. Scott Hahn, *The Lamb's Supper: The Mass as Heaven on Earth*
- Cardinal Donald Wuerl and Mike Aquilina, *The Mass: The Glory, the Mystery, the Tradition*
- Dr. Alan Schreck, *Vatican II: The Crisis and The Promise*
- Cardinal Joseph Ratzinger, *The Spirit of the Liturgy*
- Vatican II, *Sacrosanctum Concilium*

Question 44: How can you still be Catholic when Jesus came to set us free from ritual, tradition, and law?

- Mark Shea, *By What Authority? An Evangelical Discovers Catholic Tradition*
- Dr. Brant Pitre, *Jesus and the Jewish Roots of the Eucharist*
- Dr. Scott Hahn, *Swear to God*; see also *Signs of Life: 40 Catholic Customs and Their Biblical Roots*
- C.S. Lewis, *The Abolition of Man*; see also *Mere Christianity*

Question 45: How can you still be Catholic when they branded Galileo a heretic?

- Thomas Woods, *How the Catholic Church Built Western Civilization*
- Cardinal Christoph Schoenborn, *Chance or Purpose? Creation, Evolution, and a Rational Faith*
- James Hannam, *The Genesis of Science: How the Christian Middle Ages Launched the Scientific Revolution*
- Rodney Stark, *Bearing False Witness: Debunking Centuries of Anti-Catholic History*; see also *For the Glory of God: How Monotheism Led to Reformations, Science, Witch-Hunts, and the End of Slavery*
- Ronald Numbers (ed.), *Galileo Goes to Jail and Other Myths About Science and Religion*
- Pope John Paul II, *Fides et Ratio*, Encyclical Letter on Faith and Reason

Question 46 How can you still be Catholic when divorce can sometimes (sadly) be the end result of a marriage — and sometimes the only reasonable path?

- Elizabeth Marquardt, *Between Two Worlds: The Inner Lives of Children of Divorce*
- Dr. William May, *Marriage: The Rock on Which the Family Is Built*
- Dr. Jennifer Roback Morse, *Love and Economics: It Takes a Family to Raise a Village*
- Linda Waite, *The Case for Marriage*
- Pete Vere and Michael Trueman, *Surprised by Canon Law: 150 Questions Catholics Ask About Canon Law*

Question 47: How can you still be Catholic when they seem so intent on complicating a very simple message?

- F.J. Sheed, *Theology for Beginners*
- C.S. Lewis, *Mere Christianity*
- Peter Kreeft, *Jesus-Shock*

- Father Robert Spitzer, SJ, *Healing the Culture: A Commonsense Philosophy of Happiness, Freedom, and the Life Issues*
- *Catechism of the Catholic Church*

Question 48: How can you still be Catholic when they are more focused on the crucifixion of Jesus than the life of Jesus?

- Dr. Brant Pitre, *Jesus and the Jewish Roots of the Eucharist*
- Dr. Scott Hahn, *The Lamb's Supper: The Mass as Heaven on Earth*
- Pope Benedict XVI, *Jesus of Nazareth* trilogy
- Pope John Paul II, *Rosarium Virginis Mariae*

Question 49: How can you still be Catholic when the music for liturgy is so awful?

- Dr. Scott Hahn, *The Lamb's Supper: The Mass as Heaven on Earth*
- Vatican II, *Sacrosanctum Concilium*

Question 50: How can you still be Catholic when you're such a sinner?

- Cardinal Timothy Dolan, *To Whom Shall We Go?* See also *Called to Be Holy; A People of Hope.*
- Dr. Scott Hahn, *Lord, Have Mercy: The Healing Power of Confession*
- Ralph Martin, *The Fulfillment of All Desire*
- Father Thomas Dubay, *Prayer Primer: Igniting a Fire Within.* See also *Deep Conversion/Deep Prayer; Seeking Spiritual Direction: How to Grow the Divine Life Within*
- Father Reginald Garrigou-Lagrange, *The Three Conversions in the Spiritual Life*; see also *The Three Ages of the Interior Life: Prelude to Eternal Life*
- C.S. Lewis, *The Weight of Glory*

Appendix B:
Catholic Basics

The Nicene Creed

I believe in one God, the Father almighty, maker of heaven and earth, of all things visible and invisible. I believe in one Lord Jesus Christ, the Only Begotten Son of God, born of the Father before all ages. God from God, Light from Light, true God from true God, begotten, not made, consubstantial with the Father; through him all things were made. For us men and for our salvation he came down from heaven, [*At the words that follow, up to and including "and became man," all bow.*] and by the Holy Spirit was incarnate of the Virgin Mary, and became man. For our sake he was crucified under Pontius Pilate, he suffered death and was buried, and rose again on the third day in accordance with the Scriptures. He ascended into heaven and is seated at the right hand of the Father. He will come again in glory to judge the living and the dead and his kingdom will have no end. I believe in the Holy Spirit, the Lord, the giver of life, who proceeds from the Father and the Son, who with the Father and the Son is adored and glorified, who has spoken through the prophets. I believe in one, holy, catholic and apostolic Church. I confess one Baptism for the forgiveness of sins and I look forward to the resurrection of the dead and the life of the world to come. Amen.

The Apostles' Creed

I believe in God, the Father almighty, Creator of heaven and earth, and in Jesus Christ, his only Son, our Lord, [*At the words that follow, up to and including "the Virgin Mary," all bow.*] who was conceived by the Holy Spirit, born of the Virgin Mary, suffered under Pontius Pilate, was crucified, died and was buried; he descended into hell; on the third day he rose again from the dead; he ascended into heaven, and is seated at the right hand of God the Father almighty; from there he will come to judge the living and the dead. I believe in the Holy Spirit, the holy catholic Church, the communion of saints, the forgiveness of sins, the resurrection of the body, and life everlasting. Amen.

Prayers

Our Father

Our Father, who art in heaven, hallowed be thy name. Thy kingdom come, thy will be done, on earth as it is in heaven. Give us this day our daily bread, and forgive us our trespasses as we forgive those who trespass against us. And lead us not into temptation, but deliver us from evil. Amen.

Hail Mary

Hail Mary, full of grace, the Lord is with you. Blessed are you among women, and blessed is the fruit of your womb, Jesus. Holy Mary, Mother of God, pray for us sinners, now and at the hour of our death. Amen.

Glory Be

Glory be to the Father, and to the Son, and to the Holy Spirit, as it was in the beginning, is now, and ever shall be, world without end. Amen.

Morning Offering (my variation)

Oh my Jesus, I offer you through the Immaculate Heart of Mary, all of the prayers, works, joys, and sufferings of this day, in union with all the Masses offered throughout the world today, for the intentions of your Sacred Heart; in reparation for my sins; for the needs and intentions of the Holy Father;

for my family, friends, and enemies; and for the conversion of sinners everywhere, especially those prone to sin as I am prone to sin, those tempted as I am tempted, and those most in need of thy mercy. Amen.

Guardian Angel Prayer
Angel of God, my guardian dear, to whom God's love commits me here, ever this day be at my side, to light, to guard, to rule, and to guide. Amen.

Saint Michael Prayer
Saint Michael the Archangel, defend us in battle. Be our protection against the wickedness and snares of the devil. May God rebuke him, we humbly pray, and do thou, O prince of the heavenly host, by the power of God, cast into hell Satan and all the evil spirits who prowl about the world seeking the ruin of souls. Amen.

The Seven Sacraments
- Baptism
- Confession/Reconciliation/Penance
- Eucharist
- Confirmation
- Marriage
- Holy Orders
- Anointing of the Sick/Extreme Unction

The Seven Gifts of the Holy Spirit (Is 11:1-3)
- Wisdom
- Understanding
- Counsel
- Strength/Fortitude
- Knowledge
- Piety
- Fear of the Lord

Twelve Fruits of the Holy Spirit

- Charity (or love)
- Joy
- Peace
- Patience
- Benignity (or kindness)
- Goodness
- Longanimity (or long-suffering)
- Mildness
- Faith
- Modesty
- Continence
- Chastity.

The Ten Commandments (Ex 20:1-17)

Then God spoke all these words:

I am the LORD your God, who brought you out of the land of Egypt, out of the house of slavery. You shall not have other gods beside me. You shall not make for yourself an idol or a likeness of anything in the heavens above or on the earth below or in the waters beneath the earth; you shall not bow down before them or serve them. For I, the LORD, your God, am a jealous God, inflicting punishment for their ancestors' wickedness on the children of those who hate me, down to the third and fourth generation; but showing love down to the thousandth generation of those who love me and keep my commandments.

You shall not invoke the name of the LORD, your God, in vain. For the LORD will not leave unpunished anyone who invokes his name in vain.

Remember the sabbath day — keep it holy. Six days you may labor and do all your work, but the seventh day is a sabbath of the LORD your God. You shall not do any work, either you, your son or your daughter, your male or female slave, your work animal, or the resident alien within your gates. For in six days the LORD made the heavens and the earth, the sea and all that is in them; but on the seventh day he rested. That is why the LORD has blessed the sabbath day and made it holy.

Honor your father and your mother, that you may have a long life in the land the LORD your God is giving you.

You shall not kill.

You shall not commit adultery.

You shall not steal.

You shall not bear false witness against your neighbor.

You shall not covet your neighbor's house. You shall not covet your neighbor's wife, his male or female slave, his ox or donkey, or anything that belongs to your neighbor.

The Two Great Commandments (Mt 22:37-40)
You shall love the Lord, your God, with all your heart, with all your soul, and with all your mind. This is the greatest and the first commandment. The second is like it: You shall love your neighbor as yourself. The whole law and the prophets depend on these two commandments.

The New Commandment (Jn 13:34-35)
I give you a new commandment: love one another. As I have loved you, so you also should love one another. This is how all will know that you are my disciples, if you have love for one another.

The Five Precepts (*Catechism of the Catholic Church*, 2042-2043)
- You shall attend Mass on Sundays and on holy days of obligation and rest from servile labor.
- You shall confess your sins at least once a year.
- You shall receive the sacrament of the Eucharist at least during the Easter season.
- You shall observe the days of fasting and abstinence established by the Church.
- You shall help to provide for the needs of the Church.

The Works of Mercy

Corporal Works

- Feed the hungry.
- Give drink to the thirsty.
- Clothe the naked.
- Shelter the homeless.
- Visit the prisoners.
- Comfort the sick.
- Bury the dead.

Spiritual works of mercy

- Teach the ignorant.
- Pray for the living and dead.
- Correct sinners.
- Counsel those in doubt.
- Console the sorrowful.
- Bear wrongs patiently.
- Forgive wrongs willingly.

The Seven Virtues (Three Theological and Four Cardinal)

- Faith
- Hope
- Charity
- Prudence
- Temperance
- Justice
- Fortitude

The Seven Deadly Sins

- Pride
- Envy
- Wrath
- Acedia or Sloth
- Greed
- Gluttony
- Lust

Act of Contrition

Oh my God, I am sorry for my sins. In choosing to sin and in failing to do good, I have sinned against you and your Church. I firmly intend, with the help of your Son, to make up for my sins and to do as I should.

Appendix C: Glossary

Bishops — "Bishop is the title of an ecclesiastical dignitary who possesses the fullness of the priesthood to rule a diocese as its chief pastor, in due submission to the primacy of the pope."[235]

Confirmation — "A sacrament in which the Holy Ghost is given to those already baptized in order to make them strong and perfect Christians and soldiers of Jesus Christ."[236]

Connaturality — The state of sharing or partaking of the same nature; of being or becoming like another being.

Dicastery — An office in the Roman curia, or the papal court; dicasteries are analogous to the various departments and offices of the executive branch of the United States government.

Eucharist — The name given to the Blessed Sacrament of the Altar in its twofold aspect of Sacrament and Sacrifice of Mass, in which Jesus Christ is truly present under the form of bread and wine.[237]

Exegesis — "Exegesis is the branch of theology which investigates and expresses the true sense of Sacred Scripture."[238]

Hypostasis — Literally, that which lies beneath as basis or foundation. "Hypostatic union" is a theological term used with reference to the Incarnation to express the revealed truth that in Christ one person subsists in two natures, the divine and the human.[239]

Laity — "Laity means the body of the faithful, outside of the ranks of the clergy."[240]

Monstrance — "Both the name *ostensorium* and the kindred word monstrance (*monstrancia*, from *monstrare*) were originally applied to all kinds of vessels of [a] goldsmith's or silversmith's work in which glass, crystal, etc. were so employed as to allow the contents to be readily distinguished, whether the object thus honoured were the Sacred Host itself or only the relic of some saint."[241]

Pope — "The title pope, once used with far greater latitude ... is at present employed solely to denote the Bishop of Rome, who, in virtue of his position as successor of St. Peter, is the chief pastor of the whole Church, the Vicar of Christ upon earth."[242]

Priests — "The priest is the minister of Divine worship, and especially of the highest act of worship, sacrifice."[243]

United States Conference of Catholic Bishops (USCCB) — "The United States Conference of Catholic Bishops (USCCB) is an assembly of the hierarchy of the United States and the U.S. Virgin Islands who jointly exercise certain pastoral functions on behalf of the Christian faithful of the United States. The purpose of the Conference is to promote the greater good which the Church offers humankind, especially through forms and programs of the apostolate fittingly adapted to the circumstances of time and place."[244]

Permissions

in this work have been formally reviewed or approved by the United States Conference of Catholic Bishops.

Acknowledgments

There're more people to whom I owe thanks than I can possibly name, scattered across a lifetime of reading, prayer, and formation from family, friends, and yes, even enemies. I do keep you all in prayer, and hand you all over to the Divine Mercy at each Mass — I hope that serves as an ultimate thanksgiving to you all.

But special mention needs to be made of a number of people.

Thanks to Felix Carroll, my editor, who read an earlier version of the manuscript and said, "Yes! Let's publish it!" And then asked me for 10 more answers. Thanks also for your saintly patience with me, for much mentoring, and for the trust that you repose in me. It's all far more than I deserve.

Thanks to Tad and Joan (and Mary!), the Marian Press team, for their patience with my queries and their hard work on promoting this book.

Thanks, as ever, to Kathy Szpak and Curtis Bohner for layout and the cover.

Thanks to my endorsers, all of whose work and witness I deeply appreciate and respect.

Thanks to the Marian Fathers of the Immaculate Conception for my present job; for a wealth of opportunities and experiences I'd never be able to have otherwise; and for their tireless promotion of Divine Mercy, Mary Immaculate, and devotion to the Holy Souls, without which the entire Church and the world would be much poorer. Thanks to the Jesuits for one heck of an education (Go Zags!) and the TOR Franciscans for the tremendous gift that is Franciscan University of Steubenville.

Thanks to my high school classmate Art, whose comment "You're the first Catholic I've met who's ever bothered to defend their faith" is to blame for my apologetic efforts across the years, including, distantly, this book.

Thanks to Bob and Eileen, at whose home I found hospitality during my grad studies and wrote the first draft of this book; and to Betty and John, at whose home I brought this nearly to completion.

Endless thanks to my godparents, Uncle Mark and Aunt Kathy, for handing on to me the Christian faith through their words and witness; to Grandma Doumit for all her prayers, as well as her example of heroic virtue and the Catholic faith lived right; to Granddad Bob and Grandma Caryl for their love and care all my life; to Uncle Tom and Aunt Helen, for many conversations across the years; and to all who first read and gave me feedback on this manuscript. Thanks also to all of the family and friends who asked the questions that I've endeavored to answer in this book.

Thanks especially to Dad, Mom, and Jenny, without whom I have nothing much worth having. I owe y'all more than I can say.

Endnotes

[1] For more on the path to Christian perfection, see Ralph Martin, *The Fulfillment of All Desire: A Guidebook for the Journey to God Based on the Wisdom of the Saints* (Steubenville: Emmaus Road Publishing, 2006).

[2] Vatican II, Dogmatic Constitution on the Church *Lumen Gentium*, November 21, 1964, vatican.va Chapter 5

[3] Joseph Cardinal Ratzinger, *Called to Communion: Understanding the Church Today*, trans. Adrian Walker, (San Francisco: Ignatius, 1996), pp. 24-26.

[4] Pius XII, Encyclical Letter *Mystici Corporis: On the Mystical Body of Christ*, June 29, 1943, vatican.va

[5] Oscar Wilde, *A Woman of No Importance* (Arc Manor LLC, 2008), p. 82.

[6] Aristotle, *Metaphysics* 1011b25.

[7] Sally Fitzgerald, ed., *The Habit of Being: Letters of Flannery O'Connor* (Macmillan, 1988), p. 125.

[8] Vatican II, Declaration on the Relation of the Church to Non-Christian Religions *Nostra Aetate*, October 28, 1965, vatican.va, para. 2.

[9] C. S. Lewis, *The Abolition of Man* (HarperCollins, 1974), Chapter 2, The Way; Appendix—Illustrations of the Tao.

[10] Congregation for the Doctrine of the Faith, *Dominus Iesus: On the Unicity and Salvific Universality of Jesus Christ and the Church*, August 6, 2000, vatican.va.

[11] Vatican II, Dogmatic Constitution on Divine Revelation *Dei Verbum*, Chapters 1, 3:

> "God, who through the Word creates all things (see John 1:3) and keeps them in existence, gives men an enduring

witness to Himself in created realities (see Rom. 1:19-20). Planning to make known the way of heavenly salvation, He went further and from the start manifested Himself to our first parents. Then after the fall His promise of redemption aroused in them the hope of being saved (see Gen. 3:15) and from that time on He ceaselessly kept the human race in His care, to give eternal life to those who perseveringly do good in search of salvation (see Rom. 2:6-7)."

The *Catechism* (846-848) teaches:

"Outside the Church there is no salvation"
How are we to understand this affirmation, often repeated by the Church Fathers? [Cf. Cyprian, *Ep.* 73.21:PL 3,1169; *De unit.*:PL 4,509-536.) Re-formulated positively, it means that all salvation comes from Christ the Head through the Church which is his Body:

> Basing itself on Scripture and Tradition, the Council teaches that the Church, a pilgrim now on earth, is necessary for salvation: the one Christ is the mediator and the way of salvation; he is present to us in his body which is the Church. He himself explicitly asserted the necessity of faith and Baptism, and thereby affirmed at the same time the necessity of the Church which men enter through Baptism as through a door. Hence they could not be saved who, knowing that the Catholic Church was founded as necessary by God through Christ, would refuse either to enter it or to remain in it (LG 14; cf. Mk 16:16; Jun 3:5).

This affirmation is not aimed at those who, through no fault of their own, do not know Christ and his Church:

> Those who, through no fault of their own, do not know the Gospel of Christ or his Church, but who nevertheless seek God with a sincere heart, and, moved by grace, try in their actions to do his will as they know it through the dictates of

their conscience – those too may achieve eternal salvation (LG 16; cf. DS 3866-3872).

"Although in ways known to himself God can lead those who, through no fault of their own, are ignorant of the Gospel, to that faith without which it is impossible to please him, the Church still has the obligation and also the sacred right to evangelize all men" (AG 7; cf. Heb 11:6; 1 Cor 9:16).

[12] August C. Krey, *The First Crusade: The Accounts of Eye-Witnesses and Participants* (Gloucester, MA: Peter Smith, 1958).

[13] There were also spiritual incentives, though not the sort that some, including many Protestants, may think. Urban II sought to offer the warriors of Europe an easier path to doing penance for their sins than the traditional requirement: Namely, at the end of their days as lords in the world, it was expected that the leaders would give up all their power and wealth to retire to monasteries, abandon the warrior life, and lead lives of contemplation and penance for their sins. Looking at the calls for aid coming from the Eastern Roman emperor and the Christians being displaced from Jerusalem and the Holy Land, Pope Urban II put into place the crusading indulgence, which offered the complete remission of the temporal punishment due to sin if warriors "took the cross" and went on a Crusade to free their fellow Christians. In other words, if they went and fought the oppressors of their co-religionists, people were promised they could go straight to Heaven when they died, rather than spend a long time in Purgatory to suffer in reparation for their sins. His audience was receptive to the idea because of Europe's painful experience of Islam; the promise of purgation through arms rather than monastic retirement from the world; and a true sense of solidarity with other Christians, particularly those in need.

[14] *The Legacy of Jihad: Holy War and the Fate of Non-Muslims*, ed. Andrew Bostom (Amherst, NY: Prometheus Books, 2005). See especially the map inserts in the center of the book showing the expanding Islamic empire, the summary of the battles (p. 368-382), and the essay "Jihad Conquests and the Imposition of Dhimmitude—A Survey" (pp. 24-105).

[15] John Allen, *The Global War on Christians* (New York: Image, 2013), Chapter 5: The Middle East. See also Tom Heneghan, "Vat-

ican Synod Mulls Middle East Christian Exodus," Reuters, October 7, 2010, reuters.com/article/2010/10/07/us-christians-mideast-synod-idUSTRE6961GC20101007; see also Synod of Bishops Special Assembly for the Middle East, "The Catholic Church in the Middle East: Communion and Witness," Lineamenta (Vatican City, 2009), Chapter 1: The Catholic Church in the Middle East, B: The Challenges Facing Christians, vatican.va; Lawrence Solomon, "Exodus from the Arab Spring," *Globe and Mail*, October 14, 2011, theglobeandmail.com/commentary/exodus-from-the-arab-spring/article557866/.

[16] Day of Pardon, vatican.va, March 12, 2000. The text of the prayers of repentance can be found here: vatican.va/news_services/liturgy/documents/ns_lit_doc_20000312_prayer-day-pardon_en.html.

[17] Thomas Woods Jr., *How the Catholic Church Built Western Civilization* (Washington, DC: Regnery, 2005), pp. 208-211.

[18] For statements of opposition to Iraq, see John Paul II, Angelus, March 16, 2003, vatican.va; Address of Pope John Paul II to the Honorable George W. Bush, President of the United States of America, June 4, 2004, vatican.va; Gianni Cardinale, "Interview with Cardinal Joseph Ratzinger: The Catechism in a Post-Christian World," *30Days*, Issue 4, 2003, 30giorni.it/articoli_id_775_l3.htm?id=775.

[19] Paul VI, Speech to the United Nations Organization, October 4, 1965, holyseemission.org/about/paul-VI-speech-at-the-un.aspx.

[20] John W. O'Malley, *What Happened at Vatican II* (Harvard University Press, 2008), p. 264.

[21] Woods, *How the Catholic Church Built Western Civilization*.

[22] Carl Anderson and Jose Granados, *Called to Love: Approaching John Paul II's Theology of the Body*, (Random House, 2009), 202-203.

[23] Nicene-Constanipolitan Creed. See Appendix B for the full creed.

[24] Karen J. Terry, Margaret Leland Smith, Katarina Schuth OSF, James R. Kelly, Brenda Vollman, and Christina Massey, "The Causes and Context of Sexual Abuse of Minors by Catholic Priests in the United States, 1950-2010: A Report Presented to the United States Conference of Catholic Bishops by the John Jay College Research Team," May 2011, usccb.org/issues-and-action/child-and-youth-protection/upload/The-Causes-and-Context-of-Sexual-Abuse-of-Minors-by-Catholic-Priests-in-the-United-States-1950-2010.pdf. p. 2; see also "The Nature and Scope of Sexual Abuse of Minors

by Catholic Priests and Deacons in the United States 1950-2002: A Research Study Conducted by the John Jay College of Criminal Justice," City University of New York, February 2004 usccb.org/issues-and-action/child-and-youth-protection/upload/The-Nature-and-Scope-of-Sexual-Abuse-of-Minors-by-Catholic-Priests-and-Deacons-in-the-United-States-1950-2002.pdf, accessed January 19, 2012.

[25] Philip Jenkins, *The New Anti-Catholicism: The Last Acceptable Prejudice* (New York: Oxford University Press, 2003), pp. 138-141.

[26] "Dr. John Bradford, a University of Ottawa psychiatrist who has spent 23 years studying pedophilia — which is listed as an illness in the manual psychiatrists use to make diagnoses — estimates its prevalence at maybe 4% of the population. (Those attracted to teenagers are sometimes said to suffer "ephebophilia," but perhaps because so many youth-obsessed Americans would qualify, psychiatrists don't classify ephebophilia as an illness.)" In John Cloud, "Pedophilia," *Time*, January 13, 2003. time.com/time/magazine/article/0,9171,232584,00.html.

[27] Frank W. Putnam, "Ten-Year Research Update Review: Child Sexual Abuse," *Journal of the American Academy of Child and Adolescent Psychiatry*, March 2003 (Vol. 42, Issue 3) pp. 269-278, DOI: 10.1097/00004583-200303000-00006), jaacap.com/article/S0890-8567%2809%2960559-1/abstract.

[28] Terry et al, p. 2.

[29] The whole controversy within Catholicism over contraception and the encyclical letter *Humanae Vitae* reveal this plainly. For a sense of some of the consequences of the sexual revolution, see Mary Eberstadt, *Adam and Eve After the Pill* (San Francisco: Ignatius Press, 2012).

[30] Sr. Sharon Euart, RSM, JCD, "Canon Law and Clergy Sexual Abuse Crisis: An Overview of the U.S. Experience," USCCB/CLSA Seminar, May 25, 2010, old.usccb.org/canonlawseminar/documents/CanonLawandSexualAbuse-Euart.pdf.

[31] Stephen Rossetti, *Why Priests Are Happy* (Ave Maria Press, 2011).

[32] Jenkins, *The New Anti-Catholicism*, pp. 141-144.

[33] Mary Eberstadt, "How Pedophilia Lost Its Cool," *First Things*, December 2009, firstthings.com. See also Mary Eberstadt, "Pedophilia Chic," *Weekly Standard*, June 17, 1996; and Mary Eberstadt, "Pedophilia Chic Reconsidered," *Weekly Standard*, January 1, 2001.

[34] National Review Board, "A Ten Year Progress Report," June 2012, usccb.org/issues-and-action/child-and-youth-protection/upload/10-year-report-2012.pdf.

[35] The charter may be read at the USCCB's website: usccb.org/issues-and-action/child-and-youth-protection/charter.cfm.

[36] John L. Allen Jr., "Will Ratzinger's Past Trump Benedict's Present?" *National Catholic Reporter*, March 17, 2010, ncronline.org/news/accountability/will-ratzingers-past-trump-benedicts-present

[37] Michael Abrams, "The Real Story on Gay Genes: Homing in on the Science of Homosexuality—and Sexuality Itself," *Discover*, June 2007 issue, posted online June 5, 2007, discovermagazine.com/2007/jun/born-gay.

[38] "Abortion, Gay Marriage, and Porn (Bishop Barron Interview Pt. 2)," Rubin Report, January 30, 2017, youtube.com/watch?v=OYWBNMOCrlo, minute 6:30 and following. See also Fr. Donald Calloway, MIC, *No Turning Back: A Witness to Mercy* (Marian Press, 2010).

[39] G.K. Chesterton, *Orthodoxy* (New York: Image, 2001), 142-144.

[40] Vatican II, Dogmatic Constitution on Divine Revelation *Dei Verbum*, Chapters 1, 3; see also *Catechism*, 846-848.

[41] Vatican II, Dogmatic Constitution on the Church *Lumen Gentium*, Chapter V.

[42] Some background: Pope Paul VI had a group (the Papal Commission for the Study of Problems of the Family, Population, and Birth Rate) to consult on the matter of the teaching on birth control, indicating that he did, in fact, consider lifting the Church's perennial ban, or at least wanted to look at the question in light of the most recent science about human reproduction. He decided to issue the encyclical *Humanae Vitae* (*On the Regulation of Birth*) in 1968; it reiterates the Church's unchanging ban on the use of artificial contraceptives, even after a majority of the commission had given him a report that "argued that conjugal morality should be measured by 'the totality of married life,' rather than by the openness of each act of intercourse to conception. In this view, it was morally licit to use chemical or mechanical means to prevent conception as long as this was in the overall moral context of a couple's openness to children" (George Weigel, *Witness to Hope: The Biography of Pope John Paul II* (Cliff Street Books/HarperCollins, 1999), pp. 206-207). According to philosopher Dr. Janet Smith, "Several theologians,

dissenters among them, have noted that theological arguments made in the majority report were not of the quality to warrant overturning centuries of Church opposition to contraception" (Dr. Janet Smith, "*Humanae Vitae* at Twenty: New Insights into an Old Debate," in *Why Humanae Vitae Was Right: A Reader*, ed. Janet Smith [San Francisco: Ignatius Press, 1993], p. 506). A minority report was submitted, indicating that even with the invention of new methods of artificial contraception, matters had not fundamentally changed in such a way as to invalidate the perennial ban (Dr. Janet Smith, *Humanae Vitae: A Generation Later*, [Washington, DC: CUA Press, 1991], pp. 2-7) on birth control. The pope went with the arguments and information presented in the minority report and promulgated *Humanae Vitae*, prompting one of the largest controversies within the Church in her history.

[43] P. Frank-Herrmann, J. Heil, C. Gnoth, E. Toledo, S. Baur, C. Pyper, E. Jenetzky, T. Strowitzki, G. Freundl. "The Effectiveness of a Fertility Awareness Based Method to Avoid Pregnancy in Relation to a Couple's Sexual Behaviour During the Fertile Time: A Prospective Longitudinal Study," *Human Reproduction*, 2007 May; 22(5):1310-9. Epub February 20, 2007. petra.frank-herrmann@med.uni-heidelberg.de. Abstract available here: ncbi.nlm.nih.gov/pubmed/17314078.

[44] "Long-Term Effectiveness of New Family Planning Method Shown in Study," explore.georgetown.edu/news/?ID=59218. The study in question is Irit Sinai, Rebecka I. Lundgren, and James N. Gribble, "Continued use of the Standard Days Method®," *Journal of Family Planning and Reproductive Health Care*, familyplanning100097; Published Online First: August 20, 2011, doi:10.1136/jfprhc-2011-100097. Abstract available at jfprhc.bmj.com/content/38/3/150. For more information on the Standard Days method and the other methods taught by the Georgetown Institute for Reproductive Health, see irh.org/.

[45] Michael Brendan Dougherty and Pascal-Emmanuel Gobry, "Time to Admit It: The Church Has Always Been Right on Birth Control," *Business Insider*, February 8, 2012, businessinsider.com/time-to-admit-it-the-church-has-always-been-right-on-birth-control-2012-2.

[46] For evidence, see Mary Eberstadt, *Adam and Eve After the Pill* (San Francisco: Ignatius Press, 2012). See also David Halberstam, *The Fifties* (New York: Villard Books, 1993), pp. 282-294, 599-606. For a personal memoir of how the contraceptive mentality leads

to the assumptions of the sexual revolution, see Jennifer Fulwiler, *Something Other Than God: How I Passionately Sought Happiness and Accidentally Found It* (Ignatius Press, 2016).

[47] CIC, can. 1055 § 1; cf. *GS* 48 § 1, quoted in *Catechism of the Catholic Church*, 1601.

[48] Dr. Janet Smith, "Premarital Sex," *Catholic Education Resource Center*, 1998, catholiceducation.org/articles/sexuality/se0087.html. Convert Jennifer Fulwiler has identified the contraceptive culture as the source of her incomprehension of the Church's teaching on abortion. It seemed an unconscionable burden on women to expect them to bring an unwanted pregnancy to term until Fulwiler realized she had completely divorced sex from reproduction in her own mind. Her piece can be found at "A Sexual Revolution: One Woman's Journey from Pro-Choice Atheist to Pro-Life Catholic," *America*, July 7, 2008, americamagazine.org/content/article.cfm?article_id=10904.

[49] For an overview of American eugenics and their contributions to the Nazi racial policies, see Edwin Black, "The Horrifying American Roots of Nazi Eugenics," *History News Network*, November 25, 2003, hnn.us/articles/1796.html. For an academic account of forced sterilizations by state, see "Eugenics: Compulsory Sterilization in 50 American States," uvm.edu/~lkaelber/eugenics/. See also Rebecca Leung, "America's Deep, Dark Secret," *CBS News*, December 5, 2007, cbsnews.com/stories/2004/04/29/60minutes/main614728.shtml.

[50] Therese Hesketh, PhD, Li Lu, MD, and Zhu Wei Xing, MPH, "The Effect of China's One-Child Family Policy after 25 Years," *New England Journal of Medicine*, September 15, 2005 (Vol. 353), pp. 1171-1176, nejm.org/doi/full/10.1056/NEJMhpr051833.

[51] "Topic Area: Population Control," colby.edu/personal/t/thtieten/Famplan.htm; BBC, "Mass Birth-Control Programmes," *Ethics Guide*, bbc.co.uk/ethics/contraception/mass_birth_control_1.shtml.

[52] For an overview of the deep Scriptural teaching on God's spousal love for His creation, see Dr. Brant Pitre, *Jesus the Bridegroom: The Greatest Love Story Ever Told* (Image, 2014).

[53] Saint Louis-Marie de Montfort, *The True Devotion to the Blessed Virgin* (Saint Benedict Press Classics, 2006), p. 7.

[54] "We declare, pronounce, and define that the doctrine which holds

that the most Blessed Virgin Mary, in the first instance of her conception, by a singular grace and privilege granted by Almighty God,
in view of the merits of Jesus Christ, the Savior of the human race,
was preserved free from all stain of original sin, is a doctrine revealed by God and therefore to be believed firmly and constantly
by all the faithful." Pius IX, *Ineffabilis Deus*, December 8, 1854,
papalencyclicals.net.

[55] John Paul II, Apostolic Letter *Ordinatio Sacerdotalis*, May 22,
1994, para. 4, vatican.va.

[56] *Ordinatio Sacerdotalis*, para. 2.

[57] Ratzinger, *Called to Communion*, p. 24-25.

[58] Scott Hahn, *Many Are Called: Rediscovering the Glory of the Priesthood* (New York: Doubleday, 2010), especially Chapter 3, "Spiritual
Paternity: Priest as Father"; see also pp. 43-47 on the Old Testament
references to father/priests; pp. 48-49 on the New Testament's order of priests.

[59] Hahn, *Many Are Called*, pp. 41-42 on Adam as priest/father.

[60] Hahn, *Many Are Called*, pp. 43-45 on the patriarchs as priests.

[61] Hahn, *Many Are Called*, pp. 45-47 on the post-patriarchal priestly
fathers.

[62] Hahn, *Many Are Called*, pp. 47-49.

[63] *Ordinatio sacerdotalis*, para. 3

[64] Pope Francis, Papal Bull *Misericordia Vultus* (*The Face of Mercy*),
April 11, 2015, para. 1.

[65] For more on this, see Dr. Scott Hahn, *Hail, Holy Queen: The
Mother of God in the Word of God* (Image, 2006); I've also seen highly recommended Dr. Edward Sri, *Queen Mother: A Biblical Theology
of Mary's Queenship* (Emmaus Road Publishing, 2005).

[66] Ronald Rychlak, *Hitler, the War, and the Pope* (Huntington, Indiana: Our Sunday Visitor, 2000), pp. 200-201, 211.

[67] "Mother Teresa Will Set Up Homeless Shelter at Vatican," United
Press International, May 26, 1987; John Thavis, "Pope John Paul
II: A Holiness That Knew No Boundaries," *Our Sunday Visitor's The
Priest*, March 21, 2014, osv.com/Magazines/ThePriest.aspx.

[68] Carol Glatz, "Vatican Unveils Free Showers and Haircuts for the
Homeless," *Catholic Herald*, February 7, 2015, catholicherald.
co.uk/news/2015/02/07/vatican-offers-free-showers-haircuts-
and-umbrellas-to-the-homeless/.

[69] Vatican I, *Pastor Aeternus*, July 18, 1870, papalencyclicals.net.

[70] Take a look at the life and work of Blessed John Henry Cardinal Newman, the great 19th century Anglican convert to Catholicism. As an Anglican, he accepted the teachings of the great early Councils of the undivided Church before the schism between East and West as authoritative — indeed, infallible — declarations of the Christian faith See Avery Dulles, SJ, "Newman on Infallibility," *Theological Studies*, 1990 (Vol. 51), ts.mu.edu/content/51/51.3/51.3.3.pdf, p. 437. Newman recognized that the Catholic Church claimed to have an infallible teaching authority throughout her history, even if this was not explicitly defined at a Council, and believed this to be the fundamental difference between Catholicism and the humbler claims of Anglicanism (ibid., pp. 436-437). "Previous popes and councils had at times peremptorily taught certain particular doctrines, such as the Trinity, the divinity of Christ, the sacraments, grace, and eternal life, but they had not spoken about the divine assistance that enabled the Church to require faith in its word" (ibid., p. 435). "As an Anglican Newman had to ask himself on what ground he could approve this decision in the fifth century while denying the right of the great Church, in the 16th century, to condemn the Protestant positions" (ibid., p. 438).

When Newman read St. Augustine's rule for discerning the true faith in the Donatist controversies (*Securus judicat orbis terrarium*; roughly, "the whole world judges securely"), he was floored. Augustine held that the Church of his day could teach just as surely as the Church of the days of the Apostles. Newman wrote:

> The existing Church, and not simply the prior Church, was the oracle of truth. The same rule could apply for modern times and ancient. He felt bound to profess infallibility and in so doing to accept Roman Catholicism. For infallibility was, as we have seen, the distinctive trait of the Roman Church. No other church in the modern world dared to claim the gift of infallibility. If infallibility was true, the Church of Rome was the true Church (ibid., p. 438).

[71] *Lumen Gentium*, 22.

[72] Correspondence with the author, April 6, 2017. Note well — there's a great deal of discussion among solid Catholic theologians about the precise breakdown of these levels of authoritative teaching;

and a great many more subtleties and nuances remain to be delineated. But this is a good start.

[73] Father Robert Spitzer, SJ, *New Proofs for the Existence of God: Contributions of Contemporary Physics and Philosophy* (Eerdmans, 2010).

[74] Cardinal Joseph Ratzinger (later Pope Emeritus Benedict XVI), "The Feeling of Things, the Contemplation of Beauty," presented at the Rimini Meeting of Communion and Liberation, August 2002, vatican.va.

[75] Matthew Bunson, Margaret Bunson, and Stephen Bunson, *Our Sunday Visitor's Encyclopedia of Saints* (Our Sunday Visitor, 2003). For saints from the past century or so, see Ann Ball, *Modern Saints: Their Lives and Faces*, 2 volumes (TAN Books and Publishers, 1983, 1991).

[76] For his conversion alongside those of ten other former atheists, see Rebecca V. Cherico, *Atheist to Catholic: 11 Stories of Conversion* (Servant Books, 2011). For the basic account of his conversion, see "Total Conversion," *John C. Wright's Journal Musings, Reasonings, Fancies, Drollery and Apologetics from Honorary Houyhnhnm and Science Fiction Writer John C. Wright*, September 11, 2007, scifiwright.com/2007/09/total-conversion-2/; "A Question I Never Tire of Answering," *John C. Wright's Journal Musings, Reasonings, Fancies, Drollery and Apologetics from Honorary Houyhnhnm and Science Fiction Writer John C. Wright*, September 2, 2011, scifiwright. com/2011/09/a-question-i-never-tire-of-answering/#more-3997; for a moving account of his vision of Mary, see "Why I Am Not a Deist." *John C. Wright's Journal Musings, Reasonings, Fancies, Drollery and Apologetics from Honorary Houyhnhnm and Science Fiction Writer John C. Wright*, November 30, 2006, scifiwright.com/2006/11/why-i-am-not a deist/.

[77] Father Andrew Apostoli, CFR, *Fatima for Today: The Urgent Marian Message of Hope* (Ignatius Press, 2010).

[78] Ruth Harris, *Lourdes: Body and Spirit in the Secular Age* (Penguin Global, 2008); Elizabeth Ficocelli, *Lourdes: Font of Faith, Hope, and Charity* (Paulist Press, 2007).

[79] Carl Anderson and Eduardo Chavez, *Our Lady of Guadalupe: Mother of the Civilization of Love* (Doubleday Religion, 2009).

[80] Immaculee Ilibagiza, *Our Lady of Kibeho: Mary Speaks to the World from the Heart of Africa* (Hay House, 2010).

[81] See, for example, Matt Baglio, *The Rite: The Making of a Modern Exorcist* (Image, 2010); Scott Peck, *People of the Lie: The Hope for Healing Human Evil* (Touchstone, 1998); see also Peck, *Glimpses of the Devil: A Psychiatrist's Personal Accounts of Possession* (Free Press, 2009).

[82] C.S. Lewis, *The Screwtape Letters*, (HarperCollins, 2001), Letter II.

[83] Vatican II, Pastoral Constitution on the Church in the Modern World *Gaudium et Spes*, December 7, 1965, vatican.va.

[84] G. K. Chesterton, "The Chief Mourner of Marne," *Father Brown and the Church of Rome* (San Francisco: Ignatius Press, 2002), pp. 38-39.

[85] Cf. CIC, can. 976; CCEO, can. 725, cited in *Catechism of the Catholic Church*, para. 1463.

[86] George Weigel, *The Courage to Be Catholic* (Basic Books, 2002), pp. 96-100.

[87] And some of the saints, like St. Robert Bellarmine and St. Matthew the Apostle, have been bureaucrats — so there's hope!

[88] Wilde, *A Woman of No Importance*, p. 82.

[89] Ibid.

[90] Hahn, *Many Are Called*, pp. 42-44.

[91] Ibid., p. 46.

[92] William D. Miller, *Dorothy Day: A Biography* (HarperCollins, 1984), p. 198.

[93] For a basic introduction, check out Dr. Scott Hahn, *The Lamb's Supper: The Mass as Heaven on Earth* (Crown Publishing, 2002).

[94] For more, see Servais Pinckaers, *Morality: The Catholic View* (St. Augustine's Press, 2001).

[95] John Paul II, Encyclical Letter *Veritatis Splendor*, August 6, 1993, vatican.va, para. 10

[96] G.K. Chesterton, *Orthodoxy* (John Lane Company, 1909), p. 24

[97] For a book-length elaboration of the reasons we have for trusting the teaching of the Church and the promises of God, see Dr. Scott Hahn, *Reasons to Believe: How to Understand, Explain, and Defend the Catholic Faith* (Image, 2007); see also Vatican I, Chapter 3: On Faith, *Dei Filius*, April 24, 1870, papalencyclicals.net.

[98] Dr. Joseph L. Lichten, "A Question of Judgment: Pius XII and the Jews," 1963, jewishvirtuallibrary.org/jsource/anti-semitism/piusdef2.html .

[99] Beate Ruhm von Oppen, "Nazis and Christians," *World Politics*, 1969 (Vol. 21, no. 5), accessed June 18, 2007. jstor.org/stable/2009639, p. 412.

[100] Ibid., p. 413.

[101] Ibid., p. 414.

[102] Ronald Rychlak, *Hitler, the War, and the Pope* (Huntington, Indiana: Our Sunday Visitor, 2000), p. 92.

[103] Pius XII, *Summi Pontificatus*, October 20, 1939, vatican.va, para. 35-51; for a condemnation of Nazi expansionism, see para. 74.

[104] "A Question of Judgment," jewishvirtuallibrary.org/jsource/anti-semitism/piusdef2.html. For more, see the Pave the Way Foundation's document collections at ptwf.org/Projects/Education/Pope%20Pius%20XII.htm, or in Gary Krupp, *Pope Pius XII and World War II — The Documented Truth* (Pave the Way Publishing, 2010), as well as the books in Appendix A: Recommended Reading for this question.

[105] "A Question of Judgment" and Krupp, *Pope Pius XII and World War II.*

[106] *New York Times Magazine*, February 11, 1923, found in *As I Was Saying: A Chesterton Reader* (W.B. Eerdmans, 1985), p. 271.

[107] Lewis, *The Screwtape Letters*, Letter I.

[108] Mary C. Curtis, "'After-Birth Abortion': Can They Be Serious?" *Washington Post Politics: She the People*, posted March 5, 2012, the paper itself is Alberto Giubilini and Francesca Minerva, "After-Birth Abortion: Why Should the Baby Live?" *Journal of Medical Ethics*, doi:10.1136/medethics-2011-100411, Published Online First February 23, 2012, jme.bmj.com/content/early/2012/03/01/medethics-2011-100411.abstract. For more on the same, see William Saletan, "After-Birth Abortion: The Pro-Choice Case for Infanticide," Monday, March 12, 2012.

[109] See, for example, Dr. Patrick Lee, *Abortion and Unborn Human Life* (Washington, DC: Catholic University of America, 2010); Dr. Janet Smith and Dr. Christopher Kaczor, *Life Issues, Medical Choices: Questions and Answers for Catholics* (Servant Books, 2007); Dr. William May, *Catholic Bioethics and Gift of Human Life* (Our Sunday Visitor, 2008).

[110] Mother Teresa of Calcutta, Nobel Lecture, December 11, 1979, nobelprize.org.

111 Aleksandr Solzhenitsyn, *The Gulag Archipelago*, Volume 1: *An Experiment in Literary Investigation* (HarperCollins, 2007), p. 168.

112 Want to know how to do this? See Ralph Martin, *The Fulfillment of All Desire* (Emmaus Road, 2006); Fr. Reginald Garrigou-Lagrange, *The Three Conversions in the Spiritual Life* (TAN Books, 2002); Jean-Baptiste Chautard, *The Soul of the Apostolate*.

113 *Catechism of the Catholic Church*, for instance, para. 490-493; 507; 963; 966; 968-970; 2676; 2679; 2682.

114 John Paul II, *Mulieris Dignitatem: On the Dignity and Vocation of Women*, August 15, 1988, vatican.va, para. 29.

115 According to Cardinal Timothy Dolan in an interview with the late Fr. Benedict Groeschel, CFR, on *Sunday Night Prime*, women can be appointed as cardinals of the Catholic Church, since cardinals do not have to be priests. See Father Benedict Groeschel, Cardinal Timothy Dolan, "HHS Mandate," *Sunday Night Prime* February 12, 2012; for audio, ewtn.com/vondemand/audio/resolve.asp?audiofile=snl_02122012.mp3; for video, youtu.be/0DkHpaOPasU. Pope Francis has demurred, and indicates that he has no intention of making such an appointment, in an interview ("Never Be Afraid of Tenderness") with Andrea Tornielli of *La Stampa* and *Inside the Vatican*, published December 13, 2013.

116 St. Augustine, *The Confessions*, Book Nine, excerpted in *The Wisdom of Catholicism*, ed. Anton C. Pegis (Random House, 1949), pp. 58-69.

117 A term which James Joyce makes use of in *Finnegan's Wake*, but not, so far as I could find, to refer specifically to the Catholic Church. However, it does remain a great description.

118 I'd recommend especially Ralph Martin's *The Fulfillment of All Desire* as a great introduction to the spirituality of the Catholic Church. See also Bishop Robert Barron's *The Strangest Way: Walking the Christian Path*. If you have a background in philosophy or theology, Fr. Reginald Garrigou-Lagrange's *The Three Conversions in the Spiritual Life* or the massive two-volume *The Three Ages of the Interior Life: Prelude of Eternal Life* may be to your taste.

119 Congregation for the Doctrine of the Faith, *Persona humana* 9, cited in *Catechism of the Catholic Church*, 2352.

120 *Catechism of the Catholic Church*, 2352.

121 For more on all this, see Dr. Brant Pitre, *Jesus the Bridegroom: The*

Greatest Love Story Ever Told (Image, 2014).

[122] Vatican II, *Dignitatis Humanae*, December 7, 1965, vatican.va.

[123] See, for example, his addresses to the United Nations, including the ones from 1979 (vatican.va/holy_father/john_paul_ii/speeches/1979/october/documents/hf_jp-ii_spe_19791002_general-assembly-onu_en.html) and 1995 (vatican.va/holy_father/john_paul_ii/speeches/1995/october/documents/hf_jp-ii_spe_05101995_address-to-uno_en.html). For an extensive discussion of his defense and explanation of universal human rights, see the work of George Weigel in *Witness to Hope: The Biography of Pope John Paul II; The End and the Beginning: Pope John Paul II — The Victory of Freedom, the Last Years, the Legacy;* and *The Final Revolution.*

[124] See, for example, Pope John XXIII, *Pacem in Terris,* April 11, 1963, vatican.va.

[125] Pope Paul VI, *Populorum Progressio,* March 26, 1967, vatican.va.

[126] Edward Peters, *Inquisition* (New York: Free Press, 1988), p. 3.

[127] Ibid., p. 11.

[128] Henry Kamen, *The Spanish Inquisition: A Historical Revision* (New Haven: Yale University Press, 1998), p. 314.

[129] Ibid., p. 315.

[130] Ibid., pp. 316-317.

[131] Jenkins, *The New Anti-Catholicism,* 186.

[132] Kamen, p. 190.

[133] Ibid., pp. 17-18.

[134] Ibid., pp. 188-192.

[135] Universal Prayer: Confession of Sins and Asking for Forgiveness, March 12, 2000, vatican.va.

[136] Cited by Dr. Regis Martin of Franciscan University of Steubenville in a lecture attended by the author; the phrase stuck in my head, but I have no record of the date or which course it was.

[137] See *Dignitatis Humanae.*

[138] Some would say, "But isn't the Congregation for the Doctrine of the Faith the Holy Office, the Inquisition under another name?" Yes, to a certain extent, but the role of the current Congregation is the same as the role of the American Medical Association or the American Bar Association. It maintains certain standards for theologians and Catholic institutions, enforcing the internal rules of the

organization on its members. Whatever its historical ancestors, the CDF is certainly not the Inquisition of old.

[139] In English, "worship" has not always been synonymous with worship! As Jimmy Akin explains in "Hey, Your Worship. I'm Only Trying to Help" (*National Catholic Register* blog, January 15, 2010), worship has traditionally been used in England and other nations to mean "honor." ncregister.com. So a husband and a bride would say, "With my body, I thee worship"; judges and other officials would be called "your worship"; and Han Solo would call Princess Leia "your worship" in the Star Wars movies. So worship doesn't always mean "to give the adoration due to God."

[140] Carl Anderson and Jose Granados, *Called to Love: Approaching John Paul II's Theology of the Body*, (Random House, 2009), pp. 202-203.

[141] Ibid., p. 203.

[142] Declaration of Independence, July 4, 1776, archives.gov.

[143] Jenkins, Chapter 9: "Black Legends: Rewriting Catholic History," in *The New Anti-Catholicism*. For an overview of those myths from a Lutheran sociologist of religion, see Rodney Stark, *Bearing False Witness: Debunking Centuries of Anti-Catholic History* (West Conshohocken, PA: Templeton Press, 2016). I don't think Stark always understands the Catholic faith, but he certainly does a good job of debunking a number of the myths that have become what "everyone knows."

[144] Jenkins, *The New Anti-Catholicism*, p. 180.

[145] Donald Kagan, Steven Ozment, and Frank M. Turner, *The Western Heritage: Since 1300*, 7th ed. (Upper Saddle River, NJ: Prentice Hall, 2000), section on the witch hunts. To be fair to them, Stark's *Bearing False Witness* repeats this understanding of the nature of the Catholic Church's opposition to witchcraft (pp. 124-128), speaking of "Church magic" as one category alongside other categories of magic. This simply fails to understand the Catholic view of the world as a sacramental reality, mediating grace/the presence and power of God where holiness is present. Actions, places, people, or things who mediate the Holy Spirit aren't engaged in magic at all — they're dealing with the Lord, who is beyond all efforts of manipulation or control. He will do that which He has promised, but He is not one who may be bound by magic. Rather, He may be bound only by His own divine nature or commitments He has freely undertaken — for

instance, by establishing the system of Sacraments.

[146] Thomas Woods Jr., *How the Catholic Church Built Western Civilization* (Washington, DC: Regnery, 2005). For the contributions of the monks, see Chapter 3.

[147] A few works, in no particular order: Regine Pernoud, *Those Terrible Middle Ages: Debunking the Myths*, trans. Anne Englund Nash (San Francisco: Ignatius Press, 2000); James Hannam, *The Genesis of Science: How the Christian Middle Ages Launched the Scientific Revolution* (Washington, DC: Regnery Publishing, 2011); the work of Rodney Stark and Thomas Woods (cited throughout this book). For further reading, see Michael Flynn, "09:02 pm — A Thousand Years in which 'Nothing Happened': Those Terrible Middle Ages," *Mike Flynn's Journal*, October 18, 2009, m-francis.livejournal.com/101659.html; see also "10:28 pm — The Age of Unreason: Pfui," *Mike Flynn's Journal*, October 18, 2009, m-francis.livejournal.com/101929.html.

[148] Rodney Stark, *The Victory of Reason: How Christianity Led to Freedom, Capitalism, and Western Success* (Random House, 2006), p. 28.

[149] Rodney Stark, *For The Glory of God: How Monotheism Led to Reformations, Science, Witch-Hunts, and the End of Slavery* (Princeton University Press, 2003), p. 329.

[150] Ibid., p. 329.

[151] Ibid., p. 331.

[152] Ibid., p. 332. Though the enforcing brief for *Sublimus Dei* was retracted under pressure from the king of Castile and Aragon, who was mentioned in the brief, the bull was never retracted. Both bull and brief were cited as authoritative by later pontiffs. See the teaching of Popes Gregory XIV (*Cum Sicuti*, 1591), Urban VIII (*Commissum Nobis*, 1639), and Benedict XIV (*Immensa Pastorum*, 1741).

[153] Stark, *For The Glory of God*, 337.

[154] Leo XIII, *Catholicae Ecclesiae: On Slavery in the Missions*, November 20, 1890, vatican.va/holy_father/leo_xiii/encyclicals/documents/hf_l-xiii_enc_20111890_catholicae-ecclesiae_en.html.

[155] "[W]hatever insults human dignity, such as...slavery... all these things and others of their like are infamies indeed." Vatican II, *Gaudium et Spes: Pastoral Constitution on the Church in the Modern World*, December 7, 1965, vatican.va, para. 27. Keep in mind

that in some discussions, a distinction is made between "just title" slavery (i.e., the sort experienced by criminals who are imprisoned and used as a labor force) and "chattel slavery" (i.e., people treated as property, as things). The first is not necessarily condemned; the latter has been forcefully condemned. For more, see Mark Brumley, "Let My People Go: The Catholic Church and Slavery," *This Rock* (July/August 1999), pp. 16-21, catholiceducation.org/articles/facts/fm0006.html.

[156] Antonio Spadaro, SJ, "A Big Heart Open to God: The Exclusive Interview with Pope Francis," *America* Magazine, September 30, 2013.

[157] See James Loughlin, "Pope St. Celestine V," in *The Catholic Encyclopedia*, Volume 3, (New York: Robert Appleton Company, 1908), January 28, 2012, newadvent.org/cathen/03479b.htm.

[158] Vatican II, *Lumen Gentium*, 8 § 3; Cf. UR 3; 6; Heb 2:17; 726; 2 Cor 5:21.

[159] Cf. 1 Jn 1:8-10.

[160] Cf. Mt 13:24-30, cited in *Catechism of the Catholic Church*, 827, quoting Vatican II, *Lumen Gentium*, no. 8.

[161] *Catechism of the Catholic Church*, para. 2358-2359.

[162] CIC, can. 1055 § 1; cf. GS 48 § 1, quoted in *Catechism of the Catholic Church*, para. 1601.

[163] Cf. Gen 19:1-29; Rom 1:24-27; 1 Cor 6:10; 1 Tim 1:10

[164] CDF, *Persona humana* 8.

[165] *Catechism of the Catholic Church*, para. 2357.

[166] *Diary of Saint Maria Faustina Kowalska: Divine Mercy in My Soul* (Marian Press 2010).

[167] Peter John Cameron, *Benedictus: Day by Day with Pope Benedict XVI* (Ignatius Press, 2006), p. 104.

[168] Wilde, *A Woman of No Importance*, p. 82.

[169] Pope Pius IX, Apostolic Constitution *Ineffabilis Deus*, December 8, 1854, papalencyclicals.net.

[170] Ibid.

[171] Cf. DS 76; 409; 411; 801; 858; 1002; 1351; 1575; Paul VI, CPG § 12.

[172] *Catechism of the Catholic Church*, para. 1035.

[173] Cf. Mt 5:22, 29; 10:28; 13:42, 50; Mk 9:43-48.

174 Mt 13:41-42.

175 Mt 25:41, quoted in *Catechism of the Catholic Church*, para. 1034.

176 Father Andrew Apostoli, CFR, *Fatima for Today: The Urgent Marian Message of Hope* (Ignatius Press 2010), pp. 60-67.

177 *Diary of Saint Maria Faustina Kowalska*, 741.

178 *The Life of Saint Teresa of Avila by Herself,* Trans. David Lewis (Digireads, 2009), p. 164.

179 1 Jn 3:14-15.

180 Cf. Mt 25:31-46.

181 *Catechism of the Catholic Church.*, para. 1033.

182 C. S. Lewis, *The Problem of Pain* (HarperCollins, 2001), p. 130.

183 C. S. Lewis, *The Great Divorce* (HarperCollins, 2001), p. 75.

184 Ibid., pp. 124, 132-133, 135-141.

185 Barbara Freyer Stowasser, *Women in the Qur'an, Traditions, and Interpretation* (Oxford University Press, 1996), p. 13.

186 Vatican II, Dogmatic Constitution on Divine Revelation *Dei Verbum*, November 18, 1965, vatican.va, para. 11

187 *Dei Verbum*, para. 2.

188 Jordan Aumann, OP, *Christian Spirituality in the Catholic Tradition* (San Francisco: Ignatius Press, 1985), domcentral.org/study/aumann/cs/default.htm.

189 For more on this, see Mother Teresa and Brian Kolodiejchuk, *Come Be My Light: The Private Writings of the Saint of Calcutta*, (New York: Doubleday Image, 2009).

190 Robert Royal, *The Catholic Martyrs of the Twentieth Century: A Comprehensive World History* (Crossroad, 2006).

191 Brant Pitre, *The Case for Jesus: The Biblical and Historical Evidence for Christ* (New York: Image, 2016), pp. 100-101.

192 Mark Shea, *Mary, Mother of the Son* (Marytown Press, 2014), Part I, Chapters 2-3, especially pp. 30-36.

193 A useful overview is Jon Sorensen, "Was the Virgin Birth of Jesus Grounded in Paganism?" December 2, 2013, catholic.com/magazine/online-edition/was-the-virgin-birth-of-jesus-grounded-in-paganism, accessed January 27, 2017.

194 Donna Rosenberg, *World Mythology: An Anthology of the Great Myths and Epics*, Third Edition, (Lincolnwood, Illinois: NTC Publishing Group, 1994), p. 165.

[195] Mark Shea has some wonderful work on this. See Shea, *Mary, Mother of the Son*, p. 40-45.

[196] See, for instance, Dr. Brant Pitre, *The Case for Jesus* (Image, 2016).

[197] See, for example, Lee Strobel, *The Case for Christ: A Journalist's Personal Investigation of the Evidence for Jesus* (Zondervan); Pitre, *The Case for Jesus*.

[198] Millar Burrows, *The Dead Sea Scrolls* (New York: Viking Press, 1955), p. 304.

[199] Norman Geisler and Peter Bocchino, *Unshakable Foundations* (Minneapolis, MN: Bethany House Publishers, 2001), p. 256.

[200] St. Thomas Aquinas, STh I, 1, 10, ad I, in *Catechism of the Catholic Church*, 116.

[201] *Catechism of the Catholic Church*, 117.

[202] "*Lettera gesta docet, quid credas allegoria, moralis quid agas, quo tendas anagogia*"; Augustine of Dacia, *Rotulus pugillaris*, I; ed. A. Walz; *Angelicum* 6 (1929) 256, quoted in *Catechism* 118.

[203] Mark P. Shea, *Making Senses Out of Scripture: Reading the Bible as the First Christians Did* (Basilica Press, 2001).

[204] Aumann, *Christian Spirituality in the Catholic Tradition*.

[205] John W. O'Malley, *What Happened at Vatican II* (Cambridge, Massachusetts: Belknap Press of Harvard University Press, 2008), p. 74.

[206] William Fanning, "Plenary Councils of Baltimore" in *The Catholic Encyclopedia*, Volume 2 (New York: Robert Appleton Company, 1907), March 3, 2012, newadvent.org/cathen/02235a.htm.

[207] There are subtleties in the discussion of the covenants, especially when it comes to the Law given at Sinai versus the Law given in Deuteronomy, that I probably shouldn't get into here. For more on the subject, see Scott Hahn and John Bergsma, "What Laws Were Not Good: A Canonical Approach to the Theological Problem of Ezekiel 20:25-26," *Journal of Biblical Literature, 2004 (Volume 123, no. 2)*, pp. 201-218. Available here: salvationhistory.com/documents/scripture/JBL%20Ezek%2007-2004.doc.pdf.

[208] For more on the three different covenants/laws given through Moses, see Scott Hahn, *Kinship by Covenant: A Canonical Approach to the Fulfillment of God's Saving Promises* (New Haven, CT: Yale University Press, 2009), pg. 74-77; see also Hahn and Bergsma, "What Laws Were Not Good: A Canonical Approach to the

Theological Problem of Ezekiel 20:25-26."

[209] See also *Catechism* 2052-2074.

[210] Stark, *For the Glory of God: How Monotheism Led to Reformation, Science, Witch-hunts, and the End of Slavery*, pp. 163-166; he adds a few more tidbits (such as the fact that Galileo's science on the Copernican theory was not entirely defensible nor correct) in *Bearing False Witness*, pp. 163-166.

[211] Stark, *Bearing False Witness*, pp. 144-145, 150-152.

[212] George Weigel, *Witness to Hope: The Biography of Pope John Paul II* (Cliff Street Books/HarperCollins, 1999), pp. 356, 629-631.

[213] See, for instance, Corey S. Powell, "Did "Cosmos" Pick the Wrong Hero?" Discover Magazine's Out There blog, March 10, 2014, blogs.discovermagazine.com/outthere/2014/03/10/cosmos-pick-wrong-hero/#.WJYwCfLD_LI.

[214] CIC, can. 1055 § 1; cf. GS 48 § 1, cited in *Catechism of the Catholic Church*, para. 1601.

[215] As passed on by the USCCB's Committee on Divine Worship in correspondence with the author, April 4, 2017.

[216] Cf. Mk 8:34; Mt 11:29-30.

[217] Cf. Mt 19:11, cited in *Catechism of the Catholic Church*, para. 1615.

[218] Peter Vere and Michael Trueman, *Surprised by Canon Law: 150 Questions Catholics Ask About Canon Law* (Cincinnati: St. Anthony Messenger Press, 2004), pp. 116-119.

[219] Anyone who's been in the middle of a divorce or has watched a friend or family member go through a divorce can testify to this, but for further examples, see Kathy M. Kristof, "Cutting the Cost of Divorce," February 6, 2011, Personal Finance, *Los Angeles Times*, articles.latimes.com/2011/feb/06/business/la-fi-perfin-20110206.

[220] D.G. Schramm, "Individual and Social Costs of Divorce in Utah," *Journal of Family and Economic Issues*, 2006, s3.amazonaws.com/storage.nm-storage.com/marriageresourcecenter/downloads/divorcecostsstudy.pdf.

[221] David G. Schramm, PhD, "Counting the Cost of Divorce: What Those Who Know Better Rarely Acknowledge," *Family in America*, Fall 2009.

[222] C. S. Lewis, "Answers to Questions on Christianity," in *God in the Dock* (Wm. B. Eerdmans Publishing, 1994), pp. 61-62.

[223] Vatican II, *Sacrosanctum Concilium*, vatican.va, Chapter VI.

[224] Ibid., para. 112.

[225] For more, see Scott Hahn, *The Lamb's Supper: Mass as Heaven on Earth* (Random House, 1999).

[226] Eucharistic Prayer II, Third English Translation of the Roman Missal. catholic-resources.org/ChurchDocs/RM3-EP1-4.htm.

[227] *Sacrosanctum Concilium*, para. 114.

[228] Ibid., para. 116.

[229] Ibid., para. 120.

[230] Ibid., para. 120.

[231] Ibid., para. 121.

[232] G.K. Chesterton, *The Autobiography of G. K. Chesterton* (Ignatius Press, April 30, 2006), p. 324. For a free version online, see cse.dmu.ac.uk/~mward/gkc/books/163-GKC-Autobiography.txt.

[233] Knowing oneself to be a bad Catholic so as to be a good Catholic has been modeled by many of the saints and sinners in the Catholic heritage; I could list names for pages. Outstanding among them, though, is another great southern writer, Walker Percy, who once crafted a piece for *Esquire* titled "Questions They Never Asked Me So I Asked Myself," in which he describes himself as a bad Catholic (a piece that, many years later, inspired the often funny, often profound Bad Catholic blog by Marc Barnes).

[234] Cardinal Timothy Dolan, "Love, Prayers, and Best Wishes from Rome," *The Gospel in the Digital Age*, February 15, 2012, blog. archny.org/?p=2270.

[235] Alphonse Van Hove, "Bishop," *The Catholic Encyclopedia*, Volume 2 (New York: Robert Appleton Company, 1907), October 6, 2012, newadvent.org/cathen/02581b.htm.

[236] Thomas Scannell, "Confirmation," *The Catholic Encyclopedia*, Volume 4 (New York: Robert Appleton Company, 1908), October 6, 2012, newadvent.org/cathen/04215b.htm.

[237] Joseph Pohle, "Eucharist," *The Catholic Encyclopedia*, Volume 5 (New York: Robert Appleton Company, 1909), October 6, 2012, newadvent.org/cathen/05572c.htm.

[238] Anthony Maas, "Biblical Exegesis," *The Catholic Encyclopedia*, Volume 5 (New York: Robert Appleton Company, 1909), October 6, 2012, newadvent.org/cathen/05692b.htm.

[239] Edward Pace, "Hypostatic Union," *The Catholic Encyclopedia*,

Volume 7 (New York: Robert Appleton Company, 1910), October 6, 2012, newadvent.org/cathen/07610b.htm.

[240] Auguste Boudinhon, "Laity," *The Catholic Encyclopedia*, Volume 8 (New York: Robert Appleton Company, 1910), October 6, 2012, newadvent.org/cathen/08748a.htm.

[241] Herbert Thurston, "Ostensorium (Monstrance)," *The Catholic Encyclopedia*, Volume 11 (New York: Robert Appleton Company, 1911), October 6, 2012, newadvent.org/cathen/11344a.htm.

[242] George Joyce, "The Pope," *The Catholic Encyclopedia*, Volume 12 (New York: Robert Appleton Company, 1911), October 6, 2012, newadvent.org/cathen/12260a.htm.

[243] Auguste Boudinhon, "Priest," *The Catholic Encyclopedia*, Volume 12. (New York: Robert Appleton Company, 1911), October 6, 2012, newadvent.org/cathen/12406a.htm.

[244] USCCB website, "About USCCB," usccb.org/about/index.cfm.

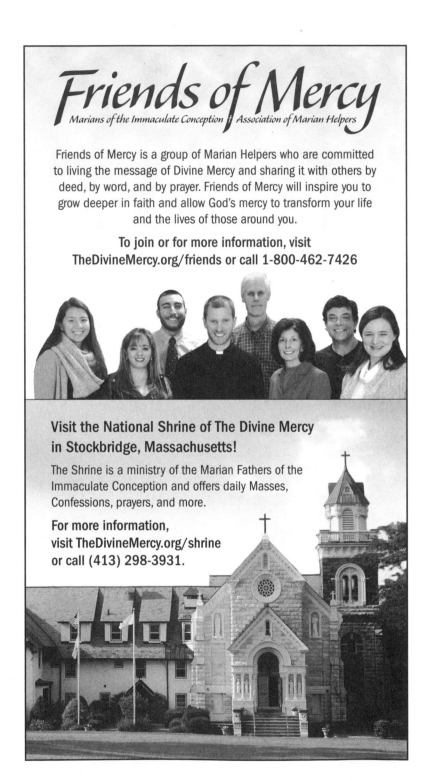

Friends of Mercy
Marians of the Immaculate Conception ⊥ Association of Marian Helpers

Friends of Mercy is a group of Marian Helpers who are committed to living the message of Divine Mercy and sharing it with others by deed, by word, and by prayer. Friends of Mercy will inspire you to grow deeper in faith and allow God's mercy to transform your life and the lives of those around you.

To join or for more information, visit TheDivineMercy.org/friends or call 1-800-462-7426

Visit the National Shrine of The Divine Mercy in Stockbridge, Massachusetts!

The Shrine is a ministry of the Marian Fathers of the Immaculate Conception and offers daily Masses, Confessions, prayers, and more.

For more information, visit TheDivineMercy.org/shrine or call (413) 298-3931.